Quantitative Syntax Analysis

Quantitative Linguistics 65

De Gruyter Mouton

Quantitative Syntax Analysis

by

Reinhard Köhler

De Gruyter Mouton

ISBN 978-3-11-027219-2
e-ISBN 978-3-11-027292-5
ISSN 0179-3616

Library of Congress Cataloging-in-Publication Data

Köhler, Reinhard.
Quantitative syntax analysis / by Reinhard Köhler.
p. cm. – (Quantitative linguistics; 65)
Includes bibliographical references and index.
ISBN 978-3-11-027219-2 (alk. paper)
1. Grammar, Comparative and general – Syntax. 2. Computational linguistics. I. Altmann, Gabriel. II. Title.
P291.K64 2012
415.01'51–dc23

2011028873

Bibliographic information published by the Deutsche Nationalbibliothek

The Deutsche Nationalbibliothek lists this publication in the Deutsche Nationalbibliografie; detailed bibliographic data are available in the Internet at http://dnb.d-nb.de.

Printing: Hubert & Co. GmbH & Co. KG, Göttingen
∞ Printed on acid-free paper

Printed in Germany

www.degruyter.com

Dedicated to Gabriel Altmann
on the occasion of his 80th birthday

Preface

Over decades, syntax has been a linguistic sub-discipline that remained almost completely untouched by quantitative methods and, on the other hand, researchers in the field of syntax remained almost unaffected by quantitative methods. One of the reasons why these two realms have been separated for so long and so thoroughly is undoubtedly the hostile attitude towards statistics among "main stream" linguists (this factor and corresponding pseudo-arguments are discussed in detail in the introduction to this volume); another one is the ignorance of the exponents of quantitative linguistics with respect to syntax (the pretexts commonly used to justify this ignorance will also turn out to be pointless). As a consequence, either camp does not know anything about the objectives and aims of the other one.

Those who are acquainted with both views on language cannot settle for the current dogmatic, unproductive situation in linguistics, which results in either the exclusion of a central linguistic field as "insignificant", or ignorance or even interdiction of the application of a large part of proven and successful scientific and mathematical concepts and methods as "inappropriate".

It is the main goal of this book to try to change this situation a little bit by giving both sides the chance to see that quantitative models and methods can indeed be successfully applied to syntax and, moreover, yield important and far-reaching theoretical and empirical results. It goes without saying that only a small part of the relevant topics and results could be presented here but I hope that the selection I made gives enough of a picture to give a useful insight into the way how quantitative linguistic thinking and research opens up new vistas in syntax as well.

R.K., Spring 2011

Contents

1 Introduction

We can hardly imagine a natural human language which would make use of lexical means only. The coding potential of such a system in which meanings are coded by lexical items only suffers from the finite, even very limited capacity of the human memory and could not meet the communication requirements of human societies. Systems of this kind, such as the traffic signs, animal "languages"[1], various technical codes and many others, provide ready-made signs (mostly indexical, partly iconic in nature) for each possible meaning and are therefore restricted to the paradigmatic coding strategy, i.e., the selection from a limited set of items.

In contrast, the *syntagmatic* strategy opens up a more effective way of coding and avoids the mentioned shortcomings. This strategy consists of combining the atomic expressions which are available in the lexicon, i.e., of collocation and ad-hoc compounding.[2] From a quantitative point of view, the first and obvious advantage of syntagmatic coding means is that they overcome the quantitative limitations of lexical coding means.

The syntactic axis, going beyond the mere concatenation by forming complex expressions out of simple ones, provides additional coding means. On the semantic side, syntax enables us to code structures instead of ideas as wholes, in particular to explicitly express predicates and propositions. Thus, the expression 'walk through a liquid' conveys much more of the conceptual structure of the corresponding concept than the atomic (short but opaque) expression 'wade'. On the side of the expression, more means become available because the arrangement of elements can (1) be made in different ways and (2) be subject to multiple restrictions. Both facts cause the existence of con-

1. Admittedly, many of these simple code systems have at their disposal a rudimentary syntax: there are combinations of traffic signs, e.g., to indicate limits of validity, and some animals combine certain patterns of sounds with certain pitch levels, e.g., in the case of warning cries to indicate what kind of animal they caution about.
2. It should be clear, of course, that a 'pure' syntagmatic coding strategy cannot exist; paradigmatic means – atomic expressions – are primary in any case.

trasts, and these can always be used to express meanings or be recycled for other functions. Any pair of elements within a syntactic construction can (1) have different distances from each other and (2) be ordered in two ways (three elements can be put into six different orders, n elements into $n!$ orders). Both types of possible differences can be used – and are used by natural languages in combination – to express meanings, together with the differentiation of word classes (parts-of-speech), morpho-syntactic and prosodic means.

There is an interesting discussion among linguists about the role of syntax with respect to the assumed uniqueness of human language as opposed to all other kinds of communication systems. It is often claimed that this uniqueness is the specific ability to express infinitely many meanings with the help of a finite set of means. Hauser, Chomsky and Fitch (2002) argue that this ability is based on recursion, i.e. on the mechanism which produces nested structures, structures with embedded structures of the same type. It seems, on the other hand, that there exist languages without any recursive structures (cf. Everett 1991). When this and other objections were raised the proponents of the recursion thesis weakened their definition of recursion, including now iterative structures. Yet, iterations, repetitive elements, are absolutely common in the world of communication systems – including inanimate systems. We will not enter this discussion however interesting it may be. This book is not based on any a priori statements about properties of language that will not immediately be tested on empirical data.

Every text – regardless of whether it consists of a single word (such as “Fire!”, “Thanks”, “Help!”, or “Password?”), a long speech, or of several printed volumes – is in every case an expression for a complex and multi-dimensionally structured, cognitive (conceptual, emotional, intentional) formation. Before a thought can be conveyed by means of linguistic material, a series of complicated processes must take place: first focussing and selecting (the choice of the aspects and elements of the cognitive structure which are to be communicated), then serializing the cognitive elements. Next in the course of linguistic coding, a combination of coding strategies is bundled. Here, the available lexical, morphological, prosodic, and syntactic means for the formation and optimisation of the expression are employed, with regards to focus (within the linguistic structure), topicalisation, speaker's coding and listener's decoding efforts, and other semantic and pragmatic requirements. The resulting complex expression should, ideally, meat several requirements at the same time, although they are in competition to each other in many cases and in many ways: the expression should enable the listener or reader to induce, as easily as possible, the structure of the concept from the linguistic structure, and at the same time cause as little effort as possible on the side of the speaker or writer. Moreover, the conditions for the way in which these criteria have to be met change from case to case. Language has developed a rich variety of coding means and has in this way become flexible enough to provide expressions appropriate in virtually any situation and for any comunication purpose.

The formal description of the syntactic structures which can be observed in natural languages has, since Chomsky, been considered as the proper mission of linguistics, and has made corresponding methodological and empirical progress. In contrast, the study of the functional dependencies and of the interrelations among syntactic units and properties, as well as between these and units and properties of other linguistic levels and extra-linguistic factors is still in its infancy. Although functional linguistics, typology, and language universals research have gathered enormous quantities of observations, plausible interpretations, and empirical generalizations, a break-through has not yet been achieved. On the one hand, these linguistic disciplines understand that the highest level of any science cannot be arrived at without scientific explanation of what has been observed and described. On the other hand, the exponents of these research fields lack the knowledge of the philosophy of science which would enable them to proceed to the explanatory level. Explanation is not possible without the help of a theory, i.e. a system made of universal laws and boundary conditions, while a law cannot be replaced by rules, patterns, typologies and classifications, or axiomatic systems (although any of these is called a "theory" in the linguistic literature).[3]

3. For a detailed treatise of fundamental concepts of the philosophy of science, cf. Bunge (1998a,b).

The triumphant advance of formal grammars as models of syntactic structures brought – alongside with advantages such as their applicability in computational linguistics etc. – severe consequences of its shady side with it. Followers of the (post-)generative school and other linguists enshrined every statement of the leading figures. In this way, dogmas arose instead of scientific skepticism, discussion and thinking.[4] These dogmas concerned central ideas of scientific research strategies, methodology, and *weltanschauung*; it remains to be seen whether they can be considered more or less obsolete or are still fully alive. The situation has changed at least in some fields, such as in computational linguistics, where devout executors of the belief in strictly formal methods as opposed to statistical ones do not have any chance to succeed, due to nothing but the properties of language itself and the corresponding failure of purely formal methods.

Nevertheless, *quantitative* – just as much as *functional* – modelling and analysis are still heavily objected to by exponents of formal linguistics, in particular in the field of syntax. Since decades, adherents as well as antagonists of a purely formal approach to language analysis cite repeatedly Chomsky's statement saying that the concept of probability is absolutely useless with respect to sentences as most of them possess an empirical probability which cannot be distinguished from zero – cf. e.g., Chomsky (1965: 10ff.; 1969). While the first camp believes any discussion about quantitative approaches – at least in the field of syntax – to be finally closed, the other camp avails itself on Chomsky's argument to prove his incompetence in the realm of statistical reasoning. However, as far as we can see, Chomsky's judgment that statistical methods are useless referred merely to the two predicates which he was interested in at that time: grammaticality and acceptability of sentences – a fact that has apparently been ignored.

Chomsky seems to have used his rejection of stochastic models as a weapon in his fight against behaviorist approaches and for his view of language as creative capability of humans. However, if grammaticality is defined as deducibility of a string in terms of a formal grammar, a statistical corpus study cannot contribute anything to determining

4. This process was mainly limited to America and Western Europe, whereas in other parts of the world, scientific pluralism could be maintained.

whether an expression is grammatical with respect to a given grammar or not. A different conception of the notion of grammaticality, however, may entail another assessment of the descriptive or even explanatory power of quantitative methods with respect to grammaticality – absolutely regardless of the probability of individual sentences or sentences types.

With respect to acceptability, the existence of interdependence with frequency is an open empirical question. Consider, e.g., the interrelation between length/complexity and frequency of syntactic construction types (Köhler 1999, Köhler and Altmann 2000); it seems at least plausible to assume that very long or complex constructions are less acceptable than shorter ones – all this depends crucially on the specific concept of acceptability.

Notwithstanding the discussion around Chomsky's statement, most individual sentences have undoubtedly a zero probability. Take, e.g., Chomsky's own example: The sentence "I live in New York" has a greater probability than the sentence "I live in Dayton, Ohio". This example shows, by the way, the important linguistic interrelation between frequency and length of linguistic expressions also on the sentence level. Few people would probably say "I live in New York, New York"; New York has a larger population, so more people have the chance to use the sentence, and, equally important, New York is familiar to much more people. All these facts interact and produce different frequencies and complexities. Sentences such as "How are you?" and "Come in!" are still more frequent. May we conclude, therefore, that statistical or other quantitative methods are principally inappropriate for studies of syntax?

Before we give an answer to this question, another mistake in Chomsky's argumentation shall be addressed here: speaking of "empirical *probabilities*" is not only a harmless, or superficial, error. Empirical observations provide access to *frequencies* – not to probabilities. And frequencies (i.e., non-zero frequencies) do exist even if a model does not assign a (theoretical) probability greater than zero to the elements under study. If a model is based on a continuous random variable or, as in the case of sentences, on a discrete random variable with an infinite domain every individual value of the variable corresponds to probability zero.[5] Anyhow, every experiment will yield an outcome where values can be observed; i.e. values with a probability equal to zero but with a frequency greater than zero. In the case of language, if a sentence has probability zero it can be uttered nevertheless. As this fact is not a specialty of syntax but a universal mathematical truth zero probabilities cannot be used as a valid argument against statistical methods.

Anyway, zero probabilities do not play any role at all with syntactic constructions below the sentence level, with syntactic units, categories, and properties. On the contrary, empirical data describing frequencies and other quantitative properties such as similarities, degrees of familiarity, complexity etc., are useful, well-proven and have even become indispensable in various fields and applications of computational linguistics and for the testing of psycholinguistic hypotheses and models. Even so, we know only little about the syntax of natural languages with respect to quantitative aspects. This fact is due not only to the former hostile attitude of most linguists in syntax research but also to the difficulties which must be faced when large amounts of relevant data are collected. Meanwhile, however, these difficulties can be partly overcome with the help of more and more powerful computers and the availability of large corpora of texts in written and oral forms. Some of the obvious quantitative properties and their lawful interrelations, which have been studied on the syntactic level so far, concern sizes of inventories, lengths and complexities of constructions, depths of embedding, positions and distances of components, and frequencies of constructions (in texts and in inventories as well as in typological respect).

The following chapters shall give an overview of concepts, definitions, models and methods, and of results of investigations on the syntactic level proper and also show some studies of syntagmatic relations and properties in a broader sense. Chapter 2 of this book gives an introduction to quantitative linguistic thinking and to the foundations of the corresponding methodology. Chapter 3 discusses quantitative

5. Consider the following example: The probability that you will observe a lightning at a specific moment of time at a given place is zero. But there are exact counts and statistics, even laws, which can be used for weather forecasts and risk calculations by insurance companies. These statistics are not based on probabilities of individual events or moments but on frequencies (and estimates of probabilities) for time and space intervals.

concepts which are specific for the syntactic level and more general concepts which also can be applied on this level; this part is concerned with the description of syntactic and syntagmatic properties and relations and their use in linguistic description. In Chapter 4 explanatory approaches are outlined. Gabriel Altmann's school of quantitative linguistics – synergetic linguistics is a branch of this school – emphasizes the need for explanation of what has been observed and described. Therefore, the highest level of quantitative syntax analysis consists of the attempt to set up universal hypotheses, which can become laws, and finally the construction of a linguistic theory in the sense of the philosophy of science, i.e. a system of laws and some other components which can not only describe but also explain why languages are as they are.

2 The quantitative analysis of language and text

2.1 The objective of quantitative linguistics

While the formal branches of linguistics use only the qualitative mathematical means (algebra, set theory) and formal logics to model structural properties of language, quantitative linguistics (QL) studies the multitude of quantitative properties which are essential for the description and understanding of the development and the functioning of linguistic systems and their components. The objects of QL research do not, therefore, differ from those of other linguistic and textological disciplines, nor is there a principal difference in epistemological interest. The difference lies rather in the ontological points of view (whether we consider a language as a set of sentences with their structures assigned to them, or we see it as a system which is subject to evolutionary processes in analogy to biological organisms, etc.) and, consequently, in the concepts which form the basis of the disciplines.

Differences of this kind form the ability of a researcher to perceive – or not – elements, phenomena, or properties in his area of study. A linguist accustomed to think in terms of set theoretical constructs is not likely to find the study of properties such as length, frequency, age, degree of polysemy etc. interesting or even necessary, and he/she is probably not easy to convince that these properties might be interesting or necessary to investigate. Zipf's law is the only quantitative relation which almost every linguist has heard about, but for those who are not familiar with QL it appears to be a curiosity more than a central linguistic law, which is connected with a large number of properties and processes in language. However, once you have begun to look at language and text from a quantitative point of view, you will detect features and interrelations which can be expressed only by numbers or rankings whatever detail you peer at. There are, e.g., dependences of length (or complexity) of syntactic constructions on their frequency and on their ambiguity, of homonymy of grammatical morphemes on their dispersion in their paradigm, the length of expressions on their age, the dynamics of the flow of information in a text on its size, the probability of change of a sound on its articulatory difficulty..., in short, in every field and on each level of linguistic analysis – lexicon, phonology, morphology, syntax, text structure, semantics, pragmatics, dialectology, language change, psycho- and sociolinguistics, in prose and lyric poetry – phenomena of this kind are predominant. They are observed in every language in the world and at all times. Moreover, it can be shown that these properties of linguistic elements and their interrelations abide by universal laws, which can be formulated in a strict mathematical way – in analogy to well-known laws of the natural sciences. Emphasis has to be put on the fact that these laws are stochastic; they do not capture single cases (this would neither be expected nor possible), they rather predict the probabilities of certain events or certain conditions in a whole. It is easy to find counter-examples to any of the examples cited above. However, this does not mean that they contradict the corresponding laws. Divergences from a statistical average are not only admissible but even necessary – they are themselves determined with quantitative exactness. This situation is, in principle, not different from that in the natural sciences, where the old deterministic ideas have been disused since long and have been replaced by modern statistical/probabilistic models.

The role of QL is now to unveil corresponding phenomena, to systematically describe them, and to find and formulate laws which explain the observed and described facts. Quantitative interrelations have an enormous value for fundamental research but they can also be used and applied in many fields such as computational linguistics and natural language processing, language teaching, optimisation of texts etc. As briefly mentioned above, QL cannot be characterised by a specific cognitive interest. QL researchers study the same scientific objects as other linguists. However, QL emphasises, in contrast to other branches of linguistics, the introduction and application of additional, advanced scientific tools. Principally, linguistics tries, in the same way as other empirical ("factual") sciences do in their fields, to find explanations for the properties, mechanisms, functions, the development etc. of language(s). It would be a mistake, of course, to think of "final" explanation which would help to conceive the "essence" of the objects.[1]

1. Cf. Popper (1957: 23), Hempel (1952: 52ff.); Kutschera (1972: 19f.)

Science strives for a hierarchy of explanations which lead to more and more general theories and cover more and more phenomena without ever being able to find an end of explanation. Due to the stochastic properties of language, quantification and probabilistic models play a crucial role in this process. In the framework of this general aim, QL has a special status only because it makes special efforts to care for the methods necessary for this purpose, and it will have this status only as long as these methods are not yet common in all the areas of language and text research. We can characterise this endeavour by two complementary aspects:

1. On the one hand, the development and the application of quantitative models and methods is indispensable in all cases where purely formal (algebraic, set-theoretical, and logical) methods fail, i.e. where the variability and vagueness of natural languages cannot be neglected, where tendencies and preferences dominate over rigid principles, where gradual changes debar the application of static/structural models. Briefly, quantitative approaches must be applied whenever the dramatic simplification, which is caused by the qualitative yes/no scale cannot be justified or is inappropriate for a given investigation.
2. On the other hand, quantitative concepts and methods are superior to the qualitative ones on principled grounds: the quantitative ones allow for a more adequate description of reality by providing an arbitrarily fine resolution. Between the two extreme poles such as yes/no, true/false, or 1/0 of qualitative concepts, as many grades as are needed can be distinguished up to the infinitely many "grades" of the continuum.

Generally speaking, the development of quantitative methods aims at improving the exactness and precision of the possible statements on the properties of linguistic and textual objects. Exactness depends, in fact, on two factors: (1) on the acuity of the definition of a concept and (2) on the quality of the measurement methods with which the given property can be determined. Success in defining a linguistic property with sufficiently crisp concepts enables us to operate it with mathematical means, provided the operations correspond to the scale level (cf. Section 2.3.3) of the concepts. Such operations help us deriving new insights which would not be possible without them: appraisal criteria, which exist at the time being only in a subjective, tentative form, can be made objective and operationalised (e.g. in stylistics), interrelations between units and properties can be detected, which remain invisible to qualitative methods, and workable methods for technical and other fields of application can be found where traditional linguistic methods fail or produce inappropriate results due to the stochastic properties of the data or to the sheer mass of them (e.g., in Natural Language Processing).

2.2 Quantitative linguistics as a scientific discipline

If asked about the reason of the success of the modern natural sciences, most scientists point out the exact, testable statements, the precise predictions, and the copious applications, which are available with their instruments and their advanced models. Physics, chemistry, and other disciplines strive, since ever, for continuous improvement of measuring methods and refined experiments in order to test the hypotheses set up in their respective theoretical fields and to develop the corresponding theories. In these sciences, counting and measuring are basic operations, whereas these methods are, in the humanities, considered as more or less useless and in any way inferior activities. No psychologist or sociologist would propagate the idea to try to do their work without the measurement of reaction times, duration of learning, protocols of eye movements, without population statistics, measurement of migration, without macro and micro census. Economics is completely based on quantitative models of the market and its participants. Phonetics, the science which investigates the material-energetic manifestation of speech, could not investigate anything without the measurement of the fundamental quantities like sound pressure, length (duration) and frequency (pitch). Other sciences are not yet advanced enough to integrate measurement and applications of mathematics as basic elements into their body of instruments. In particular, in linguistics, the history of quantitative research is only 60 years old, and there are still only very few researchers who introduce and use these methods, although in our days, the paradigm of the natural sciences and the history of their successes could serve as a signpost. This situation is the reason why all the activities which make an effort to improve the methodological and epistemological inventory of linguistics are subsumed under the term "Quantitative Linguistics", which may underline the necessity to develop and to introduce specific linguistic methods and models in analogy to those in the natural sciences. This special term, hopefully, can be abandoned in the near future, for the exponents of QL have, in principle, the same scientific aims as the rest of the linguists.

As opposed to formal mathematics and logics, the quantitative methods of mathematics did not establish themselves in linguistics at the same speed although they appeared not later than the formal ones. Systematic studies on the basis of statistical counting were conducted as early as in the first half of the 19th century – studies which have not yet been fully evaluated. The first researcher to try to derive quantitative findings from theoretical, mathematically formulated models of language was George Kingsley Zipf (1902–1950). His pioneering work is now considered as the cornerstone of QL.

Early modern linguistics, in the time after the seminal contribution of de Saussure, was mainly interested in the structure of language. Consequently, linguists adopted the qualitative means of mathematics: logics, algebra and set theory. The historical development of linguistics and a subsequent one-sided emphasis on certain elements in the structuralist achievements resulted in the emergence of an absolutely static concept of system, which has prevailed until our days. The aspects of systems which exceed structure, viz. functions, dynamics, or processes, were disregarded almost completely. To overcome this flaw, the quantitative parts of mathematics (e.g., analysis, probability theory and statistics, function theory, differential and difference equations) must be added to the qualitative ones, and this is the actual aim of QL.

2.3 Foundations of quantitative linguistics

The fact that language can adequately be analysed only by means of quantitative methods follows from epistemological, heuristic, and methodological considerations (cf. also Altmann and Lehfeldt 1980: 1ff.). The phenomena of reality themselves are neither qualitative nor quantitative, neither deterministic nor stochastic, neither ordered nor chaotic. These criteria are not properties of the world (or language) but of our scientific concepts and methods of analysis, which we use to approximate the observable facts by creating understandable models. These models are relative; their properties depend on the stage of development of a science. Historical evidence, however, shows that scientific progress can be measured in terms of the precision of the concepts. Significant, escalating progress in the history of science has always been connected to the introduction of quantitative concepts into a discipline.

2.3.1 Epistemological aspects

The possibilities to derive empirical statements about language(s) are extremely limited. Direct observation of 'language' is impossible and introspection (a commonly applied method) cannot provide more than heuristic contributions and does not possess the status of empirical evidence (even if the contrary is often claimed in linguistics). Only linguistic behaviour is available as a source of scientific data – in the form of oral or written text, in form of psycho-linguistic experiments, or from other kinds of observations of behaviour in connection with the use of language. Confusion in this respect arises if we forget that language in the sense of the structuralist *langue* is an abstraction of speech in the sense of the structuralist *parole*.

Furthermore, the situation is aggravated, in the same way as in other empirical sciences, by the fact that we never dispose of complete information on the object under study. On the one hand, this is because only a limited part or aspect of the object is accessible. This may be the case because the object is principally infinite (such as the set of all texts or all sentences) or because it cannot be described in full for practical reasons (such as the set of all words of a language at a given time). On the other hand, very often we lack the complete information about the number and kinds of all factors which might be relevant for a given problem and we are therefore unable to give a full description.

Only mathematical statistics enables us to find valid conclusions in spite of incomplete information, and indeed with objective, arbitrary reliability. Let us consider at this point an example (Frumkina 1973: 172ff.), which concerns the description of the use of the definite article 'the' in English. If you try to set up deterministic rules you will, at first, fail to cover the majority of usage types. More rules and more conditions will improve the result but still a lot of cases will remain uncovered. The more additional rules and conditions are set up, the less additional cases will be covered by them. Finally, you would have to set up individual rules for every new type of usage you meet and still be uncertain if all relevant criteria have been found. A statistical approach tackles the problem in a different way. It considers the occurrence of the definitive article as a random event (i.e., following a stochastic law in accordance with a set of conditions) and makes it possible to arrive at an arbitrary number of correct predictions. The effort to achieve the correct predictions increases with the reliability the researcher selects in advance. Thus, mathematical statistics provides us with a conceptual and methodological means to enter deeper layers of the complex structure of reality and to better understand the object of our interest.

2.3.2 Heuristic benefits

One of the most elementary tasks of any science is to create some order within the mass of manifold, diverse, and unmanageable data. Classification and correlation methods can give indications to phenomena and interrelations not yet known before. A typical example of a domain where such inductive methods are very common is corpus linguistics, where huge amounts of linguistic data are collected and could not even be inspected with the bare eye. However, it should be stressed that inductive, heuristic means can never replace the step of forming hypotheses. It is impossible to 'find' units, categories, relations, or even explanations by data inspection – statistical or not. Even if there are only a few variables, there are principally infinitely many formulae, categories, or other models which would fit in with the observed data. Data cannot tell us which of the possible properties, classifications, rules, or functions are appropriate in order to represent the hidden structures, mechanisms, processes, and functions of human language (processing). Purely inductive investigations may result not only in irrelevant statements, numbers or curves, but also in misleading ones. Languages, for example, are rich of elements with a complex history where nested processes and changing influences and conditions formed structures and shapes which cannot be understood by e.g., simply counting or correlating surface phenomena, i.e., without having theoretically justified hypotheses.

The scientific value of heuristic statistical methods may be illustrated by a metaphor: You will see different things if you walk, ride a bike, go by car, or look down from a plane. Statistics is a vehicle which can be used at arbitrary 'velocity' and arbitrary 'height', depending on how much overview you wish for and how detailed you want to look at a linguistic 'landscape'.

2.3.3 Methodological grounds

Any science begins with categorical, qualitative concepts, which divide the field of interest in as clearly as possible delimited classes in order to establish some kind of order within it. This first attempt at creating some order is always rather crude: one can, on the basis of qualitative concepts, state that two or more objects are, or are not, identical with respect to a given property. With P for the property under consideration, and A and B for two objects, this can be expressed formally as:

$$P(A) = P(B) \quad \text{or} \quad P(A) \neq P(B).$$

A linguistic example of this kind of concepts is the classical category of part-of-speech. It is possible to decide whether a word should be considered as a noun or not. All the words which are classified as nouns are counted as identical with respect to their part-of-speech property. Repetition of this procedure for all postulated parts-of-speech yields a categorical classification. Every statement which is based on qualitative concepts (categories) can be reduced to dichotomies, i.e. the assignment to binary sets (with exactly two values, such as {true, false}, {1,0}, {yes, no}). This kind of concept is fundamental and indispensable but it does not suffice any more as soon as a deeper insight into the object of interest is desired.

Comparison with respect to identity is too crude to be useful for most scientific purposes and has to be upgraded by methods which enable gradual statements. This possibility is provided by comparative (ordinal-scale) concepts – the simplest form of quantitative concepts. They allow us to determine that an object possesses more, or less, of a given property than another one, or the same amount of it – formally:

$$P(A) > P(B), \quad P(A) = P(B) \quad \text{or} \quad P(A) < P(B).$$

Applying this kind of concept yields a higher degree of order, viz. a ranking of the objects with respect to a given property. A linguistic example of this is grammatical acceptability of sentences.

The highest degree of order is achieved with the help of metrical concepts, which are needed if the difference between the amounts of a given property, which objects *A* and *B* possess, plays a role. In this case, the values of the property are mapped to the elements of an appropriate set of numbers, i.e. a set of numbers in which the relations between these numbers correspond to the relations between the values of the properties of the objects. In this way, specific operations such as subtraction correspond to specific differences or distances in the properties between the objects – formally:

$$P(A) - P(B) = d,$$

where *d* stands for the numerical value of the difference. This enables the researcher to establish an arbitrarily fine conceptual grid within his field of study. Concepts which allow distances or similarities between objects to be determined are called interval-scale concepts. If another feature is added, viz. a fixed point of reference (e.g. an absolute zero) ratio-scaled concepts are obtained, which allow the operation of multiplication and division, formally:

$$P(A) = aP(B) + d.$$

The mathematical relation represents the relation between the objects with respect to property *P* if the numbers *a* and *b* are determined appropriately. Only the latter scale enables to formulate how many times object *A* has more of some property than *B*. Often, quantitative concepts are introduced indirectly. Quantification can start from established (or potential) quantitative concepts and then add the needed features. One has to make sure that the conceptual scale is chosen properly, i.e. the concepts must be formed according to the mathematical operations which correspond to the properties and relations of the objects. The polysemy of words may serve as a linguistic example of an indirectly introduced quantitative concept. Polysemy is originally a qualitative concept in traditional linguistics which identifies or differentiates words with respect to ambiguity.

Taking this as a starting point, a quantitative variant of this concept can easily be created: it may be defined as the number of meanings of a linguistic expression; the values admitted are cardinal numbers in the interval $[1,\infty)$, i.e. the smallest possible value is 1 whereas an upper limit cannot be specified. This is a well-defined ratio-scale concept: using basic mathematical operations, differences in polysemy between words can be expressed (e.g. word x has three meanings more than word y) and even the ratio between the polysemy of two words values can be specified (e.g. word v has twice as many meanings as word w), since we have a fixed reference point – the minimum polysemy 1.

Only by means of concepts on higher scales, i.e. quantitative ones, is it possible to pose deeper-reaching questions and even to make corresponding observations. Thus, without our quantitative concept of polysemy no-one could even notice that there is a lawful relation between the number of meanings of a word and its length (cf. p. 22).

Another step in the procedure of quantification (the establishing of quantitative concepts) is operationalisation, which determines the correspondence between a theoretical concept and its empirical counterpart. One has to decide how observation, (identification, segmentation, measurement etc.) has to be done in accordance with the theoretical model. In our example of polysemy, so far, no clarification has been done as to how the number of meanings of a word should be determined. There may be many ways to operationalise a theoretical concept; in our case a dictionary could be consulted or a text corpus could be used where the number of different usages of a word could be determined etc.

A common way to introduce quantitative concepts into linguistics and philology is forming indices – the definition of mathematical operations to map properties onto relations between numbers. The most familiar indices in linguistics are the morphological indices introduced by Greenberg (1960); many other typological indices can be found in (Altmann and Lehfeldt 1973). Forming correct indices is far from trivial – cf. Altmann and Grotjahn (1988) for a systematic presentation of corresponding methods and problems.

2.4 Theory, laws, and explanation

Science does not confine itself to observe phenomena, to describe these observations, and to apply the collected knowledge. The highest aim of any science is the *explanation* of the phenomena (which also opens up the possibility to predict them). The attempt to find universal laws of language and text, which enable us to provide explanations for the observed phenomena and interrelations, consists in the search for general patterns. From such patterns, we can derive which phenomena, events, and interrelations are possible on principled grounds and which of them are not, and under which conditions the possible ones can appear. There is probably not a single a priori promising strategy for such a quest and therefore, in the course of history, different approaches have been followed. Historically, the first known attempt to explain linguistic phenomena by means of laws in analogy to the natural sciences ("according to Euclid's method") is the fascinating work by the Benedictine monk Martin Sarmiento (1695–1737; cf. Pensado 1960).

As opposed to this early work, the attempts of the neogrammarians to formulate universal sound laws are better known. However, their endeavour failed for methodological reasons (as we know today). They lacked the needed quantitative concepts, in particular the concept of stochastic laws, and so they had to surrender to the many exceptions they encountered.

Noam Chomsky also understood the need for explanation in linguistics. He, however, developed a formal *descriptive* device without any explanative power. In this school, the quest for explanation ends before it has really begun. The "why" question is answered here quickly by the assumption of an innate "universal grammar", whose origin is then claimed to be outside of linguistic research but rather a part of biological evolution (cf. e.g. Chomsky 1986). This treatment of linguistic explanation left behind the well-known classification of descriptions into "observational", "descriptive", and "explanative" *adequacy*. An excellent critique of Chomskyan linguistics with respect to its fundamental flaws and defects in its theoretical background and of its immunisation against empirical counterevidence can be found in Jan Nuyts' analysis (1992).

Other examples of linguistic approaches which strive for explanation can be found in the work of Dressler et al. (1987), the exponents of "Natural morphology", who also have to fail – at least in the current stage of this approach. Their main problem consists in the nature of the explanatory instances they employ: they refer to postulated properties such as "naturalness" instead of referring to laws, which prevents the approach from being able to derive the observed phenomena as results of a logical conclusion.

The quest for models with explanatory power can follow two principally opposed strategies of research. It is possible, on the one hand, to go the inductive way, as usual in language typology and universals research: one looks for common properties of all known languages (cf. Croft 1990; Greenberg 1966). Such properties might be useful as starting points for the research on the laws which are responsible for them. The inductive method, however, brings with it an inherent disadvantage. Even after looking at a very large number of languages which all share a common feature without a single exception, one cannot exclude the possibility that one (or even all) of the languages not yet inspected differ from the others in the given aspect. But it is impossible to investigate literally all languages (including all the languages of the past which are not more accessible and all languages in the future). Consequently, inductive methods, i.e. conclusions on the basis of not more than currently available data, possess only little value as one has to face the possibility of falsifying results of a new study, which would cause the complete inductive construction to collapse.[2]

2. Remember the famous example of generalizations in logics: "All swans are white".

The other strategy is the deductive one: starting from given knowledge, i.e. from laws or at least from plausible assumptions (i.e. assumptions which are not isolated speculations but reasonable hypotheses logically connected to the body of knowledge of a science) one looks for interesting consequences (i.e. consequences which – if true – contribute new knowledge as much as possible, or – if false – show as unambiguously as possible that the original assumptions are wrong), tests their validity on data and draws conclusions concerning the theoretically derived assumptions.

There is no linguistic theory as of yet. The philosophy of science defines the term "theory" as a system of interrelated, universally valid laws and hypotheses (together with some other elements; cf. Altmann 1993, 3ff.; Bunge 1967) which enables to derive explanations of phenomena within a given scientific field. As opposed to this definition, which is generally accepted in all more advanced sciences, in linguistics, the term "theory" has lost its original meaning. It has become common to refer with it arbitrarily to various kinds of objects: to descriptive approaches (e.g. phoneme "theory", individual grammar "theories"), to individual concepts or to a collection of concepts (e.g. Bühler's language "theory"), to formalisms ("theory" in analogy to axiomatic systems such as set theory in mathematics), to definitions (e.g. speech act "theory"), to conventions (X-Bar "theory") etc. In principle, a specific linguistic terminology concerning the term "theory" could be acceptable if it only were systematic. However, linguists use the term without any reflection for whatever they think is important, which leads to confusion and mistakes. Some linguists (most linguists are not educated with respect to the philosophy of science, as opposed to most scientists working in the natural sciences) associate – correctly – the term "theory" with the potential of explanation and consequently believe – erroneously – that such "theories" can be used to explain linguistic phenomena.

Thus, there is not yet any elaborated linguistic theory in the sense of the philosophy of science. However, a number of linguistic laws have been found in the framework of QL, and there is a first attempt at combining them into a system of interconnected universal statements, thus forming an (even if embryonic) theory of language: synergetic linguistics (cf. Köhler 1986, 1987, 1993, 1999). A second approach was recently presented (Wimmer and Altmann 2005), which combines the mathematical formulations of most of the linguistic laws known today as special cases of a unified approach in form of differential or difference equations. Both approaches furnish the same results.

A simple example will illustrate the explanation of a linguistic phenomenon: one of the properties of lexical units (in the following, we use also the simpler term "word" instead of "lexical unit" but this does not mean that we refer only to one-word expressions), which is studied since a long time (Zipf 1949, Guiter 1974). As is well known, many words correspond to more than one meaning. The cited works, among others, found that there is a relation between the number of meanings of a word and its length: the shorter a word the more meanings. There are, of course, many exceptions to this generalisation, as is the case with most linguistic phenomena. As we have seen, explanation is possible only with the help of an appropriate universal law from which the phenomenon to explain can logically be derived. There is, in fact, such a law (cf. Altmann, Beőthy, and Best 1982). It says that the number of meanings of a lexical unit is a function of the length of the given unit and can be expressed by the formula

$$B = AL^{-s},$$

where B denotes the number of meanings, L the length and s and A are empirical constants. This law is, according to Altmann, a consequence of Menzerath's law, which states a functional dependence between the length of a linguistic construction (e.g., a sentence) and the lengths of its immediate components (clauses in the case of sentences). A critical discussion and an alternative derivation of this equation can be found in (Köhler 1990a: 3f.).

After establishing an explanative relation between a law (or a hypothesis) and the phenomenon under investigation, one has to test whether the theoretical statement holds if confronted with the linguistic reality. For such a test, appropriate data must be collected. In the case of our example, the question rises as to how the quantities "polysemy" or "number of meanings" on the one hand and "length" on the other hand have to be measured. An answer to such a question is called "operationalisation". Any theoretical concept may correspond to several different operationalisations depending on the circumstances and purposes of the investigation. A simple (but for a number of reasons not very satisfying) solution for the quantity "polysemy" is to count the number of meanings of each word in a dictionary. word length can be measured in terms of the number of phonemes or letters, syllables and morphs. In most QL studies, word length is measured in term of the number of syllables it consists of.

In this way, a table is set up in which for each word the polysemy and length values are taken down. The words themselves are not needed. According to the law, polysemy is the dependent variable. Therefore, the value pairs are arranged in the order of the length values. It goes without saying that the table will contain, as a rule, more than one polysemy value for a given length value and vice versa. As we are interested in the general behaviour of the data – in other words: the tendency – we may calculate, for each of the length values, the average polysemy; the corresponding results are represented in Table 2.1.

Table 2.1: Observed (f_i) and expected (Np_i) values of polysemy of words with length x_i in a German corpus

x_i	f_i	Np_i	x_i	f_i	Np_i
3	5.0000	5.0485	15	1.1071	1.3308
4	4.6316	3.9779	16	1.2037	1.2615
5	4.2740	3.3066	17	1.0789	1.1998
6	3.6981	2.8430	18	1.0333	1.1443
7	2.6000	2.5022	19	1.0357	1.0941
8	1.8938	2.2402	20	1.0000	1.0486
9	1.5943	2.0319	21	1.1429	1.0071
10	1.7537	1.8621	22	1.1111	0.9690
11	1.4215	1.7207	23	1.0000	0.9340
12	1.3853	1.6010	24	1.2000	0.9016
13	1.2637	1.4983	25	1.0000	0.8716
14	1.2658	1.4091	26	1.0000	0.8438

Figure 2.1 shows the theoretically predicted function in form of a solid line and the mean polysemy values (y-axis) for the individual length values (x-axis).

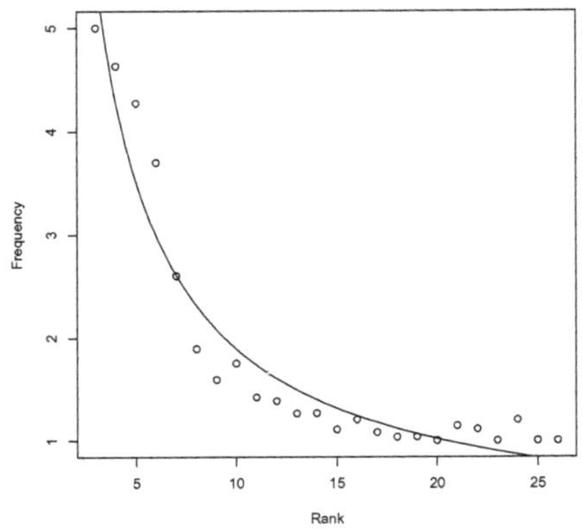

Figure 2.1: Observed and calculated values from Table 2.1

The data represent German words in a 1-million corpus. Now, an empirical test of significance can be conducted, which checks whether the deviations of the data marks from the theoretically given line may be considered as insignificant fluctuations or results of the crude measurement method or have to be interpreted as significant. Significant deviations would mean that the hypothesis has to be rejected. In our case, however, the corresponding test (which we will not present here) yields a confirmation of the law.

In general, we can differentiate three kinds of language and text laws: (1) functional laws (among them the relation between length and polysemy and Menzerath's law), (2) distribution laws (such as Zipf's law) and (3) developmental laws (such as Piotrowski's law), which model the dynamics of a linguistic property over time.

2.5 Conclusion

In Sections 2.1 to 2.4, the most salient reasons for the introduction of quantitative concepts, models, and methods into linguistics and the text sciences, and to apply them in the same way as the more advanced sciences, in particular the natural sciences, employ them for ages, were presented and discussed. Besides the general arguments, which are supported by the accepted standards from the philosophy of science and which are cross-disciplinarily valid, in linguistics, the following considerations are of central interest:

1. The phenomena of language and text cannot be described exactly and completely by means of qualitative concepts alone. Those cover merely extreme cases, which may be captured sufficiently well for a given purpose using categorical concepts.
2. Limitation to the toolbox of qualitative means results in a principal inability to even detect the majority of linguistic and textual properties and interrelations.
3. A fully established conceptual and methodological apparatus is essential for the advancing to higher levels of research by more precise and deeper looking analyses, by modelling interrelations and mechanisms, and finally by formulating universal laws and setting up a linguistic theory.
4. Even if – just in order to discuss the argument – qualitative methods would suffice to describe the linguistic phenomena, the attempt at explaining them, i.e. the first steps to theory construction, would unveil the quantitative characteristics of language-external instances. Criteria such as success of communication, appropriateness of linguistic means for a given purpose, memory capacity, disturbances in the acoustic channel, ability to differentiate acoustic features, communicative efficiency (economy versus security of transmission) etc., are doubtlessly comparative (ordinal) or metric quantities. Hence, the bonds and dependences between external boundary conditions, the global and the local system variables have automatically to be analysed with quantitative means. Moreover, who would dare to deny the quantitative character of such central properties of language systems as inventory size (on each level of linguistic analysis), unit length, depth of embedding, complexity, position, age, frequency, polysemy, contextuality, semantic transparency, iconicity and many more?

3 Empirical analysis and mathematical modelling

3.1 Syntactic units and properties

Units and properties are, of course, conceptual models; consequently, they cannot be found in the object of investigation[1] but are rather a result of definition (cf. e.g. Altmann 1993; 1996). We therefore have to define the corresponding concepts before we can perform an investigation of any kind. Some units and properties which are widely used originate rather from pre-theoretical intuition than from theory-guided considerations (e.g. *word*, on the syntactic level of *sentence*) even if one or more operationalisations for a concrete analysis exist. Early studies on sentence length, e.g., were based on an intuitive idea as to what a sentence is; length measurement became nevertheless possible because this concept was operationalised in terms of the number of words between certain separators (full stops etc.).

Definitions are neither true nor false – they cannot be assigned a truth value. The definition of a concept is a matter of convention, i.e., every researcher may define his or her concepts in the way most appropriate from the point of view of the theoretical framework in which the concept plays a role, and of the purpose the given investigation aims at. Hence, a definition can prove (or fail to prove) to be promising, appropriate, or successful but never be true. Clearly defined concepts are the most important prerequisite for a well-formulated scientific hypothesis (cf. Bunge 2007: 51ff., 253ff.) and for determining or measuring a property. In very much the same way as units cannot be found by means of observation, properties too must be defined; properties are not inherent features of objects but attributes which come into (conceptual) existence as a consequence of a theoretical framework. Thus, in the framework of a grammar based on constituency,

1. There are, in fact, researchers who believe 'new linguistic units' can be found by means of intensive corpus studies. It should be clear, however, that this is a fundamental confusion between model and reality. Any unit is conventional, not only meter, kilogram and gallon but also our linguistic units such as phoneme, syllable etc.

non-terminal nodes and certain relations (such as being the mother node) exist whereas such nodes and relations do not exist in a word grammar like dependency grammar, and the strata of Lamb's, (1966) stratification grammar have no counterpart in other grammar conceptions. Similarly, a property with the name of complexity can, but need not, be defined in each of these models of syntax , but these complexities are quite different properties. The complexity of a constituency structure can, e.g., be defined as the number of immediate constituents or as the sum of the nodes under the given one; in dependency grammar, the complexity of a stemma, could be defined, among others, as the number of complements of the central verb, the number of direct and indirect dependents, etc.

Thus, the definition of a unit or a property constitutes its meaning with respect to a theoretical framework and is formed with regard to a specific hypothesis (cf. Altmann 1996). Then, the concept (unit, property, or other relation) must be operationalised, i.e., a procedure must be given how the concept has to be applied to observable facts. This procedure can consist of criteria as to how to identify, segment, count, or measure a corresponding phenomenon. Suppose a researcher has set up a hypothesis about sentence length in texts on the background of some psycholinguistic assumptions. Before the length of the first sentence can be determined it must be clear whether length should be measured in terms of physical length in cm or inches (an operationalisation which is, e.g., useful in content analysis when the prominence of an expression in press media is scrutinized), in seconds (duration of oral speech), in the number of letters, phonemes, syllables, morphs, words, phrases, clauses etc.

Units and properties which have been used for quantitative syntactic analyses up to now include, but are not limited to:

- sentence length in terms of the number of words, in terms of the number of clauses, and of length motifs;
- clause length in terms of words and of motifs;
- complexity of syntactic constructions in terms of the number of immediate constituents and in terms of the number of words (terminal nodes);
- frequency of syntactic construction types;

- position of syntactic constructions in the sentence and in the mother construction;
- depth of embedding of syntactic constructions (various operationalisations, cf. Section 4.1.1;
- information of syntactic constructions;
- frequency and direction of dependency types;
- length of dependency chains;
- frequency of valency patterns;
- distribution of the number of complements;
- distribution of part-of-speech;
- distribution of semantic roles;
- size of inventories;
- typological distribution of part-of-speech systems;
- ambiguity and flexibility of part-of-speech systems;
- efficiency of part-of-speech systems;
- efficiency of grammars.

3.2 Quantitation of syntactic concepts and measurement

There are familiar and general concepts which seem to have a quantitative nature as opposed to those just as well familiar ones which seem to be of qualitative nature. Transforming qualitative concepts into quantitative ones usually is called 'quantification', a better term might be 'quantitation', a term introduced by Bunge (see below). Examples of 'naturally' quantitative concepts are length and duration, whereas noun and verb are considered as qualitative ones. The predicates quantitative and qualitative, however, must not be mistaken as ontologically inherent in the objects of the world. They are rather elements of the individual model and the methods applied (cf. Altmann 1993). In the Introduction, we mentioned the concept of grammaticality, which can be considered as a qualitative or as a quantitative one where a sentence is allowed to be more, or less grammatical than another one. There are numerous examples of linguistic properties which are used either in a qualitative or a quantitative sense, depending on the given purpose of the study, the method applied, and the guiding hypothesis behind an investigation. Moreover, any qualitative property can be transformed into a quantitative one – except a single one: existence.[2] There are, clearly, non-quantitative concepts such as class membership (this kind of concept is the very basis of, e.g., formal sciences) but once "we realize that it is not the subject matter but our ideas concerning it that are the subject of numerical quantification no insurmountable barriers to quantitation remain" (Bunge 1998b: 228). Consequently, fuzzy sets have been introduced where membership is defined as a number in the interval $[0, 1]$.

The general advantage of quantitative concepts over qualitative ones has been discussed in Chapter 2. Here, we should pay attention to concepts which belong to the syntactic level of linguistic analysis. Concepts such as length and complexity are automatically considered as quantitative ones and it is taken for granted that the corresponding quantities can be measured. Others, e.g. ambiguity, do not easily come into mind as quantitative properties, since formal (or 'structural') linguistics is interested in structure and does not focus on other questions. From a quantitative point of view, when ambiguity is addressed the very first idea is to ask "how ambiguous?" The second one is "how can ambiguity be measured?" or "how can the ambiguity of structure S_1 be compared to the ambiguity of structure S_2?" A straightforward answer is easily found in this case: a perfect measure of ambiguity is the number of different interpretations a structure can be attributed to. The transformation of a qualitative or categorical concept into a quantitative one, i.e., creating a new concept which takes numbers as values instead of categories, is often called *quantification*. Bunge (1998b: 217) coined the term *quantitation* to avoid confusion with the logical concept of introducing a quantifier ("quantor") into a logical formula. Other terms are *metrification* and *metricisation*.

Not so easily determined is, in many cases, the *procedure* of counting. In the case of ambiguity, we would have to give a precise definition of the concept of interpretation and to predetermine the criteria which allow deciding whether an interpretation is identical to another one or not. This is again the step which is called *operationalisation* (cf. p. 18) of a concept. Concept definition and concept operationalisation are indispensable prerequisites of any measurement. There are

2. I am not absolutely sure about this either.

always several different operationalisations of one and the same concept. "word length" is an example of a concept which has been operationalised in many ways, of which each one is appropriate in another theoretical context. Thus, word length has been measured in the number of sounds, phonemes, morphs, morphemes, syllables, inches, and milliseconds in phonetic, phonological, morphological, and content analytical studies (the latter for the sake of comparison of newspapers with respect to the weights of topics). Operationalisations do not possess any truth value, they are neither true nor false or wrong; we have to find out which one is the most promising one in terms of hypothetical relations to other properties.

Counting is the simplest form of measurement and yields a dimensionless number; a unit of measurement is not needed for this procedure. Linguistics investigates only discrete objects (as opposed to, e.g., phonetics where continuous variables are measured); therefore, the measurement of a fundamental linguistic property is always performed by counting these objects. Fundamental properties are not composed of other ones (e.g., velocity is measured in terms of length units divided by time units whereas length and duration are fundamental properties; linguistic examples of composed properties are Greenberg's, (1957; 1960) and Krupa's, (Krupa 1965; Krupa and Altmann 1966) typological indices, e.g., the number of prefixes divided by the number of all morphemes in a language). Indices are popular measures in linguistics; however, they must not be used without some methodological knowledge (cf. e.g. Altmann and Grotjahn 1988: 1026ff.).

3.3 The acquisition of data from linguistic corpora

Empirical research in quantitative linguistics relies on availability of large amounts of linguistic data in form of dictionaries or corpora, depending on the aims of the intended studies. Quantitative studies on the syntactic level have been severely constricted by the lack of appropriate data; it took until the last decade to change this situation and to produce large text collections with more information than part-of-speech tags. Today, several syntactically annotated corpora exist and can be used for a wide range of investigations.

There is a number of problems connected to the work with corpora, regardless of the object and purpose of a linguistic investigation. One of them is the lack of interfaces for quantitative questions. There are dozens of tools and portals which can be used to find examples of specific words, combinations of features, structures etc., but not a single one for typical quantitative questions such as "which is the distribution of word length in prose texts in this corpus?" or "give me the dependence of mean syntactic complexity of a constituent on its depth of embedding". We should not hope that interfaces of this kind will be developed because there are infinitely many questions of this sort, and the implementation of programs that can answer only a few of them would take too much time and effort. The only solution to this problem is to write own programs to extract the required data. But this solution bears two other problems: (1) many corpora are not accessible to 'foreign' programs because the owners fear data burglary and (2) there is no general standard as to how corpora should be structured and notated.[3] There are ways to overcome these problems (cf. Köhler 2005a) but they exist only in the form of proposals. For now, there is no other way than to write individual programs for most questions and most corpora.

Among syntactically annotated corpora, some similarities can be found; there is only a limited number of principles. The following sections will show some examples of the most common formats of syntactically annotated corpora.

3.3.1 Tagged text

The following is an extract of tagged text from one of the notational versions of the Pennsylvania Treebank:

```
[ Pierre/NNP Vinken/NNP ]
,/,
[ 61/CD years/NNS ]
```

3. Cf. http://www.ldc.upenn.edu/annotation/ where you can find an overview of the most popular annotation tools.

```
old/JJ ,/, will/MD join/VB
[ the/DT board/NN ]
as/IN
[ a/DT nonexecutive/JJ director/NN Nov./NNP 29/CD ]
./.
[ Mr./NNP Vinken/NNP ]
is/VBZ
[ chairman/NN ]
of/IN
[ Elsevier/NNP N.V./NNP ]
,/,
[ the/DT Dutch/NNP publishing/VBG group/NN ]
./.
```

3.3.2 Tree banks[4]

This commonly used structuring of corpora can be exemplified by another notational version of the Pennsylvania Treebank[5], which provides, in addition to part-of-speech tags, a flat syntactic analysis in form of bracketed and labelled constituents:

```
( (S (NP-SBJ (NP Pierre Vinken)
             ,
             (ADJP (NP 61 years)
                   old)
             ,)
     (VP will
         (VP join
             (NP the board)
```

4. The term ‘tree bank’ is often used as a name for syntactically annotated corpora in general.
5. http://www.cis.upenn.edu/~treebank/home.html

```
             (PP-CLR as
                   (NP a nonexecutive director))
             (NP-TMP Nov. 29)))
     .))
((S (NP-SBJ Mr. Vinken)
    (VP is
       (NP-PRD (NP chairman)
               (PP of
                  (NP (NP Elsevier N.V.)
                      ,
                      (NP the Dutch publishing
                         group)))))
     .))
```

As can be seen, indenting is often used to facilitate the inspection of the syntactic structure.

3.3.3 Column structure

Structuring the information in columns is yet another way of representing a corpus. The example has been taken from the Susanne Corpus, which organises each running word token in a line of its own together with technical and linguistic annotations[6]:

```
A01:0010a   -   YB       <minbrk>   -        [Oh.Oh]
A01:0010b   -   AT       The        the      [O[S[Nns:s.
A01:0010c   -   NP1s     Fultcn     Fulton   [Nns.
A01:0010d   -   NNL1cb   County     county   .Nns]
A01:0010e   -   JJ       Grand      grand    .
A01:0010f   -   NN1c     Jury       jury     .Nns:s]
A01:0010g   -   VVDv     said       say      [Vd.Vd]
```

[Continued on next page]

6. Cf. Sampson (1995)

[Continued from previous page]

```
A01:0010h - NPD1  Friday           Friday          [Nns:t.Nns:t]
A01:0010i - AT1   an               an              [Fn:o[Ns:s.
A01:0010j - NN1n  investigation    investigation   .
A01:0020a - IO    of               of              [Po.
A01:0020b - NP1t  Atlanta          Atlanta         [Ns[G[Nns.Nns]
A01:0020c - GG    +<apos>s         -               .G]
A01:0020d - JJ    recent           recent          .
A01:0020e - JJ    primary          primary         .
A01:0020f - NN1n  election         election        .Ns]Po]Ns:s]
A01:0020g - VVDv  produced         produce         [Vd.Vd]
A01:0020h - YIL   <ldquo>          -               .
A01:0020i - ATn   +no              no              [Ns:o.
A01:0020j - NN1u  evidence         evidence        .
A01:0020k - YIR   +<rdquo>         -               .
A01:0020m - CST   that             that            [Fn.
A01:0030a - DDy   any              any             [Np:s.
A01:0030b - NN2   irregularities   irregularity    .Np:s]
A01:0030c - VVDv  took             take            [Vd.Vd]
A01:0030d - NNL1c place            place           [Ns:o.Ns:o]Fn]Ns:o]
                                                      Fn:o]S]
A01:0030e - YF    +.               -               .O]
A01:0030f - YB    <minbrk>         -               [Oh.Oh]
A01:0030g - AT    The              the             [O[S[Ns:s.
A01:0030h - NN1c  jury             jury            .Ns:s]
A01:0030i - RRR   further          far             [R:c.R:c]
A01:0030j - VVDv  said             say             [Vd.Vd]
A01:0030k - II    in               in              [P:p.
A01:0030m - NNT1c term             term            [Np[Ns.
A01:0030n - YH    +<hyphen>        -               .
A01:0030p - NN1c  +end             end             .Ns]
A01:0040a - NN2   presentments     presentment     .Np]P:p]
A01:0040b - CST   that             that            [Fn:o.
A01:0040c - AT    the              the             [Nns:s101.
A01:0040d - NNL1c City             city            .
A01:0040e - JB    Executive        executive       .
A01:0040f - NNJ1c Committee        committee       .
```

[Continued on next page]

[Continued from previous page]

```
A01:0040g - YC    +,             -         .
A01:0040h - DDQr  which          which     [Fr[Dq:s101.Dq:s101]
A01:0040i - VHD   had            have      [Vd.Vd]
A01:0040j - JB    over<hyphen>all overall  [Ns:o.
A01:0050a - NN1n  charge         charge    .
A01:0050b - IO    of             of        [Po.
A01:0050c - AT    the            the       [Ns.
A01:0050d - NN1n  election       election  .Ns]Po]Ns:o]
A01:0050e - YC    +,             -         .Fr]Nns:s101]
A01:0050f - YIL   <ldquo>        -         .
A01:0050g - VVZv  +deserves      deserve   [Vz.Vz]
A01:0050h - AT    the            the       [N:o.
A01:0050i - NN1u  praise         praise    [NN1n&.
A01:0050j - CC    and            and       [NN2+.
A01:0050k - NN2   thanks         thank     .NN2+]NN1n&]
A01:0050m - IO    of             of        [Po.
A01:0050n - AT    the            the       [Nns.
A01:0060a - NNL1c City           city      .
A01:0060b - IO    of             of        [Po.
A01:0060c - NP1t  Atlanta        Atlanta   [Nns.Nns]Po]Nns]Po]N:o]
A01:0060d - YIR   +<rdquo>       -         .
A01:0060e - IF    for            for       [P:r.
A01:0060f - AT    the            the       [Ns:103.
A01:0060g - NN1c  manner         manner    .
A01:0060h - II    in             in        [Fr[Pq:h.
A01:0060i - DDQr  which          which     [Dq:103.Dq:103]Pq:h]
A01:0060j - AT    the            the       [Ns:S.
A01:0060k - NN1n  election       election  .Ns:S]
A01:0060m - VBDZ  was            be        [Vsp.
A01:0060n - VVNv  conducted      conduct   .Vsp]Fr]Ns:103]P:r]
                                               Fn:o]S]
A01:0060p - YF    +.             -         .O]
```

The example above is the complete first sentence of text A01 from the Susanne corpus. The organisational and linguistic information for each word-form is given in six columns: The first column (reference field) gives a text and line code, the second (status field) marks abbreviations, symbols, and misprints; the third gives the word tag according to the Lancaster tagset, the fourth the word-form from the raw text, the fifth the lemma, and the sixth the parse. In lines A01:0040j and A01:0050d, for example, the :o's mark the NP "the over-all ... of the election" as logical direct object, the brackets with label Fr in lines A01:0060h and A01:0060n mean that "in which ... was conducted" is a relative clause.

3.3.4 Feature-value pairs

A fourth alternative consists of elements associated with one or more pairs of names and values of properties. The currently most popular variant is the notation as XML files, which allows a consequent hierarchical formalisation of all kinds of information a document might need. The following example shows the beginning of a text from the German lemmatized and syntactically annotated *taz* corpus[7].

```
<?xml version="1.0" encoding="iso-8859-1"?>
<!DOCTYPE corpus SYSTEM "corpus.dtd">
<corpus>
<article>
<header>
<copyright>
Copyright © contrapress media GmbH
</copyright>
<identifier>
T990226.149 TAZ Nr. 5772
</identifier>
<page>
15
</page>
<date>
26.02.1999
</date>
<length>
```

7. A newspaper corpus set up and maintained by the Institute of Computational Linguistics at the University of Trier, Germany.

```
298 Zeilen
</length>
<texttype>
Interview
</texttype>
<author>
Maximilian Dax
</author>
</header>
<body>
<headings>
<title>
<token lemma="@quot;" wclass="$(" type="open">
"
</token>
<token wclass="PDS" lemma="d">
Das
</token>
<token wclass="VVFIN" lemma="nennen">
nenne
</token>
<token wclass="PPER" lemma="ich">
ich
</token>
<token wclass="NN" lemma="Selbstreferenz">
Selbstreferenz
</token>
<token wclass="$." lemma="!">!
</token>
<token lemma="@quot;" wclass="$(" type="close">
"
</token>
</title>
<subtitle>
<clause complete="+">
```

The example shows that corpora and documents may be enriched by meta-information such as text title, author, publishing date, copyright etc. Annotation categories are not implicit as in the examples in Sections 3.3.1 to 3.3.3 but explicitly given in form of feature-value pairs. As XML was chosen as mark-up language the structure of the document including annotation is defined in a corresponding DTD (document type definition) in a separate file:

```
<!-- Corpus-DTD Version 1 -->
<!ENTITY % textabschnitt "iwp | clause | token | fnm">
<!ENTITY % satzabschnitt "clause | token | fnm | syntax">
<!ELEMENT corpus     (article)+ >
<!ELEMENT syntax     ((%satzabschnitt;)*) >
<!ELEMENT article    (header, body)>
<!ELEMENT header     (copyright, identifier, page, date,
                      length, texttype, author*)>
<!ELEMENT copyright  (#PCDATA)>
<!ELEMENT identifier (#PCDATA)>
<!ELEMENT page       (#PCDATA)>
<!ELEMENT date       (#PCDATA)>
<!ELEMENT length     (#PCDATA)>
<!ELEMENT texttype   (#PCDATA)>
<!ELEMENT author     (#PCDATA)>
<!ELEMENT body       (headings*, text)>
<!ELEMENT headings   (title, subtitle*)>
<!ELEMENT title      ((%satzabschnitt;)*)>
<!ELEMENT subtitle   ((%satzabschnitt;)*)>
<!ELEMENT text       ((%textabschnitt;) | subtitle)*>
<!ELEMENT clause     ((%satzabschnitt;)*)>
<!ELEMENT token      (#PCDATA)>
<!ELEMENT fnm  (token)>
<!ELEMENT iwp  (token*)>
<!ATTLIST token
          lemma   CDATA #IMPLIED
          wclass  CDATA #IMPLIED
```

```
          type    CDATA #IMPLIED
>
<!ATTLIST clause
          complete   CDATA #IMPLIED
>
<!ATTLIST syntax
          cat        CDATA #REQUIRED
          position   CDATA #IMPLIED
>
```

3.3.5 Others

There are many other solutions (we consider here only pure text corpora of written language. The variety of structures and notations is by a magnitude greater if oral, sign language, or even multimedia corpora are included). We will illustrate here only one more technique, viz. a mixed form of annotation. The example is an extract from one of the notational versions of the German Saarbrücken Negra Korpus.[8]

```
o %% word  tag   morph  edge  parent  secedge  comment
o #BOS  1   1  985275570 1
o Mögen  VMFIN 3.Pl.Pres.Konj HD 508
o Puristen  NN Masc.Nom.Pl.* NK 505
o aller  PIDAT *.Gen.Pl NK 500
o Musikbereiche  NN Masc.Gen.Pl.* NK 500
o auch  ADV -- MO 508
o die  ART Def.Fem.Akk.Sg NK 501
o Nase  NN Fem.Akk.Sg.* NK 501
o rümpfen   VVINF -- HD 506
o  ,  $, -- -- 0
o die  ART Def.Fem.Nom.Sg NK 507
```

8. www.coli.uni-saarland.de/projects/sfb378/negra-corpus

```
o Zukunft  NN Fem.Nom.Sg.* NK 507
o der  ART Def.Fem.Gen.Sg NK 502
o Musik  NN Fem.Gen.Sg.* NK 502
o liegt  VVFIN 3.Sg.Pres.Ind HD 509
o für  APPR Akk AC 503
o viele  PIDAT *.Akk.Pl NK 503
o junge  ADJA Pos.*.Akk.Pl.St NK 503
o Komponisten  NN Masc.Akk.Pl.* NK 503
o im  APPRART Dat.Masc AC 504
o Crossover-Stil  NN Masc.Dat.Sg.* NK 504
o .  $. -- -- 0
o #500 NP -- GR 505
o #501 NP -- OA 506
o #502 NP -- GR 507
o #503 PP -- MO 509
o #504 PP -- MO 509
o #505 NP -- SB 508
o #506 VP -- OC 508
o #507 NP -- SB 509
o #508 S -- MO 509
o #509 S -- -- 0
```

Here, morphological information is given in columns whereas syntactic relations are to be found at the end of each sentence, pointed to by numbered marks in the lines. A notational variant of this and other tree banks is the TIGER format, which, together with corresponding software, provides a very comfortable graphical user interface.[9]

Researchers, confronted with this situation – missing standards, varying structures, tagsets and annotations, occasional changes of all this made by the creators of a corpus due to new interests or just changing popularity of tools – may be tempted to claim standardisation efforts. In fact, there are always initiatives towards a standardisation of corpus ‘formats’, and corresponding transformation tools are created.

9. www.ims.uni-stuttgart.de/projekte/TIGER/TIGERSearch/doc/html/TigerXML.html

However, as experience teaches us, any currently ‘modern format’ will be tomorrow’s ‘obsolete’ or ‘legacy’ format, and new initiatives will arise. The real problem is that there *is* no universal format for all kinds of data and information and for all kinds of research interest. Moreover, large numbers of corpora will never be touched for ‘modernisation’ because the owners cannot, or do not want to, invest the effort. And even more importantly, they may have invested a lot of time, money, and effort in the creation of software tools specific to just that currently used format and would now have to change them too – without any benefit to themselves. As a consequence, as long as there are no universal interfaces on the basis of the concept of “corpus as an abstract data structure” (cf. Köhler 2005), empirical research in quantitative linguistics will always rely on programming tools which must be individually adapted to the given question (scientific hypothesis or technical application) and the given corpus.

When syntactic information is to be acquired, special emphasis is recommended for the selection of algorithms and data structures applied in the program. More often than not, programmers try to treat an annotated corpus just as a stream of symbols, a decision which may lead to overly complicated dynamic pointer structures and convoluted, hence expensive and error-prone programs while simple concepts from automata theory might have helped creating small, safe, and fast-running programs. The situation is, of course, ideal if the linguist has enough knowledge of programming theory and practice to do the job without any help, but this is not always the case. Non-linguist programmers should, therefore, be carefully introduced into the nature of the data (e.g., that the data need not be parsed because they represent the result of parsing; instead, a push-down automaton controlled by the opening and closing brackets in the data will do in most cases).

3.4 Syntactic phenomena and mathematical models

3.4.1 Sentence length

Sentence length, measured in terms of the number of words, has been an object of quantitative studies since the end of the 19th century. The first researcher to statistically and methodically investigate this property was, as far as we know, L.A. Sherman (1888). He tried to find systematic differences among the mean sentence lengths of texts and authors hoping to be able to contribute in this way to the field of rhetoric. Most work on sentence length was devoted to stylistics (stylometry) until in the beginning of the 20th century interest grew in the search for adequate models of sentence length distribution. Best (2005) gives an account of the development over these years: several probability distributions were proposed, most of which lacked theoretical justification and linguistic interpretability or failed to agree with empirical data. Williams (1939) proposed the lognormal distribution, whereas Sichel (1971; 1974) favoured the composed Poisson distribution; both solutions are good descriptive models of sentence length data but fail to be useful in terms of theoretical interpretability.

With the advent of modern quantitative linguistics, a theory-driven approach was propounded (Altmann 1988b), based on the general assumption that the relative difference between the probabilities of neighbouring length classes is a function of the probability of the first of the two given classes. Thus, if the observed sentence length, sentence have been pooled into class $x = 1$ (say, sentence lengths from 1 to 5), class $x = 2$ (sentence lengths from 6 to 10) etc., the probability of sentences of lengths 11 to 15 (class $x = 3$) will depend on the probability of class $x = 2$, and the probability of this class will, in turn, depend on the probability of the preceding class $x = 1$. This specific function is composed of factors and terms which represent the influences of speakers, of hearers, and of text parameters. In its most general form the function takes account also of the effects of intervening levels of linguistic analysis depending on how sentence length, sentence is measured (directly in terms of clauses or indirectly e.g., in terms of words or phrases). These considerations and their mathematical formulation yields the 1-displaced negative binomial distribution (3.1) if sentence length is measured in terms of the number of clauses and the 1-displaced negative hyper-Pascal distribution (3.2) if the measurement is indirect:

$$P_x = \binom{k+x-2}{x-1} p^k q^{x-1}, \; x = 1,2,\ldots \qquad (3.1)$$

$$P_x = \frac{\binom{k+x-2}{x-1}}{\binom{m+x-2}{x-1}} q^{x-1} P_1 \,, \; x = 1,2,\ldots \tag{3.2}$$

These theoretical probability distributions are very satisfactory from a linguistic point of view and proved to fit the corresponding data with good results. The models are useful not only for scientific purposes but also for practical applications such as authorship attribution, text classification, the measurement of text comprehensibility, forensic linguistics etc. – cf. Kelih and Grzybek (2005), Kelih et al. (2005).

3.4.2 Probabilistic grammars and probabilistic parsing

Statistical information has impressively proved its usefulness particularly for the automatic syntactic analysis (parsing) of linguistic mass data. This kind of information can be used for

1. Assigning probabilities to sequences of symbols, i.e. to word strings and sentences (language model);
2. Narrowing down the parser's search space to the *n* best hypotheses (increase of efficiency);
3. Selecting the best structural description out of the set of alternative ones (disambiguation).

The simplest method for incorporating statistical information is the assignment of probabilities to the elementary objects of syntax, i.e. to rules or trees. These probabilities are either approximated on the basis of relative frequencies of these objects in a parsed corpus (treebank) or using appropriate techniques such as the EM algorithm. In this way, a probabilistic variant can be generated for any conventional type of grammar: there are, e.g. probabilistic context-free grammars, probabilistic Tree Adjoining Grammars, stochastic HPSG, etc. Furthermore, syntactic structures can be generated exclusively on the basis of statistical information about selected lexical and syntactic relations (dependency, lexical head, head-complement, head-adjunct, etc.) or can combine this information with the syntactic information that is available in form of rules or elementary trees.

We will not elaborate on this topic in this book as there exists sufficient literature about probabilistic grammars and probabilistic parsing and a wealth of publications from computational linguistics, where the application of quantitative methods such as probabilistic modelling and the use of stochastic techniques has become routine (cf. e.g. Naumann 2005a,b).

3.4.3 Markov chains

The 1950s and 1960s were characterised by pure enthusiasm for – on the one hand – and strict refusal of information theoretical models on the other hand. In this period also Markov Chains were discussed as means for models on the sentence level (cf. Miller and Selfridge 1950, Miller and Chomsky 1963, Osgood 1963). In particular, their psycholinguistic adequacy was a controversial subject. The following example of text generation on the basis of a Markov model is cited from Miller and Chomsky (1963):

(1) road in the country was insane especially in dreary rooms where they have some books to buy for studying Greek

Not all the arguments that played central roles at that time were sound and substantive; unproved statements and dogmas are everything that prevailed until today. But one thing is sure: one of the characteristic properties of syntactic structures, viz. recursive embedding, cannot be captured by means of pure Markov Chains. This kind of stochastic process can, of course, be enriched by mechanisms for recursive embedding and other forms can be constructed such as cascaded Markov Chains but these constructs are not Markov Chains any more so that the original debate may be considered pointless. Nevertheless, in applications of computational linguistics "*Hidden Markov Chains*" play an important role not only for phonetic-phonological speech recognition but also as simple probabilistic grammar models in various kinds of natural language processing.

3.4.4 Word classes

Words can, of course, be classified on the basis of a large number of different criteria. If we want to investigate words as elements of syntactic constructions, pure syntactic criteria should be taken as a basis. We will consider here parts-of-speech as such a system of word classes although in most cases (in computational linguistics as well as in corpus linguistics and often in quantitative linguistics, too) traditional part-of-speech classifications fail to satisfy clear and consequent, exhaustive and unambiguous criteria. For our purposes, we will put emphasis on methodological aspects; therefore, we can disregard these problems to some extent.

Numerous observations in quantitative linguistics show that the proportions between part-of-speech frequencies differ between individual texts, even between texts of one and the same author. Table 3.1 contains the numbers of occurrences (f_x) of traditional parts-of-speech in two German texts, written by Peter Bichsel: *Der Mann, der nichts mehr wissen wollte* (Text 1), and *Und sie dürfen sagen, was sie wollen* (Text 2).[10]

Table 3.1: Frequencies of parts-of-speech in two texts by Peter Bichsel

Text 1			Text 2		
Part-of-speech	Rank	f_x	Part-of-speech	Rank	f_x
Verb (V)	1	313	Noun (N)	1	229
Pronoun (PRON)	2	262	Verb (V)	2	172
Adverb (ADV)	3	193	Determiner (DET)	3	144
Noun (N)	4	163	Pronoun (PRON)	4	132
Conjunction (CONJ)	5	150	Adjective (ADJ)	5	120
Determiner (DET)	6	104	Adverb (ADV)	6	89
Adjective (ADJ)	7	56	Preposition (PREP)	7	80
Preposition (PREP)	8	45	Conjunction (CONJ)	8	79
Interjection (Int)	9	1			

The table shows that not only the absolute frequencies of the parts-of-speech differ among the texts but also the rank orders: in the first text, verbs are the most frequent words whereas the second text has

10. The data were taken from Best (1997).

more nouns than verbs etc. Best (1997) determined the frequencies of parts-of-speech in ten narrative German texts and obtained the following ranks:

Table 3.2: Ranks of parts-of-speech in ten texts

Text	N	V	ADJ	ADV	DET	PRON	PREP	CONJ
1	4	1	7	3	6	2	8	5
2	1	2	5	6	3	4	7	8
3	1	2	7	3	4	5	6	8
4	3	1	7	2	5	4	8	6
5	1	2	5	3	4	6	7	8
6	1	2	8	3	4	5	6	7
7	3	1	5	4	7	2	8	6
8	1	2	5	7	3	4	6	8
9	1	2	4	7	6	3	8	5
10	2	1	7	4	5	3	8	6

Table 3.2 seems to suggest that the rank orders of the parts-of-speech differ considerably among the texts, which could be interpreted as an indicator that this is a suitable text characteristic for, e.g., text classification or stylistic comparison. However, valid conclusions can only be drawn on the basis of a statistical significance test, as the differences in the table could result from chance as well. An appropriate test is Kendall's (cf. Kendall 1939) concordance coefficient. We will identify the texts by $j = 1, 2, 3, \ldots, m$ and the word classes by $i = 1, 2, 3, \ldots, n$. t will stand for the individual ranks as given in the cells of the table and T_i for the sum of the ranks assigned to a word class.

Kendall's coefficient W can be calculated as

$$W = \frac{12 \sum_{i}^{n} (T_i - \bar{T})^2}{m^2(n^3 - n) - mt} \tag{3.3}$$

where

$$\bar{T} = \frac{1}{n} \sum_{i=1}^{n} T_i$$

and

$$t = \sum_{j=1}^{m} \sum_{k=1}^{s_j} (t_{jk}^3 - t_{jk}) ,$$

where s_j is the number of equal ranks among word classes in a text:

$$s_j = \sum_k t_{jk} .$$

In our case, equal ranks are very unlikely. Best (1997) calculated W for Table 3.2 and obtained $W = 0.73$ and $\chi^2 = 51.17$ with 7 degrees of freedom; the differences between the ranks are significant and cannot be regarded as a result of random fluctuations. An alternative, which should be preferred at least for small values of m and n, is a significance test using the F-statistic

$$F = (m-1)W/(1-W) ,$$

which is asymptotically distributed like F with $v_1 = n - 1 - (2/m)$ and $v_2 = v_1(m-1)$ degrees of freedom[11] and is reported to be more reliable than χ^2.

A deeper analysis of such data can be achieved by studying the frequency distributions instead of the ranks only. The first to set up a hypothesis on the proportion of word class frequencies was Ohno (cf. Mizutani 1989); he assumed that these proportions are constant over time in a language. A number of researchers presented attempts at modelling these distributions by means of theoretical probability distributions. In many cases, the Zipf-Alekseev distribution[12] yielded good results (Hammerl 1990). Schweers and Zhu (1991) showed that the negative hypergeometric distribution is more flexible and can be fitted to data from several languages. Best (1997) applies another method, which was developed by Altmann (1993). Instead of a probability distribution, a functional approach is used. Frequency y of a rank x is predicted by the formula

11. Cf. Legendre (2011).
12. Sometimes erroneously called "Zipf-Dolinsky distribution".

$$y_x = \frac{\binom{b+x}{x-1}}{\binom{a+x}{x-1}} y_1, \; x = 1,2,\ldots,k. \tag{3.4}$$

Here, degrees of freedom do not play any role; goodness-of-fit is tested with the help of the determination coefficient.

Best obtained very good results for the ten texts under study. The determination coefficients varied from $0.9008 \leq R^2 \leq 0.9962$; just one of the texts yielded a coefficient slightly below 0.9: Günter Kunert's *Warum schreiben?* yielded $R^2 = 0.8938$. The absolute (f_r) and relative ($f_{r\%}$) empirical frequencies of one of the texts – Peter Bichsel's *Der Mann, der nichts mehr wissen wollte* – are presented in colummns 3 and 4 of Table 3.3; the last column gives the theoretical relative frequencies ($\hat{f}_{r\%}$) as calculated by means of formula (3.4), the corresponding determination coefficient is $R^2 = 0.9421$.

Table 3.3: Frequencies of parts-of-speech in Peter Bichsel's *Der Mann, der nichts mehr wissen wollte*

Part of speech	Rank	f_r	$f_{r\%}$	$\hat{f}_{r\%}$
Verb (V)	1	313	24.32	24.32
Pronoun (PRON)	2	262	20.36	18.62
Adverb (ADV)	3	193	15.00	14.39
Noun (N)	4	163	12.67	11.21
Conjunction (CONJ)	5	150	11.60	8.81
Determiner (DET)	6	104	8.08	6.97
Adjective (ADJ)	7	56	4.35	5.56
Preposition (PREP)	8	45	3.50	4.46
Interjection (INT)	9	1	0.08	3.60

Recently, an alternative has been proposed in (Popescu, Altmann and Köhler 2009). It is similar to the aforementioned one in that the model has the form of a function but it is based on the assumption that linguistic data are, in general, composed of several layers ('strata'). In the case of word class frequencies, these strata could reflect influences of, say grammatical, thematic, and stylistic factors. For each of the possible strata, a term with specific parameters is introduced in the formula. The relation between rank and frequency is assumed to be exponential, i.e., with a constant relative rate of (negative) growth, cf. function (3.5). The constant term (here 1) corresponds to the smallest frequency.

$$f_r = 1 + \sum_{i=1}^{k} A_i \exp(-r/r_i) \tag{3.5}$$

We present and use the model here in a modified and simpler form, cf. formula (3.6).

$$y = ae^{bx} + ce^{dx} \tag{3.6}$$

Fitting this model to the data in Table 3.3 yields, with a determination coefficient of $R^2 = 0.9568$, an even better result than model (3.5) although only the first exponential term was used (cf. Figure 3.1).

There is a very easy way to determine the number of terms needed for a data set: those terms whose parameters are identical with the parameters of a preceding term are superfluous. Also the fact that the determination coefficient does not change if a term is removed is a perfect indicator.

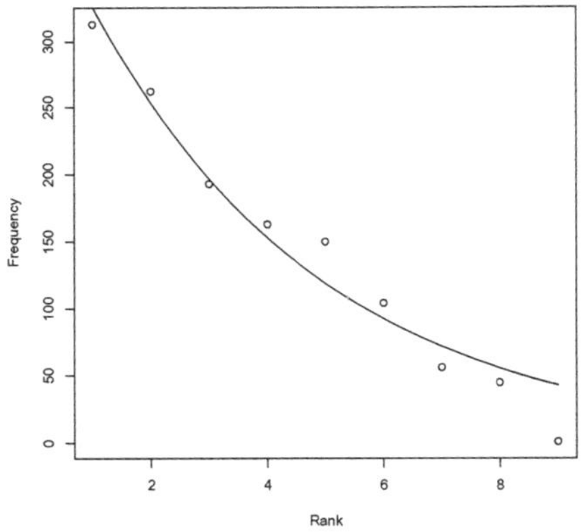

Figure 3.1: Plot of function (3.6) as fitted to the data in Table 3.3

A recent study in which the model (3.5) was tested on data from 60 Italian texts can be found in Tuzzi, Popescu and Altmann (2010, 116ff.). More studies of part-of-speech distributions in texts have been published by several authors, among them Best (1994, 1997, 1998,

2000, 2001), Hammerl (1990), Schweers and Zhu (1991), Zhu and Best (1992), Ziegler (1998, 2001), Ziegler and Altmann (2001).

Now, we will present an example where more than one exponential term is needed. The syntactically annotated corpus of Russian[13] differentiates relatively few parts-of-speech; e.g., all kinds of non-inflecting word classes are tagged as "PART" (particle).

Therefore, it seems likely that the distribution of these tags displays more than one stratum. For a randomly chosen text from the corpus, we obtain the rank-frequency distribution shown in Table 3.4.

Table 3.4: Rank-frequency distribution of the parts-of-speech in a Russian text

Rank	1	2	3	4	5	6	7	8	9
Frequency	182	63	54	50	19	14	11	10	4

Fitting model (3.5) with one, two, three, and four exponential terms yields the better values of the determination coefficient the more terms we use (cf. Table 3.5).

Table 3.5: Adjusted coefficients of multiple determination (ACMD) and estimated parameters of function 3.6 with one to four exponential terms

Number of exponential terms		1	2	3	4
ACMD		0.9322	0.9752	0.9702	0.9942
	a_1	326.7518	135.2902	9105.0244	−7487.1539
	b_1	−0.6619	−0.3662	−0.1266	−1.1530
	a_2		34849502.6000	−8999.6489	1627.4647
	b_2		−12.9334	−0.1253	−0.8643
	a_3			431819.9600	6072.0465
	b_3			−8.4131	−1.6684
	a_4				1686.3195
	b_4				−0.8637

13. SYNTAGRUS: A Corpus of Russian Texts Syntactically Annotated with Dependency Trees, developed by the Laboratory of Computational Linguistics of the Institute for Problems of information Transfer of the Russian Academy of Sciences, Moscow.

Figures 3.2a–3.2d offer plots of function (3.6) with varying numbers of exponential terms as fitted to the data from Table 3.4: the figures show very clearly the stratification of the data and also the stepwise improvement of the function behaviour with respect to the configuration of the data elements.

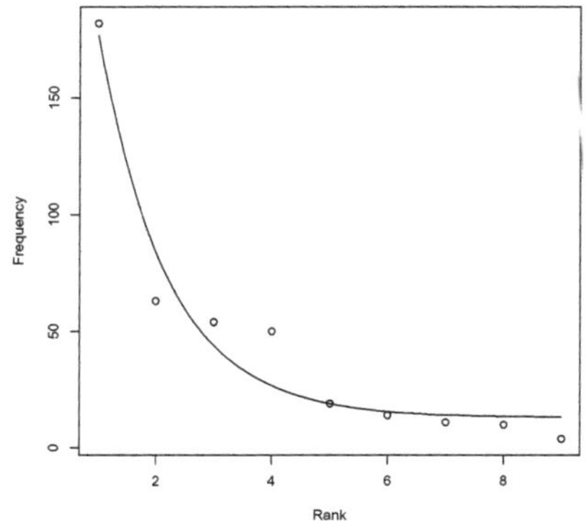

(a) One term

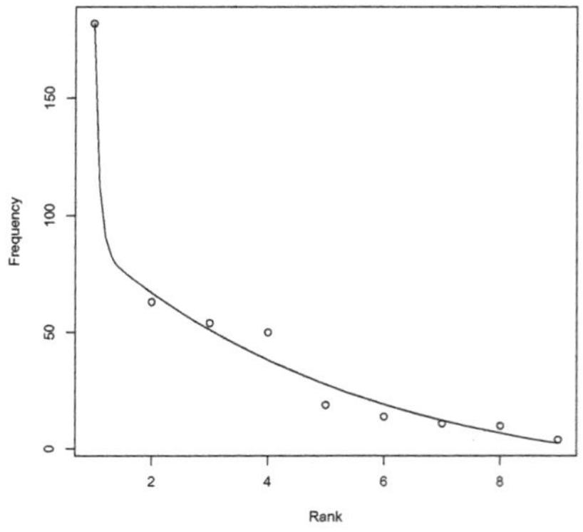

(b) Two terms

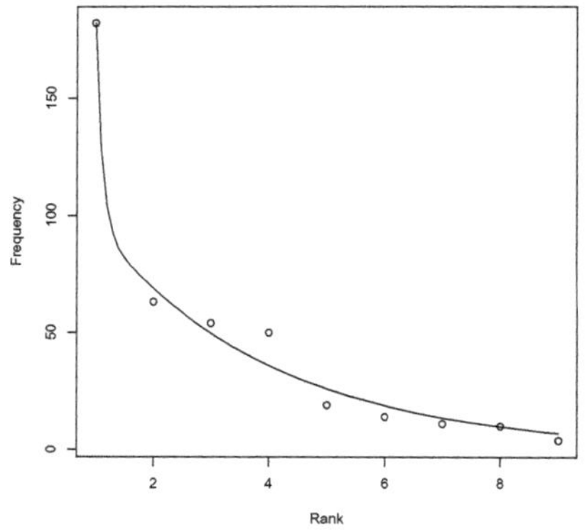

(c) Three terms

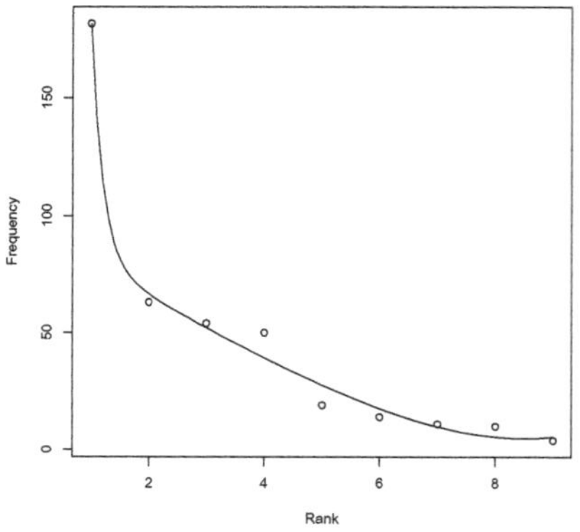

(d) Four terms

Figure 3.2: Plot with varying numbers of exponential terms

However, although the fourth exponential term brings another improvement of the determination coefficient and a smoother fit of the function to the data there are important reasons why to reject the model with four terms:

1. It is determined by eight parameters while it describes just nine data elements whence the model has almost no descriptive advantage over the original data.[14]
2. We see that in the four terms variant a_2 and a_4 as well as b_2 and b_4 respectively are almost identical, a sign of redundancy.
3. We should be warned that an "abnormal" deviation from a model may be caused by modifications of the text after its completion either by the author himself or by editors, which could be considered as a case of manipulated data.

In general, models with more than three parameters (even if you have hundreds or thousands of data elements) are seldom useful in linguistics because already for two or three empirically determined parameters it may be hard to find plausible linguistic interpretations. As a rule, a model with an additional parameter which gives a better result than another model with fewer parameters need not be the better one. A small improvement of the goodness-of-fit characteristic is of little value if you have no idea what the extra parameter stands for. In our case, the situation is different insofar as model (3.5) or (3.6), respectively, is a (well grounded) series of two-parameter functions where the pair-wise addition of parameters does not introduce any principally new aspects. Nevertheless, a trade-off between the two criteria – improvement of the goodness-of-fit on the one hand and number of parameters on the other – might lead to prefer the model version with only two components.

Another problem with a focus on word classes was raised by Vulanović (cf. Vulanović 2008a,b; Vulanović and Köhler 2009); he investigates part-of-speech systems of languages from a typological point of view. Besides the questions as how to classify part-of-speech systems in the languages of the world, the development of a measure of efficiency of such systems are in the focus of Vulanović's research (Vulanović 2009).

Recently, a comprehensive cross-linguistic study of three properties of part-of-speech (in the following: PoS) systems in 50 languages was conducted departing from a classification of PoS systems as defined in

14. We must not forget, however, that the model is theoretically founded. Its main purpose is not to just describe a single data set but infinitely many data and, even more importantly, it does not only describe but it *explains* the behaviour of the data.

Hengeveld et al. (2004). The features considered were (1) the number of propositional functions a word class can express, (2) the number of lexeme classes in the PoS system, and (3) the presence or absence of fixed word order and morphological or syntactic markers, which are used to possibly disambiguate between the propositional functions in three contexts: the head of the predicate phrase vs. the head of the referential phrase, the head of the referential phrase vs. its modifier, and, finally, the head of the predicate phrase vs. its modifier (ibd., 304).

Table 3.6 shows the cross-linguistic sample with the classification[15] from Hengeveld et al. (HRS-type) and the features under study, where n = number of propositional functions, l = number of lexical classes, P&R = presence or absence of markers which distinguish predicate phrase and referential phrase, RefPh = presence or absence of markers which distinguish head and modifier of referential phrases, PredPh = presence or absence of markers which distinguish head and modifier of the predicate phrase; the table is taken from (Vulanović and Köhler 2009).

For all languages with the same values of n and l in Table 3.6, for which a plus or a minus is recorded in the relevant feature-column, the proportion y of languages with a plus is calculated. The data set obtained for each feature consists of ordered triples (n, l, y).

15. The question marks in Table 3.6 indicate classificational uncertainties in Hengeveld et al. (2004); see also the discussion in Vulanović and Köhler (2009).

Table 3.6: Cross-linguistic sample of 50 languages

n	*l*	Language	HRS type	P&R	RefPh	PredPh
	1	Samoan	1	+	+	+
	2	Mundari	1.5	+	+	+
	2	Hurian	2	+	+	+
	2	Imbabura Quechua	2	+	+	+
	2	Warao	2	+	+	+
	3	Turkish	2.5	+	+	+
	3	Ket	3	+	+	+
	3	Miao	3	+	+	+
	3	Ngiti	3	+	+	–
	3	Tidore	3	+	+	+
	4	Lango	3.5	+	+	+
	4	Abkhaz	4	–	–	+
	4	Arapesh	4	+	–	–
	4	Babungo	4	+	+	+
4	4	Bambara	4	+	+	+
	4	Basque	4	–	–	+
	4	Burushaski	4	–	–	–
	4	Georgian	4	–	+	+
	4	Hittite	4	+	–	+
	4	Hungarian	4?	–	+	+
	4	Itelmen	4	+	–	+
	4	Japanese	4	+	+	+
	4	Nama	4	–	+	+
	4	Ngalakan	4	–	–	+
	4	Polish	4	–	–	–
	4	Kayardild	4.5?	–	–	–
	4	Koasati	4.5	–	+	–
	4	Nasioi	4.5	–	–	+
	4	Paiwan	4.5	+	+	+
	4	Pipil	4.5	–	–	–
	4	Sumerian	4.5	+	–	+
	4	Garo	?	+	+	+
	1	Tagalog	?	+	+	
	3	Alamblak	5	–	–	
	3	Berbice Dutch	5	+	+	
	3	Guaraní	5	–	+	
	3	Kisi	5	+	+	
3	3	Oromo	5	+	+	
	3	Wambon	5	+	+	
	3	Gude	5.5	–	+	
	3	Mandarin Chinese	5.5	+	+	
	3	Nung	5.5	–	+	
	3	Tamil	5.5	–	+	
	3	West Greenlandic	5.5	–	+	
	2	Hixkaryana	6	–		
	2	Krongo	6	–		
2	2	Navaho	6	+		
	2	Nivkh	6	+		
	2	Nunggubuyu	6	–		
	2	Tuscarora	6.5	–		

Then, a three-dimensional generalization of the Piotrowski-Altmann law[16] is fitted to the data:

$$y = \frac{1}{1 + e^{an+bl+c}}. \tag{3.7}$$

Figure 3.3 displays the data given in Table 3.6 and the graph of function (3.7) in the case when y represents an average value for all three features, P&R, RefPh and PredPh.

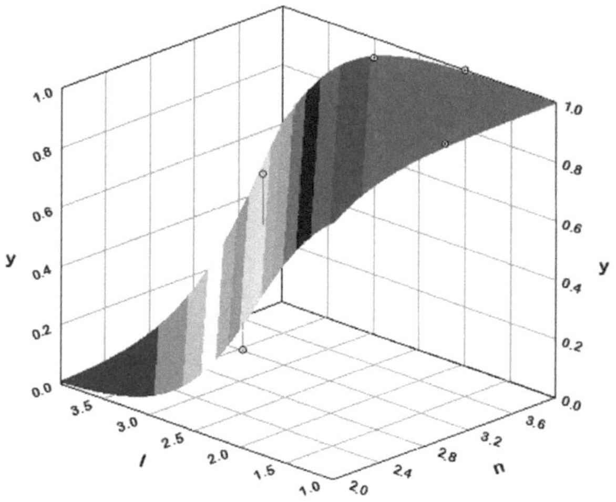

Figure 3.3: Plot of function 3.6 as fitted to the data resulting from Table 3.4. The diagram is taken from Vulanović and Köhler (2009).

Vulanović and Köhler (2009: 300) interpret this result as follows:

> The choice of the equation [...] is based on the following theoretical considerations. On the one hand, there are highly flexible languages of type 1, which have the greatest need for disambiguation between the four propositional functions. It is to be expected that each language of this kind has either fixed word order or a grammatical marker, or both, in all three contexts of interest. Therefore, the value of y should be 1 for this PoS system type. On the other hand, ambiguity is not theoretically possible in rigid languages. It

16. Piotrowski or Piotrowski-Altmann law is the name of the logistic function in quantitative linguistics. It is a model that has been confirmed by all applications to changes of the use of linguistic units over time (cf. Altmann 1983; Altmann et al. 1983).

is to be expected that they use fixed word order or markers even less if they have fewer propositional functions, like in type 6.5. In this type, y should be 0 in the P&R context. Moreover, if n is fixed and l increases, the need for disambiguation is diminished and y should therefore decrease. The other way around, if l is fixed and n increases, then there are more propositional functions to be disambiguated with the same number of lexeme classes, which means that increasing y values should be expected. In conclusion, y values should change in a monotonous way from one plateau to the other one, which is why this model was considered.

Moreover, the model could as well capture the diachronic development of languages from one extreme state towards the other pole; this hypothesis could be tested on data from languages of which descriptions from different periods of time exist.

3.4.5 Frequency spectrum and rank-frequency distribution

The frequency structure of a text or a corpus with respect to syntactic constructions can be determined in the same way as the frequency structure with respect to words by means of the well-known word frequency distributions.

Theoretical probability distributions usually are favored as a model when frequency structures are studied. With linguistic data, however, which often consist of thousands or more of data units specific problems may arise with distributional models. Such large samples can cause the Chi-square goodness-of-fit test to become unreliable or even fail in cases where a corresponding hypothesis may be confirmed on smaller data sets. Sometimes, the C statistics can be used instead but it may fail, too.

Yet, probability distributions are just one of the applicable mathematical model types. Another approach which is less problematic is the use of functions. This kind of model is tested by means of the determination coefficient in the same way as in case of hypotheses which model interrelations between two or more regular variables. This test does not depend on degrees of freedom and is stable also with extremely large data sets. In the following, probability distributions are applied where possible, in some cases, functions are used instead.

Figure 3.4: (Simplified) structure of a sentence beginning in the Susanne corpus

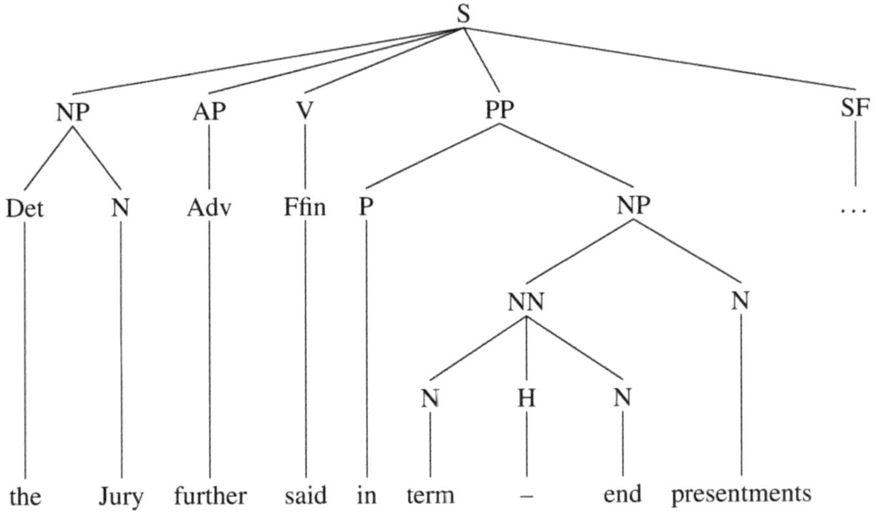

Rank-frequency distributions and the other variant, frequency spectra, have become known as "Zipf's Law" although this term is inappropriate in most cases because a large number of different mathematical models, as well as theoretical derivations, exist; only a specific version is due to Zipf.

Word frequency distributions have theoretical implications and they have found a wide field of applications. We will show here that this holds also for frequency distributions of syntactic units. In Köhler and Altmann (2000), frequency counts were conducted on data from the English Susanne and the German Negra corpus (cf. Section 2.3) in the following way: on all levels of embedding, the sequence of the immediate constituents of a given construction, as a pattern, was registered and considered as a basic unit, regardless of how the constituents were structured themselves. As an example consider the structure in Figure 3.4, where the pattern of immediate constituents (PIT) of the sentence (`S`) is `NP-AP-V-PP-SF`, and the PIT of the first `NP` is `Det-N`.

The number of PIT's with a given frequency x was counted in the entire corpus, which yielded a sample size of 10870 PIT's. The frequency distribution (spectrum) of all PIT's in the Negra-Korpus is shown in Figure 3.5. Fitting of the Waring distribution to the Negra data yielded a very good fit: $\chi^2_{DF=203} = 153.89, P(\chi^2) = 0.9958, C = 0.0142$, with parameter values $b = 0.7374$ and $n = 0.3308$. Since both criteria, $P(\chi^2)$ and C, show good values, the hypothesis that the frequency spectrum of syntactic constructions follows the Waring distribution is supported by the data. Figure 3.5 illustrates the results: both axes are logarithmic (X: frequency class, Y: number of occurrences).

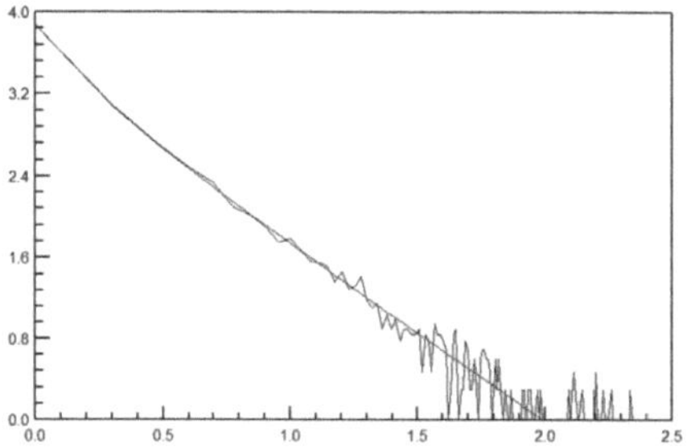

Figure 3.5: Fit of the Waring distribution to the Negra data

The observed distributions resemble the familiar word rank-frequency distributions and spectra; however, they are even much steeper than those. Both display a monotonously decreasing, very skew shape, a fact that has methodological consequences for the treatment of linguistic data. The skew distribution of unit frequency has direct and indirect effects on the distributions of other properties such as length, polysemy (ambiguity) etc. Symmetric distributions do practically not occur in linguistics, and even the expected deviations of observed data from the theoretical distributions and functions do not necessarily follow a normal distribution. Hence, regular methods and statistical tests from statistics textbooks are not automatically applicable to linguistic data.[17] Now we can see that the same kind of phenomenon appears also on the syntactic level.

Let us take a closer look at the top of the frequency spectrum. The details are as follows: of the 4621 different types of constituents with 90821 tokens, 2710 types occur only once; 615 of the rest occur twice; 288 types occur three times, 176 four times, etc. (cf. Table 3.7).

17. A fact which seems to be unknown in corpus linguistics and statistical natural language processing (with very few exceptions). Therefore, an unknown but certainly huge number of conclusions in these fields are likely to be invalid.

Table 3.7: The first four classes of the frequency spectrum (Susanne corpus)

Frequency of constituent type	Number of occurrences	Percentages
1	2710	58.6
2	615	13.3
3	288	6.2
4	176	3.8

In other words, around 60% of all the constituent types (or rules) correspond to but a single occurrence; 13% are used only two times. Just about 20% of all constituent types can be found more often than four times in a corpus. There is some practical potential in these findings. In analogy to word frequency studies, results may be useful for language teaching, the definition of basic and minimal inventories, the compilation of grammars and the construction of parsing algorithms, the planning of text coverage, estimation of effort of (automatic) rule learning, characterisation of texts etc.

It seems clear that grammarians have no idea how the effort which must be invested in setting up enough rules to cover a given percentage of text is affected by the distribution we presented here.

3.4.6 Frumkina's law on the syntactic level

One of the basic kinds of word repetition in texts is their distribution in text blocks (cf. Altmann 1988: 174ff.): a text is segmented into adjacent passages of equal size; in each block, the frequency of the given word is counted.

Frumkina (1962) was the first to investigate the number of blocks with x occurrences of a given word, where x is considered a random variable. She started from the assumption that the Poisson distribution is an appropriate model of the corresponding probability; other authors (for details cf. Altmann 1988: 75) used the normal and the log-normal distributions.

Later, a theoretical derivation of the negative hypergeometric distribution was given, empirically tested, and baptised Frumkina's law by

Altmann (Altmann and Burdinski 1982; Altmann 1988: 175ff.). Meanwhile, many investigations of data from several languages have been conducted, and all of them have confirmed the negative hypergeometric distribution together with its special cases (the Poisson, binomial and negative binomial distributions) as an appropriate model of the frequency of occurrence of words in text blocks.

In Köhler (2001), a hypothesis was set up and tested which predicted the validity of the same law for the repetition of syntactic elements. However, a repetition pattern of identical elements was not expected; instead, construction types and the occurrence of instances of syntactic categories were taken as entities. Hřebíček (1998) had proposed a similar kind of study in connection with investigations concerning the Menzerath-Altmann law. Consequently, the segmentation of blocks and the definition of the appropriate block size have also to be based on the occurrence of categories regardless of the fact that they do not define unambiguous text positions in terms of terminal elements (words). In this first study, two kinds of categories were considered: clause types (viz. relative, infinitival, participle clauses) and function types (logical direct, indirect, and prepositional objects).

The text corpus used was again the Susanne corpus (cf. Sampson 1995). The corpus, or rather the grammar according to which the texts were analysed and tagged, differentiates the following clause types:

```
Complement Function tags

s logical subject
o logical direct object
i indirect object
u prepositional object
e predicate complement of subject
j predicate complement of object
a agent of passive
S surface (and not logical) subject
O surface (and not logical) direct object
G "guest" having no grammatical role within its tagma
```

```
Adjunct Function tags

p place
q direction
t time
h manner or degree
m modality
c contingency
r respect
w comitative
k benefactive
b absolute

Other Function tags

n participle of phrasal verb
x relative clause having higher clause as antecedent
z complement of catenative
```

In the first case – the frequency analysis of clause types – two alternative block definitions were applied:

1. each syntactic construction was counted as a block element,
2. only clauses were considered as block elements.

In the second case, each functionally interpreted construction, i.e. each function tag in the corpus, was counted as a block element. As the results presented in the next section show, the hypothesis that the categories analysed are block-distributed according to Frumkina's law was confirmed in all cases.

In order to form a sufficiently large sample, the complete Susanne corpus (cf. Section 2.3) was used for each of the following tests. As types of syntactic constructions are more frequent than specific words, smaller block sizes were chosen – depending on which block elements were taken into account, 100 or 20, whereas a block size of at least several hundred is common for words. The variable x corresponds to the frequencies of the given syntactic construction, and F gives the number of blocks with x occurrences.

For the first of the studies[18], all syntactic constructions were considered block elements; the negative binomial distribution with its parameters k and p was fitted to the data. The resulting sample size was 1105 with a block size of 100 elements. The details are shown in Table 3.8, and illustrated in Figure 3.6.

Table 3.8: Present and past participle clauses: fitting the negative binomial distribution

x_i	f_i	Np_i	x_i	f_i	Np_i
0	92	90.05	7	31	28.26
1	208	198.29	8	7	13.56
2	226	241.31	9	6	6.13
3	223	214.67	10	2	2.64
4	142	155.77	11	1	1.09
5	102	97.72	12	1	0.70
6	64	54.89			

$k = 9.4115,\ p = 0.7661$
$\chi^2 = 8.36,\ DF = 9,\ P(\chi^2) = 0.50$

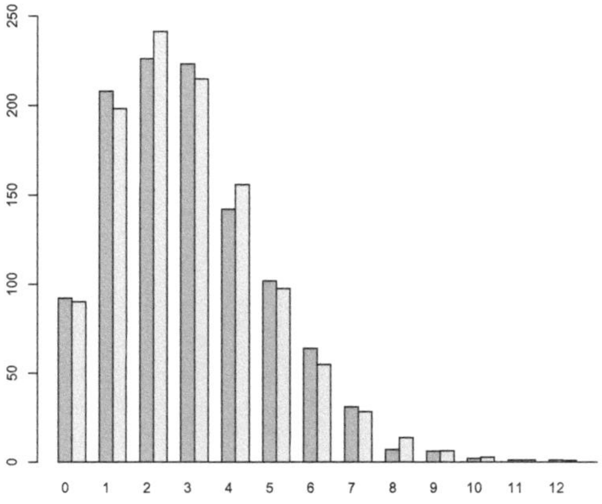

Figure 3.6: Plot of the distribution in Table 3.8

18. All calculations were performed with the help of the Altmann-Fitter (Altmann 1994).

Next, clauses were taken as block elements. As present and past participle clauses were counted, block size 20 was chosen. Table 3.9 and Figure 3.7 present the results of fitting the negative binomial distribution to the data (sample size: 976).

Table 3.9: Present and past participle clauses

x_i	f_i	Np_i	x_i	f_i	Np_i
0	55	54.26	7	37	35.02
1	143	139.78	8	17	17.68
2	205	194.66	9	3	8.34
3	181	194.26	10	5	3.76
4	148	155.53	11	1	1.58
5	102	106.12	12	1	1.04
6	78	64.03			

$k = 12.3413, p = 0.7912$
$\chi^2 = 9.33, DF = 10, P(\chi^2) = 0.50$

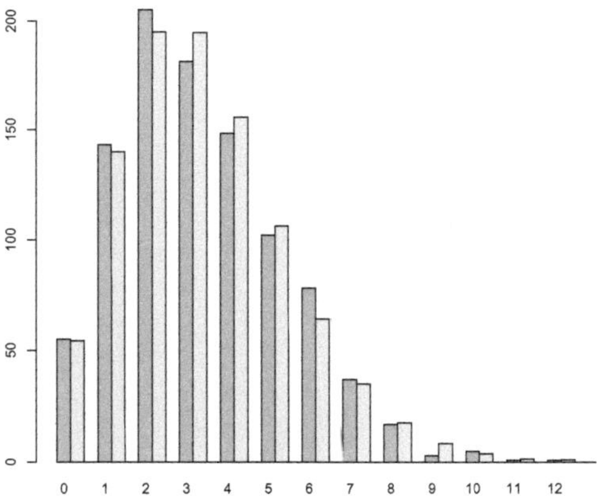

Figure 3.7: Plot of the distribution in Table 3.9

The number of blocks with x occurrences of relative clauses was investigated with all syntactic constructions as block elements. Block size was 100 in this case, sample size 1105, the hypothesis tested was again the negative binomial distribution. Table 3.10 and Figure 3.8 give the corresponding results.

Table 3.10: Number of blocks with x occurrences of relative clauses

x_i	f_i	Np_i	x_i	f_i	Np_i
0	368	376.54	5	17	16.17
1	366	352.73	6	4	5.87
2	208	208.95	7	2	2.03
3	94	99.78	8	1	0.68
4	44	41.93	9	1	0.32
$k = 3.7781$, $p = 0.0750$					
$\chi^2 = 2.08$, $DF = 5$, $P(\chi^2) = 0.84$					

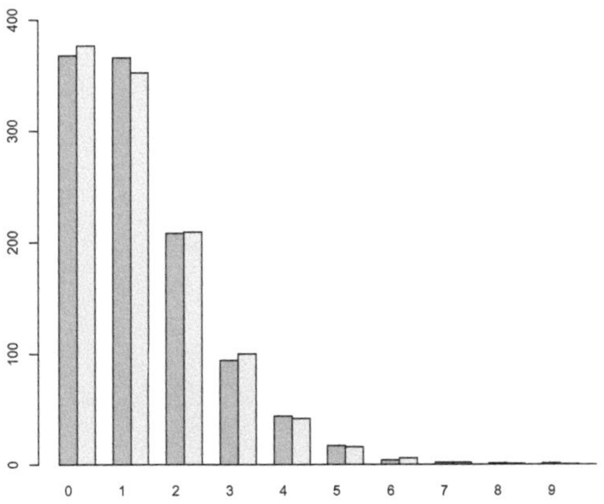

Figure 3.8: Plot of the distribution in Table 3.10

The next test of the negative binomial distribution concerns relative clauses with clauses as block elements. With a block size of 30, a sample size of 651 was obtained (cf. Table 3.11 and Figure 3.9).

Table 3.11: Number of blocks with *x* occurrences of relative clauses

x_i	f_i	Np_i	x_i	f_i	Np_i
0	105	113.44	6	12	17.06
1	170	164.23	7	11	8.24
2	165	145.31	8	5	3.81
3	92	101.33	9	3	1.7
4	57	61.15	10	1	1.28
5	30	33.46			

$k = 4.4941$, $p = 0.6779$
$\chi^2 = 8.84$, $DF = 8$, $P(\chi^2) = 0.36$

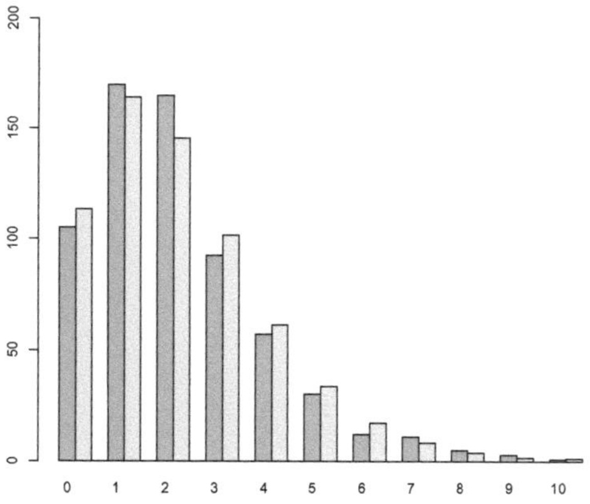

Figure 3.9: Plot of the distribution in Table 3.11

This time, infinitival clauses were scrutinized. All syntactic constructions served as block elements; the sample size was therefore again 1105. See Table 3.12 and Figure 3.10 for the results of fitting the negative binomial distribution to the data.

Table 3.12: Number of blocks with x occurrences of infinitival clauses

x_i	f_i	Np_i	x_i	f_i	Np_i
0	271	264.03	5	30	30.02
1	323	332.99	6	13	12.02
2	248	247.97	7	3	4.52
3	147	141.96	8	3	2.44
4	67	69.05			

$k = 5.5279$, $p = 0.7719$
$\chi^2 = 1.44$, $DF = 6$, $P(\chi^2) = 0.96$

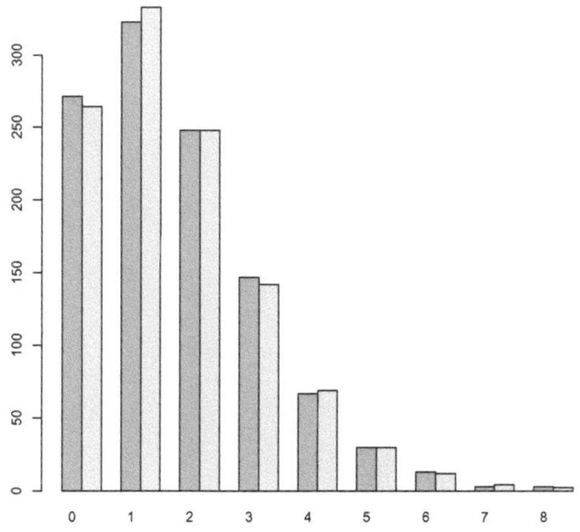

Figure 3.10: Plot of the distribution in Table 3.12

Fitting the negative binomial distribution to the number of blocks with x occurrences of infinitival clauses with clauses as block elements (block size 100 (sample size 1105), yielded the results shown in Table 3.13 and illustrated in Figure 3.11.

Table 3.13: Number of blocks with x occurrences of infinitival clauses

x_i	f_i	Np_i	x_i	f_i	Np_i
0	186	184.80	7	5	5.05
1	275	278.59	8	1	1.76
2	231	235.37	9	0	0.58
3	156	146.86	10	0	0.18
4	76	75.41	11	0	0.06
5	33	33.73	12	1	0.02
6	12	13.59			

$k = 8.2771,\ p = 0.8179$

$\chi^2 = 0.045,\ DF = 6,\ P(\chi^2) = 0.98$

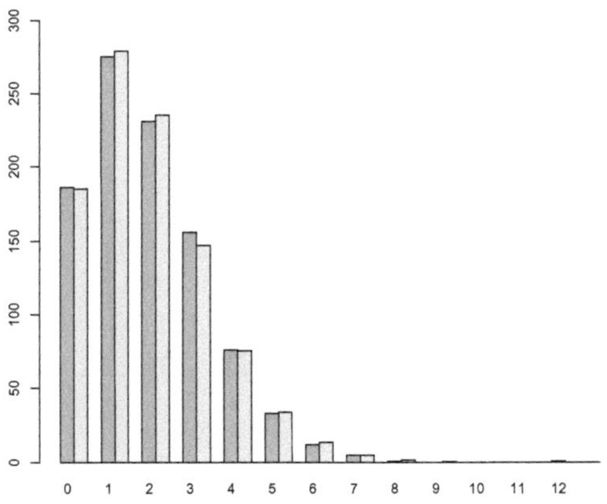

Figure 3.11: Plot of the distribution in Table 3.13

Prepositional objects yielded a somewhat less excellent yet nevertheless good result when the negative binomial distribution was tested with all syntactic constructions as block elements (block size 100, sample size 461), as can be seen from Table 3.14 and Figure 3.12.

Table 3.14: Number of blocks with x occurrences of prepositional clauses

x_i	f_i	Np_i	x_i	f_i	Np_i
0	58	57.5	6	15	18.64
1	101	98.22	7	13	9.92
2	98	100.39	8	1	5.03
3	88	79.64	9	5	2.46
4	56	54.08	10	2	2.13
5	24	33.01			

$k = 5.0853,\ p = 0.6641$
$\chi^2 = 11.08,\ DF = 8,\ P(\chi^2) = 0.20$

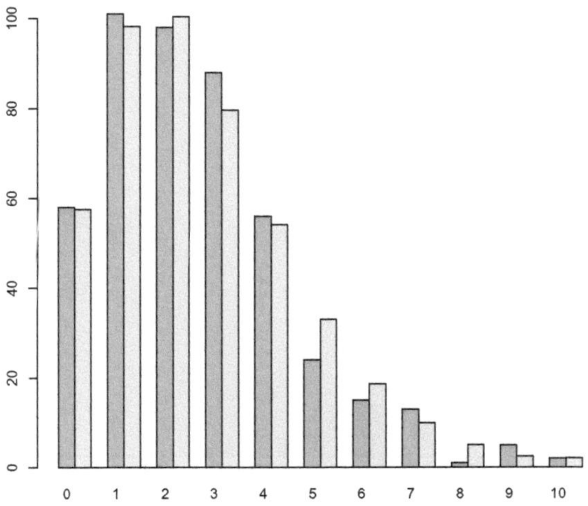

Figure 3.12: Plot of the distribution in Table 3.12

With the same block elements and the same block size as above, indirect objects were studied (sample size 461). The negative binomial distribution yielded a very good result, cf. Table 3.15 and Figure 3.13.

Table 3.15: Number of blocks with x occurrences of an indirect object

x_i	f_i	Np_i
0	298	296.92
1	109	108.73
2	34	37.05
3	14	12.31
4	5	4.04
5	0	1.32
6	1	0.63

$k = 1.1613,\ p = 0.6846$
$\chi^2 = 1.17,\ DF = 3,\ P(\chi^2) = 0.76$

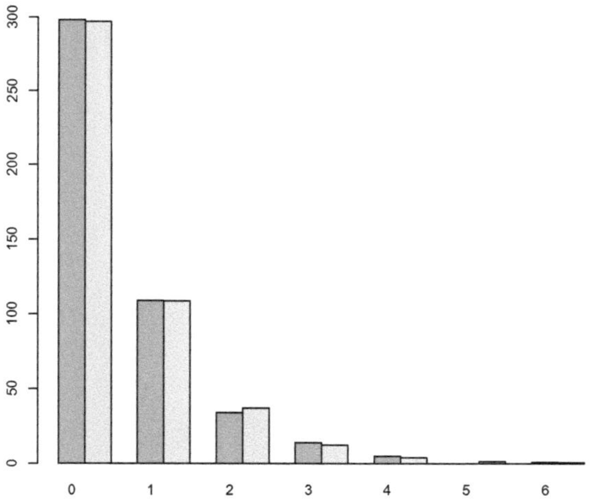

Figure 3.13: Plot of the distribution in Table 3.15

The more general negative hypergeometric distribution was required for logical direct objects; this distribution has three parameters (K, M, n). Sample size was 2304 (all syntactic constructions as block elements), block size was 20. The results can be seen in Table 3.16 and Figure 3.14.

Table 3.16: Number of blocks with x occurrences of a logical direct object

x_i	f_i	Np_i	x_i	f_i	Np_i
0	76	76.23	6	198	191.05
1	245	240.32	7	86	88.43
2	397	408.83	8	30	30.88
3	497	487.46	9	5	7.34
4	451	446.56	10	4	0.90
5	315	326.00			

$K = 19.8697, M = 6.9199, n = 10$
$\chi^2 = 1.45, DF = 6, P(\chi^2) = 0.96$

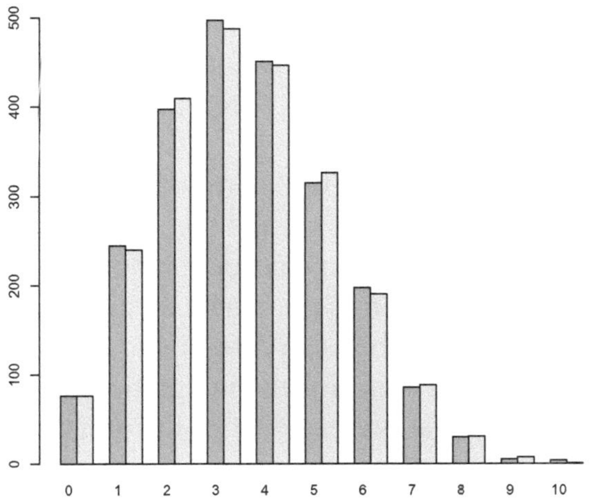

Figure 3.14: Plot of the distribution in Table 3.16

These results show that not only words but also categories on the syntactic level abide by Frumkina's law. In all cases (with the exception of the logical direct object) the negative binomial distribution could be fitted to the data with good and very good χ^2 values. In all these cases, the negative binomial distribution yielded even better test statistics than the negative hypergeometric distribution. Only the distribution of the logical direct object differs inasmuch as the more general distribution, the negative hypergeometric with three parameters, turns out to be the better model, with $P(\chi^2) = 0.9627$.

If future investigations – of other construction types and of data from other languages – corroborate these results, we can conclude that

1. Frumkina's law, which was first found and tested for words, can be generalised (as already supposed by Altmann) to possibly all types of linguistic units;
2. the probability of occurrence of syntactic categories in text blocks can be modelled in principally the same way as the probability of words.

However, for words, all four possible distributions are found in general (the negative hypergeometric as well as its special limiting cases, the Poisson, the binomial, and the negative binomial distributions). As both distributions found in this study for syntactic constructions are waiting time distributions, a different theoretical approach may be necessary.

At present, full interpretation or determination of the parameters is not yet possible. Clearly, block size and the simple probability of the given category have to be taken into account but we do not yet know in which way. Other factors, such as grammatical, distributional, stylistic, and cognitive ones are probably also essential.

Another open question concerns the integration of Frumkina's law, which reflects the aggregation tendency of the units under study, into a system of text laws together with other laws of textual information flow. A potential practical application of these findings is that certain types of computational text processing could profit if specific constructions or categories can be differentiated and found automatically by their particular distributions (or, by the fact that they do not follow expected distributions) – in analogy with text characteristic key words.

3.4.7 Type Token Ratio

In a similar way as described in the preceding section, the TTR index, which is also well-known from regularities on the word level, can be taken as an archetype for an analogous study on the syntactic level. In Köhler (2003a,b), corresponding investigations were performed; as opposed to the case of Frumkina's law, however, a different mathematical model than the one used for word TTR is needed here.

The simplest way of looking at the relation between types and tokens of a linguistic entity is the ratio of the number of types in a text and the number of tokens; the latter is identical with text length measured in terms of running entities, e.g. words. Traditionally, this index was used by philologists as a stylistic characteristic of texts, text sorts, or authors, and believed to represent vocabulary richness in a way which enabled them to compare texts to each other and even to identify individual authors in cases of disputed authorship. This approach is problematic for several reasons; the most important ones are (1) that this kind of TTR index depends heavily on the individual text length and (2) that the statistical properties of the index are unknown, which makes comparison on the basis of significance tests of observed differences absolutely impossible.

These and other reasons led a number of researchers to investigate the dynamics of vocabulary growth in the course of the texts instead of using a single number as a measure of a whole text. The corresponding procedure is simple, too: At each text position, i.e. token by token, the number of types which occurred until the given position is determined. The series of pairs of token and type numbers constitute the empirical function, which can, of course, be represented by a curve (cf. Fig 3.15). Several approaches to arrive at a theoretical mathematical model of the type-token relation were presented (cf. Altmann 1988a: 86f.); we will illustrate only one of them, viz. the direct derivation of a function from theoretical textological considerations. The most interesting and at the same time most successful approach can be formulated as a simple differential equation which represents the assumption that new elements are introduced into a text at a constant relative increase rate (Tuldava 1980; Altmann, ibd.):

$$\frac{dT}{T} = b\frac{dL}{L}, \tag{3.8}$$

where L stands for text position (i.e. number of tokens), T – the number of types accumulated at this position, and b is an empirical parameter, which represents the growth rate of the text under study. The solution to this differential equation is the function (3.9):

$$T = aL^b. \tag{3.9}$$

Parameter a has the value 1 if – as in most cases – types and tokens are measured in terms of the same unit because the first token is always also the first type and because for $L = 1$, $1^b = 1$.

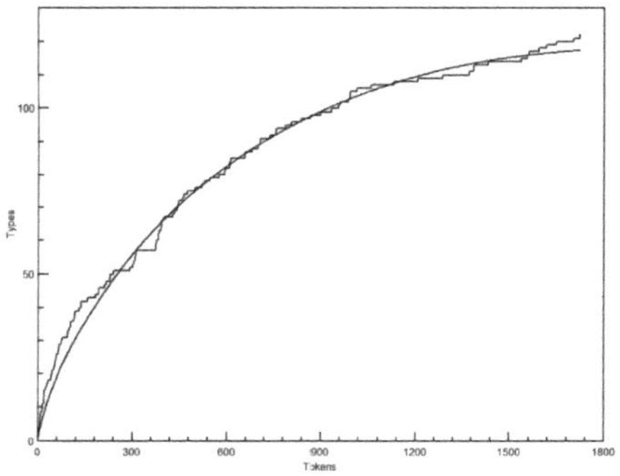

Figure 3.15: Empirical type-token function with matching theoretical curve (smooth line)

In this section we will show that analogous behaviour can be observed on the syntactic level. We choose again the Susanne corpus as data source and register begin and end of sentences, clauses, and phrases at each text position. Type-token counts of these items in the texts of the corpus yield in fact curves similar to the ones known from vocabulary growth and statistical tests confirm good fits of the mathematical model (3.9) to the data ($R^2 \approx 0.9$). But visual inspection (cf. Figure 3.16) suggests that there is a systematic deviation from what we expect and the values of parameter a (which should have[19] a value of $a \approx 1$) are too large (e.g. $a = 4.0958$ for text A01).

19. Text positions of syntactic structures are defined on the basis of the beginnings of any of the structures which are taken into account – no matter whether other structures interrupt them (discontinuities) or are embedded substructures.

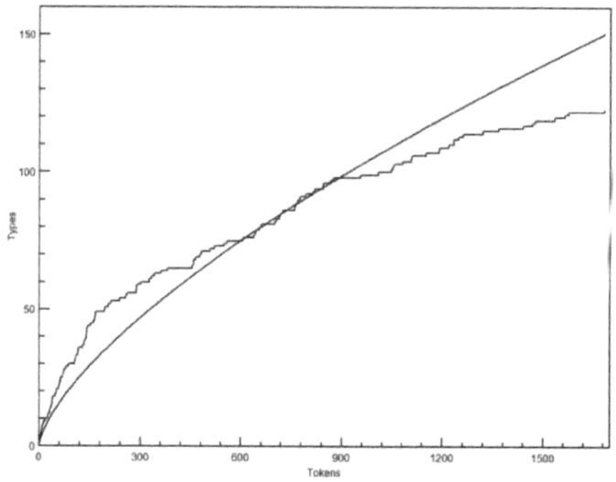

Figure 3.16: TTR of syntactic constructions in text A01 of the Susanne Corpus; the smooth line represents the hypothesis $T = L^b$

We have therefore to reject the hypothesis that syntactic units abide by formula (3.9). There are apparent reasons for a different behaviour of elements of this level, the most conspicuous being the difference in inventory sizes. While languages have inventories of millions of words, there are much less syntactic categories and much less syntactic construction types (by a factor of, say 1000), whence saturation (or put differently, exhaustion of the inventory) in the course of a text is much faster. Consequently, the coefficient b, which is responsible for the velocity of type increase, must be larger (which should arise automatically when the parameters are estimated from the data) and a retardation element is needed to balance the increased velocity in the beginning of the curve by a decelerating effect (which requires a modification of the model). Formula (3.8) can easily be modified correspondingly, yielding (3.10).

$$\frac{dT}{T} = b\frac{dL}{L} + c, \; c < 0. \tag{3.10}$$

The additional term, the additive constant c, is a negative number, of course. This approach, and its solution, function (3.11), are well-known in linguistics as Menzerath-Altmann law. It goes without saying that this identity is a purely formal one because there is neither identity in the theoretical derivation nor in the object of the model.

$$T = aL^b e^{cL}, \; c < 0. \tag{3.11}$$

The modified formula is not appropriate as a general model of syntactic TTR behaviour because it can take a non-monotonous, unimodal form. It provides, however, a suitable model of the mechanisms we are presently interested in. With $L = 1$ and $T = 1$, as required by the circumstances, a becomes e^{-c}:

$$T = e^{-c} L^b e^{cL} = L^b e^{c(L-1)}, \quad c < 0. \tag{3.12}$$

Fitting of this function with its two parameters to the data from the Susanne corpus yielded the results shown in Table 3.17: Subsequent to the text number, values for parameters a and b are given, as well as the number of syntactic constructions (f) and the coefficient of determination (R^2). As can be seen in Table 3.17, and as also becomes evident from the diagrams (cf. Figures 3.17a– 3.17c), the determination coefficients perfectly confirm the model.

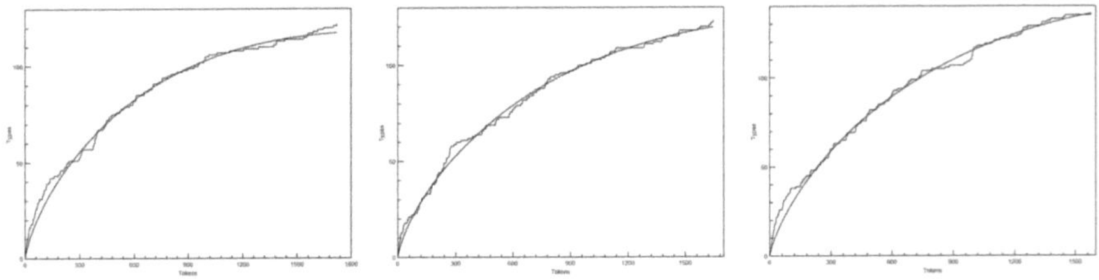

(a) Text N06 *(b)* Text N08 *(c)* Text G11

Figure 3.17: Fitting of function (3.12) to the type/token data from three different texts, taken from the Susanne corpus (cf. Table 3.17)

A general aim of quantitative linguistics is, after finding a theoretically justified and empirically corroborated model of a phenomenon, to determine, as far as possible, the parameters of the model. In most cases, parameter values cannot be determined on the basis of the theoretical model, i.e., from the linguistic hypothesis. But sometimes we can narrow down the possible interpretations of a parameter or even give a clear meaning and a procedure to find its value (cf. p. 81 where we show such a case in connection with syntactic function tag TTR).

As a first step, we can check whether the parameters of a model show any interdependence. At a first glance, the values of b and c in Table 3.17 seem to be linearly interrelated. Many empirical studies in

Table 3.17: Fitting function (3.12) to the type/token data from 56 texts of the Susanne corpus

Text	b	a	f	R^2	Text	b	a	f	R^2
*A*01	0.7126	−0.000296	1682	0.9835	*G*13	0.7080	−0.000315	1661	0.9763
*A*02	0.7120	−0.000350	1680	0.9681	*G*17	0.7610	−0.000382	1715	0.9697
*A*03	0.7074	−0.000321	1703	0.9676	*G*18	0.7781	−0.000622	1690	0.9705
*A*04	0.7415	−0.000363	1618	0.9834	*G*22	0.7465	−0.000363	1670	0.9697
*A*05	0.6981	−0.000233	1659	0.9884	*J*01	0.7286	−0.000478	1456	0.9641
*A*06	0.7289	−0.000430	1684	0.9603	*J*02	0.6667	−0.000246	1476	0.9714
*A*07	0.7025	−0.000204	1688	0.9850	*J*03	0.7233	−0.000491	1555	0.9762
*A*08	0.7110	−0.000292	1646	0.9952	*J*04	0.7087	−0.000378	1627	0.9937
*A*09	0.6948	−0.000316	1706	0.9784	*J*05	0.7283	−0.000468	1651	0.9784
*A*10	0.7448	−0.000474	1695	0.9691	*J*06	0.7154	−0.000504	1539	0.9902
*A*11	0.6475	−0.000112	1735	0.9612	*J*07	0.7147	−0.000353	1550	0.9872
*A*12	0.7264	−0.000393	1776	0.9664	*J*08	0.7047	−0.000287	1523	0.9854
*A*13	0.6473	−0.000066	1711	0.9765	*J*09	0.6648	−0.000286	1622	0.9870
*A*14	0.6743	−0.000187	1717	0.9659	*J*10	0.7538	−0.000590	1589	0.9322
*A*19	0.7532	−0.000456	1706	0.9878	*J*12	0.7188	−0.000333	1529	0.9878
*A*20	0.7330	−0.000487	1676	0.9627	*J*17	0.6857	−0.000393	1557	0.9385
*G*01	0.7593	−0.000474	1675	0.9756	*J*21	0.7157	−0.000589	1493	0.9461
*G*02	0.7434	−0.000417	1536	0.9895	*J*22	0.7348	−0.000466	1557	0.9895
*G*03	0.7278	−0.000323	1746	0.9938	*J*23	0.7037	−0.000334	1612	0.9875
*G*04	0.7278	−0.000323	1746	0.9938	*J*24	0.7041	−0.000294	1604	0.9958
*G*05	0.7406	−0.000391	1663	0.9809	*N*01	0.7060	−0.000239	2023	0.9863
*G*06	0.7207	−0.000318	1755	0.9515	*N*02	0.7050	−0.000314	1981	0.9527
*G*07	0.7308	−0.000423	1643	0.9106	*N*03	0.7308	−0.000410	1971	0.9656
*G*08	0.7523	−0.000469	1594	0.9804	*N*04	0.7291	−0.000339	1897	0.9854
*G*09	0.7312	−0.000490	1623	0.9351	*N*05	0.7143	−0.000314	1944	0.9770
*G*10	0.7255	−0.000413	1612	0.9863	*N*06	0.7245	−0.000368	1722	0.9920
*G*11	0.7304	−0.000296	1578	0.9928	*N*07	0.7170	−0.000295	1998	0.9748
*G*12	0.7442	−0.000358	1790	0.9903	*N*08	0.7327	−0.000387	1779	0.9506

the literature (in psychology, sociology, and sometimes also in linguistics) apply correlation analysis and use one of the correlation coefficients as an indicator of an interdependence of two variables but this method has severe methodological and epistemological disadvantages. We use regression analysis instead to test the hypothesis of a linear dependence $b = mc + d$ of one of the parameters on the other one. The resulting coefficient of determination yielded 0.6261 – an unsatisfying statistic.

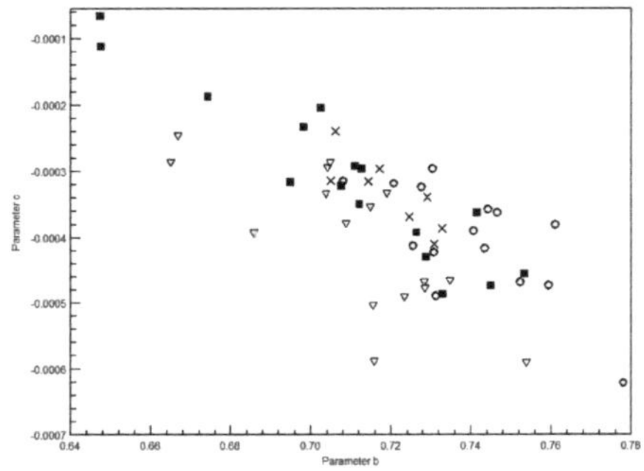

Figure 3.18: Interdependence of the parameters *b* and *c*; the symbols represent the four text sorts in the corpus

We cannot conclude that there is a linear relation between *b* and *c* although the data points in Figure 3.18 display a quasi-linear configuration. At least, they seem to form groups of points which might roughly indicate the text sort a text belongs to. Maybe a refined version of analysis can contribute to text classification using e.g. discriminant analysis.

Another kind of syntactic information, which is provided by some corpora, consists of syntactic function annotation. We will demonstrate on data from the Susanne corpus that also this kind of tag shows a specific TTR behaviour. The Susanne corpus differentiates the following tags for syntactic functions:

```
"Complement Function tags"

s logical subject
o logical direct object
i indirect object
u prepositional object
e predicate complement of subject
j predicate complement of object
a agent of passive
S surface (and not logical) subject
O surface (and not logical) direct object
G "guest" having no grammatical role within its tagma
```

```
"Adjunct Function tags"

p place
q direction
t time
h manner or degree
m modality
c contingency
r respect
w comitative
k benefactive
b absolute

"Other Function tags"

n participle of phrasal verb\index{sub}{verb}
x relative clause\index{sub}{clause} having higher
     clause as antecedent
z complement of catenative.
```

Each occurrence of one of these function tags was considered a token (and hence in the sequence as a text position). The function tags can be found in the last column of the Susanne representation and are marked by a ":" prefix. The following lines show two examples: the nominal phrase "several minutes" in lines `N12:0010c` to `N12:0010d` is marked as logical subject of the sentence ("`:s`") and the prepositional phrase in lines `N12:0010m` to `N12:0020c` as directional ("`:q`"):

```
N12:0010a -YB <minbrk>-[Oh.Oh]
N12:0010b -CSn When when [O[S[Fa:t[Rq:t.Rq:t]
N12:0010c -DA2q several several [Np:s.
N12:0010d -NNT2 minutes minute .Np:s]
N12:0010e -VHD had have [Vdf.
```

```
N12:0010f -VVNv passed pass .Vdf]
N12:0010g -CC and and [Fa+.
N12:0010h -NP1m Curt Curt [Nns:s.Nns:s]
N12:0010i -VHD had have [Vdef.
N12:0010j -XX +n<apos>t not .
N12:0010k -VVNi emerged emerge .Vdef]
N12:0010m -II from from [P:q.
N12:0020a -AT the the [Ns.
N12:0020b -NN1c livery livery .
N12:0020c -NN1c stable stable .Ns]P:q]Fa+]Fa:t]
N12:0020d -YC +,-.
```

Formula (3.9) is inappropriate for this kind of phenomenon, similarly to the TTR of syntactic constructions. The function is too flat and fails to converge (cf. Figure 3.19). But here we cannot use function (3.12) instead, because the estimated parameters form a curve which decreases at the end of a text. A potential alternative is Orlov's function (cf. equation (3.13), the form which Baayen and Tweedie (1998) use to model the dependence of word TTR on text length L).

$$T = \frac{Z}{\log(pZ)}\frac{L}{L-Z}\log(L/Z), \tag{3.13}$$

where (in our notation) T is the number of types, p and Z are parameters, which have to be estimated from the data. Z is the so-called "Zipf's size", i.e. the text length which guarantees the best fit of Zipf's law to the word frequency data, and p is the maximum relative frequency in the given text.

Fitting is quite successful with respect to the coefficient of determination. However, some of the parameter values question the model: In 36 of 64 cases, the parameter estimation of p yields a number larger than 1, which is not compatible with the role of this parameter as a relative frequency; parameter Z, which is expected to stand for Zipf's size is estimated too low (by a factor of 10.000). This model cannot be adopted for our purposes, at least if we want to maintain the interpretation of the parameters.

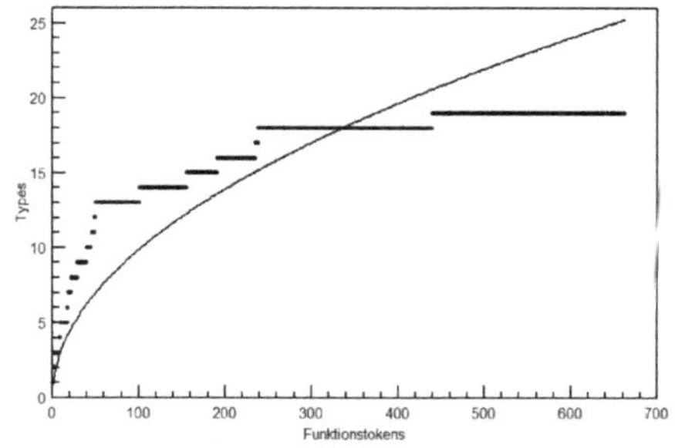

Figure 3.19: The TTR of the syntactic functions in text A01 of the Susanne Corpus. The smooth line represents formula (3.16); the steps correspond to the data. The diagram shows quite plainly the small size of the inventory and the fact that it takes longer and longer until a new type is encountered, i.e., that the inventory is soon exhausted

The fact that an inventory size of 23 syntactic functions is again smaller (by the factor 10) than that of the syntactic constructions, would appear to indicate that the differential equation must be modified once more. In equation (3.14) the additive term takes, instead of a constant, the form of a function of the inventory size:

$$\frac{dT}{T} = \frac{b}{L(aL+b)}dL = \left(\frac{1}{L} - \frac{b}{a+bL}\right) dL. \tag{3.14}$$

The general solution to this equation is

$$T = \frac{kL}{aL+b}. \tag{3.15}$$

The limit of this general solution when $L \to \infty$ is 1/a, whence $k = 1$. And with $T = 1$ at $L = 1$, the solution reduces to

$$T = \frac{L}{aL-a+1}. \tag{3.16}$$

This is one of the rare cases where the parameter of a model does not have to be fitted to (estimated from) the data but can be determined according to the theoretical model as the inverse value of the inventory size. This approach (we owe the idea to Gabriel Altmann) is successful also in the case of musicological entities, where inventories (of pitch, quantized duration and intensity values) are similarly small as compared to 'text' length – cf. Köhler and Martináková-Rendeková (1998: 532ff.).

Table 3.18 shows the text length (L), the parameter values for parameter a, and the coefficients of determination (R^2) for all the 64 texts of the Susanne corpus. The model can be considered as (preliminarily) confirmed for two reasons: in particular because the parameter a was estimated as if we had no prior theoretical knowledge, and the results conform remarkably to the theoretically expected value of $1/22 = 0.045$. The second reason is the acceptability of the values of the coefficient of determination, which vary from excellent over good to a few cases of moderate goodness-of-fit.

Figures 3.20a and 3.20b reveal the reason for the differences in the goodness-of-fit indicators. Figure 3.20a shows a good fit (with $R^2 = 0.9872$), Figure 3.20b one of the worst ($R^2 = 0.8001$).

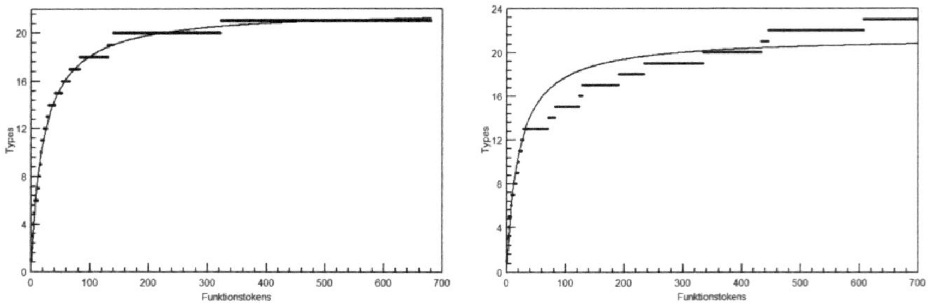

(a) Text J10 *(b)* Text G10

Figure 3.20: TTR curve of syntactic function tags in two texts

Apparently, the problem is not due to the model but to the possibly rather individually deviating dynamics of texts. The same phenomenon can be found with words. From a practical point of view, this behaviour does not appear as a problem at all but as the most interesting (in the sense of applicable) thing about TTR. There are, indeed, numerous approaches which aim at methods which can automatically find conspicuous spots in a text such as change of topic. At this moment, however, we cannot yet foresee whether syntactic TTR can also provide information about interpretable text particularities.

Table 3.18: Fitting results for the type/token data from 64 analyzed texts of the Susanne corpus

Text	L	a	R^2	Text	L	a	R^2
A01	662	0.0489849540	0.8154	J01	450	0.0525573198	0.8943
A02	584	0.0438069462	0.8885	J02	490	0.0546573995	0.7604
A03	572	0.0507712909	0.7864	J03	626	0.0487327361	0.9288
A04	586	0.0499810773	0.9143	J04	600	0.0495446316	0.7189
A05	689	0.0471214463	0.8454	J05	627	0.0494539833	0.7360
A06	606	0.0494782896	0.8710	J06	485	0.0489399240	0.8264
A07	574	0.0527951202	0.8790	J07	454	0.0552605334	0.9417
A08	662	0.0502591550	0.7711	J08	533	0.0524191848	0.9130
A09	584	0.0518121222	0.8823	J09	501	0.0533087860	0.6123
A10	680	0.0478617568	0.8461	J10	680	0.0457068572	0.9872
A11	634	0.0485004978	0.7371	J12	550	0.0482407944	0.9531
A12	755	0.0459426502	0.8825	J17	533	0.0481818730	0.9731
A13	649	0.0501875414	0.8679	J21	594	0.0541457400	0.8541
A14	648	0.0464558815	0.8262	J22	612	0.0463024776	0.9220
A19	649	0.0493071760	0.8436	J23	552	0.0432459279	0.8461
A20	624	0.0458766957	0.8109	J24	515	0.0446497495	0.8538
G01	737	0.0477366253	0.9260	N01	944	0.0489100905	0.8557
G02	607	0.0457507156	0.9130	N02	865	0.0471130146	0.9440
G03	626	0.0536206547	0.6775	N03	816	0.0516965940	0.8091
G04	747	0.0481523657	0.8106	N04	850	0.0463222091	0.9661
G05	647	0.0469292783	0.9481	N05	901	0.0462508508	0.8734
G06	768	0.0477997546	0.8849	N06	852	0.0461673635	0.9802
G07	630	0.0484196039	0.8955	N07	843	0.0494920675	0.8584
G08	648	0.0491887687	0.8849	N08	786	0.0489330857	0.8516
G09	625	0.0438939268	0.9534	N09	888	0.0478592744	0.9355
G10	698	0.0467707658	0.8001	N10	843	0.0460366103	0.9342
G11	686	0.0509721363	0.8889	N11	803	0.0514264265	0.9478
G12	804	0.0460735510	0.9615	N12	943	0.0447647419	0.8857
G13	667	0.0458765632	0.7797	N13	847	0.0438540668	0.9543
G17	738	0.0466041024	0.9631	N14	926	0.0489875139	0.8825
G18	613	0.0423246398	0.9346	N15	776	0.0468495400	0.8345
G22	685	0.0519459779	0.8216	N18	912	0.0454862484	0.8826

3.4.8 Information content

In Köhler (1984), a model of the human language processing mechanism was presented, which was designed for the derivation of the well-known Menzerath-Altmann law – cf. e.g., Altmann (1980), Altmann and Schwibbe (1989), Prün (1994), and Section 4.1.3 – from assumptions on properties of the human language processing mechanism. We call this model the "register hypothesis".

The Menzerath-Altmann law predicts for all levels of linguistic analysis that the (mean) size of the components of a linguistic construction is a function of the size of the given construction, measured in terms of the number of its components. This function, viz. $y = Ax^{-b}e^{-cx}$, where y denotes the component size, and x the size of the construction, has been confirmed on data from many languages, text genres, and styles. The basic idea of the register hypothesis can be characterized by two assumptions:

1. There is a special "register" – such as the hypothetical short term memory but not necessarily identical to it – for language processing, which has to serve two requirements: (1) it must store, on each level, the components of a linguistic construction under analysis until its processing has been completed, and, at the same time, (2) it must hold the result of the analysis – the structural information about the connections among the components, i.e. the connections between nodes and the types of the individual relations as well as – on the lowest level – pointers or links to lexical entries. This register has a limited and more or less fixed capacity (cf. Figure 3.21).
2. The more components the construction is composed of, the more structural information must be stored. However, the resulting increase in structural information is not proportional to the number of components, because there are combinatorial restrictions on each level (phonotactics, morphotactics, syntax, lexo- and semotactics), and because the number of possible relations and types of relations decreases with the number of already realized connections.

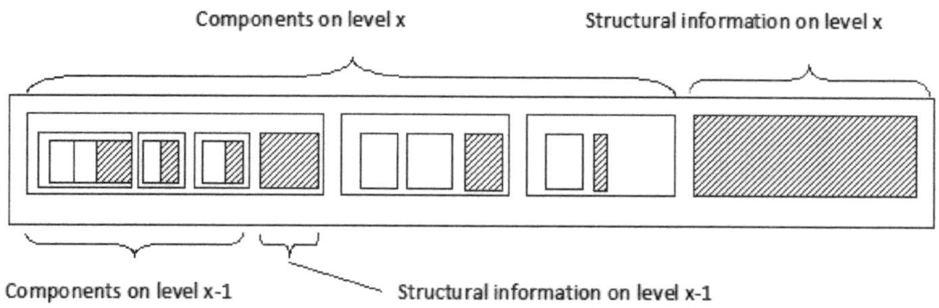

Figure 3.21: Language processing register: the more components, the more structural information on each level

A consequence of these two assumptions is that the memory space which is left in the register for the components of a construct depends on the number of the components, which means that there is, on each level, an upper limit to the length of constructs, and that with increasing structural information there is less space for the components, which must, in turn, get shorter.

As is well known, the Menzerath-Altmann law has been tested successfully on a large number of languages, different text types, various authors and styles, whereas the attempt at explaining this law with the register hypothesis is untested so far. At the time when this hypothesis was set up, there was no realistic chance to empirically determine from large samples the amount of structural information and its increase with growing size of the constructions – at least on the syntactic level, the most significant one for this question. The availability of syntactically annotated linguistic corpora makes it possible now to collect quantitative data also on this level and to investigate whether there is in fact an increasing amount of structural information in the sequence of the constituents of a construct, and whether the increase decreases 'from left to right' in a way which is compatible with the register hypothesis.

First data which could provide corresponding evidence were collected, evaluated, and published in Köhler (1999). In this paper, all sentences which occur in the Susanne corpus were investigated in the following way. At each position of a given sentence, from left to right, the number of possible alternatives was determined. This was done first with respect to structural alternatives, then with respect to functional alternatives.

Suppose, as an example, that a nominal phrase can begin with a determiner, a pronoun, a proper noun, and, say, five other constituents. Then, at position 1 of this construction type, 8 alternatives can be realized. Next, the number of alternatives at position 2 is counted and so forth. However, since we are not interested in the behaviour of individual construction types, the number of alternatives is determined with respect to position but regardless of the construction type. It is important to underline that the number of alternatives was counted conditionally, i.e. with respect to the realization of a component at the previous position.

The result of this investigation was that the number of (structural as well as functional) alternatives decreases with the position from left to right – with an exception at the second position of the sentence (which is plausible for English because this is where the finite verb must be expected with high probability).

Figure 3.22 shows the dependence of the logarithm of the number of alternatives at a given position in the sentence, since the logarithm can be used as a measure of information with respect to the alternatives.

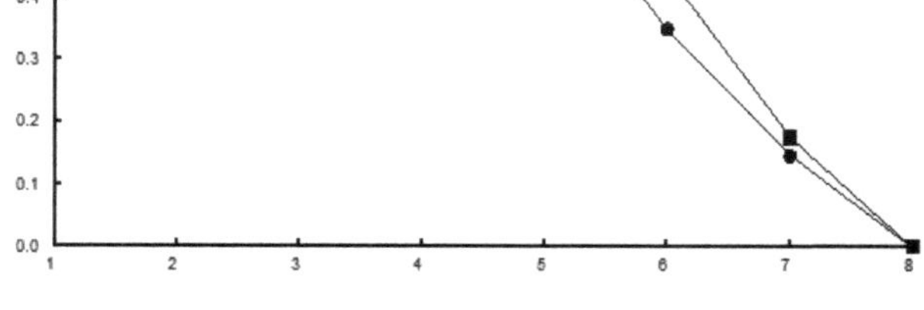

Figure 3.22: Logarithm of the number of alternatively possible constituent types and functions in dependence on the position (separately calculated for an individual text)

Figure 3.23 shows the logarithm of the numbers of alternatives when not only the sentence level is taken into account but, recursively, all the more than 100000 constructions in the corpus are analyzed and the alternatives are counted unconditionally, i.e. regardless of the component type at the preceding position, which has been done in the present study.

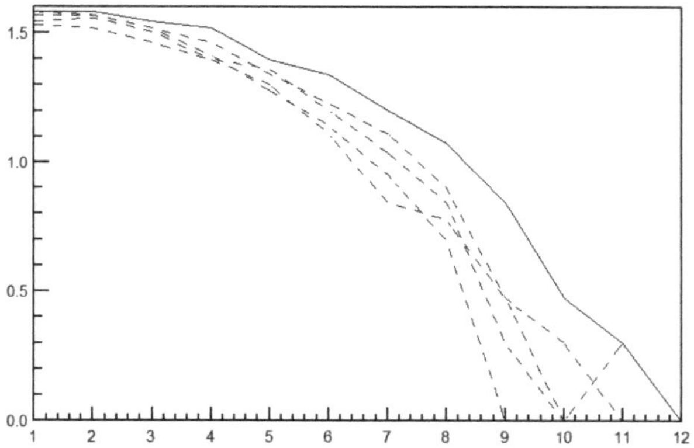

Figure 3.23: Logarithm of the number of alternatively possible constituent types in dependence on the position in the entire Susanne corpus (solid line) and in the four text types included in the corpus (dashed lines)

Both findings support the register hypothesis: with increasing position, i.e. with growing size of a construction, the structural information which has to be stored while processing the construction increases, while the amount of additional information decreases with each step. The logarithm of the number of alternatives, however, may not be the best measure of information, because it does not take into account that the individual alternatives may have a different probability. Thus, a situation where there are three alternatives, one of which has probability 0.98 and the others 0.01 each, is associated with much less information than a situation where all three alternatives are equally likely to be realized. The Tables on pp. 88ff. show the frequency and probability distributions of the structural alternatives at the positions in all constituents in the Susanne corpus; the symbols for the constituents as used in the corpus are explicated in Table 3.19.

Table 3.19: Symbols used for constituent types occurring in the Susanne corpus

Clause and phrase symbols			
S	Main clause	V	Verb group
F	Clause	N	Noun phrase
T	Participle, infinitive and other clauses	J	Adjective phrase
		R	Adverb phrase
W	*With* clause	P	Prepositional phrase
A	Special as clause	D	Determiner phrase
Z	Reduced relative	M	Numeral phrase
L	Misc. verbless clause	G	Genitive phrase

Terminal symbols			
a	Determiner, possessive pronoun	m	Number
b	*in order* introducing infinitive	n	Noun
c	Conjunction	p	Personal, interrogative, relative pronoun
d	Adjectival indeterm. Pronoun	r	Postnominal modifier
e	Existential there	t	Infinitival *to*
f	Affix, formula, code	u	interjection
g	*'s* genitive	v	verb
i	Preposition	x	*not*
j	Adjective	y	Hyphen etc.
l	Pre-co-ordinator	z	letter

The individual columns of the following table give the absolute frequencies (f) and relative frequencies ($\hat{p}$) of the constituent types (SC) at the indicated positions. Each column displays at the bottom the sum of the frequencies and the negentropy of the frequency distribution ($-H$). The head rows give the positions and the overall frequency of constituents (tokens) at the given position. The first column of each position sub-table gives the symbols of the constituents (cf. Table 3.19 above), the second one the frequency, and the third one the estimated probability of the constituent. The bottom rows give the entropy values which correspond to the frequency distributions given on p. 88ff.

Pos. 1			**Pos. 2**			**Pos. 3**			**Pos. 4**		
SC	*f*	$\hat{p}$	*SC*	*f*	$\hat{p}$	*SC*	*f*	$\hat{p}$	*SC*	*f*	$\hat{p}$
v:	16482	0.1630	N:	19943	0.2793	n:	7481	0.2432	P:	4321	0.3013
i:	15487	0.1531	n:	18655	0.2612	P:	5821	0.1892	N:	2727	0.1902
a:	14681	0.1452	V:	7567	0.1060	V:	5105	0.1660	n:	1380	0.0962
N:	7080	0.0700	v:	5232	0.0733	N:	4588	0.1491	F:	1136	0.0792
n:	6965	0.0689	j:	4836	0.0677	v:	1448	0.0471	T:	1131	0.0789
c:	6654	0.0658	P:	2834	0.0397	T:	1322	0.0430	R:	964	0.0672
r:	5887	0.0582	T:	1573	0.0220	R:	1287	0.0418	V:	826	0.0576
p:	5747	0.0568	R:	1528	0.0214	F:	1219	0.0396	S:	620	0.0432
V:	4813	0.0476	m:	1207	0.0169	J:	749	0.0243	J:	534	0.0372
j:	3637	0.0360	J:	1000	0.0140	j:	628	0.0204	v:	176	0.0123
d:	3249	0.0321	r:	798	0.0112	m:	145	0.0047	D:	88	0.0061
t:	1769	0.0175	F:	677	0.0095	D:	139	0.0045	j:	68	0.0047
R:	1572	0.0155	d:	667	0.0093	i:	131	0.0043	M:	53	0.0037
m:	1436	0.0142	x:	666	0.0093	S:	115	0.0037	Q:	46	0.0032
D:	1012	0.0100	g:	660	0.0092	M:	91	0.0030	W:	35	0.0024
P:	760	0.0075	i:	630	0.0088	r:	87	0.0028	I:	34	0.0024
G:	688	0.0068	p:	546	0.0076	f:	57	0.0019	A:	34	0.0024
S:	410	0.0041	a:	544	0.0076	L:	36	0.0012	m:	31	0.0022
T:	387	0.0038	D:	473	0.0066	d:	36	0.0012	r:	31	0.0022
I:	380	0.0038	f:	316	0.0044	Q:	33	0.0011	f:	30	0.0021
J:	353	0.0035	M:	306	0.0043	c:	31	0.0010	Z:	25	0.0017
F:	344	0.0034	c:	153	0.0021	Z:	30	0.0010	L:	21	0.0015
f:	284	0.0028	e:	141	0.0020	I:	27	0.0009	i:	8	0.0006
Q:	272	0.0027	S:	140	0.0020	A:	24	0.0008	p:	4	0.0003
M:	186	0.0018	I:	67	0.0009	e:	22	0.0007	a:	4	0.0003
e:	139	0.0014	G:	43	0.0006	p:	21	0.0007	U:	3	0.0002
l:	98	0.0010	O:	42	0.0006	W:	19	0.0006	e:	2	0.0001
C:	91	0.0009	z:	35	0.0005	z:	17	0.0006	x:	2	0.0001
x:	74	0.0007	A:	29	0.0004	x:	15	0.0005	G:	1	0.0001
O:	58	0.0006	l:	27	0.0004	G:	14	0.0005	c:	1	0.0001
L:	39	0.0004	Q:	20	0.0003	a:	11	0.0004	z:	1	0.0001
u:	33	0.0003	L:	17	0.0002	g:	5	0.0002	d:	1	0.0001
A:	28	0.0003	W:	12	0.0002	u:	5	0.0002	u:	1	0.0001
z:	14	0.0001	b:	10	0.0001	O:	2	0.0001			
b:	10	0.0001	u:	8	0.0001	l:	1	0.0000			
B:	10	0.0001	t:	7	0.0001						
W:	6	0.0001	Z:	5	0.0001						
U:	3	0.0000	X:	1	0.0000						
$\sum$	101138		$\sum$	71415		$\sum$	30762		$\sum$	14339	
$-H$	2.6199		$-H$	2.2359		$-H$	2.1711		$-H$	2.1774	

Pos. 5 SC	f	$\hat{p}$	**Pos. 6** SC	f	$\hat{p}$	**Pos. 7** SC	f	$\hat{p}$	**Pos. 8** SC	f	$\hat{p}$
P:	1516	0.3031	P:	369	0.2795	P:	65	0.2265	S:	14	0.2258
N:	798	0.1596	S:	253	0.1917	S:	63	0.2195	N:	13	0.2097
F:	637	0.1274	F:	202	0.1530	N:	55	0.1916	F:	12	0.1935
S:	577	0.1154	N:	193	0.1462	F:	49	0.1707	T:	7	0.1129
T:	531	0.1062	T:	127	0.0962	T:	20	0.0697	P:	5	0.0806
R:	320	0.0640	R:	76	0.0576	R:	12	0.0418	R:	4	0.0645
n:	171	0.0342	J:	23	0.0174	r:	3	0.0105	I:	2	0.0323
J:	133	0.0266	n:	16	0.0121	J:	3	0.0105	A:	1	0.0161
V:	113	0.0226	A:	12	0.0091	V:	3	0.0105	f:	1	0.0161
D:	32	0.0064	W:	10	0.0076	I:	3	0.0105	V:	1	0.0161
A:	25	0.0050	V:	9	0.0068	A:	3	0.0105	J:	1	0.0161
I:	22	0.0044	I:	7	0.0053	L:	2	0.0070	L:	1	0.0161
W:	21	0.0042	M:	6	0.0045	f:	2	0.0070			
M:	20	0.0040	Q:	3	0.0023	W:	2	0.0070			
L:	19	0.0038	D:	3	0.0023	Q:	1	0.0035			
Q:	15	0.0030	L:	3	0.0023	m:	1	0.0035			
Z:	11	0.0022	Z:	2	0.0015						
f:	8	0.0016	f:	2	0.0015						
v:	8	0.0016	x:	1	0.0008						
r:	8	0.0016	O:	1	0.0008						
j:	6	0.0012	m:	1	0.0008						
m:	6	0.0012	u:	1	0.0008						
c:	2	0.0004									
x:	1	0.0002									
e:	1	0.0002									
Σ	5001		Σ	1320		Σ	287		Σ	62	
$-H$	2.1112		$-H$	2.004		$-H$	1.9876		$-H$	2.0512	

Pos. 9 SC	f	$\hat{p}$	**Pos. 10** SC	f	$\hat{p}$	**Pos. 11** SC	f	$\hat{p}$	**Pos. 12** SC	f	$\hat{p}$
S:	3	0.2727	N:	4	0.6667	N:	3	0.7500	N:	1	1.0000
N:	3	0.2727	f:	1	0.1667	I:	1	0.2500			
I:	1	0.0909	F:	1	0.1667						
f:	1	0.0909									
m:	1	0.0909									
M:	1	0.0909									
F:	1	0.0909									
Σ	11		Σ	6		Σ	4		Σ	1	
$-H$	1.7987		$-H$	0.8676		$-H$	0.5623		$-H$	0.0000	

We will use these negentropy values as given at the bottom of each column as a measure of information which could be more appropriate than the simple logarithm because it takes the distribution of the probabilities into account. Here, the logarithm with basis e is used: entropy H is defined here as

$$H = -\sum_{i} p_i \ln p_i. \tag{3.17}$$

For the sake of simplicity, *negentropy* $(-H)$ is used. In Figure 3.24, negentropy is shown as a function of the position.

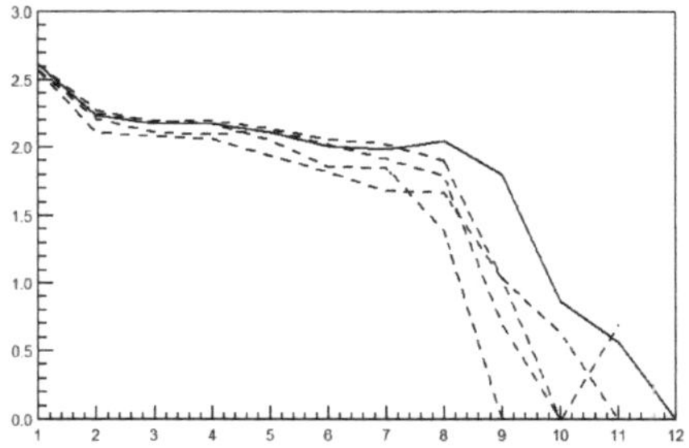

Figure 3.24: Negentropy associated with the number and probability of possible constituents at a given position in the Susanne corpus (solid line) and in the four text types included in this corpus (dashed lines)

As can be seen, in the entire corpus as well as in the four text types (the same holds for individual texts), this measure of information displays also an (almost) monotonous decrease with the position but a more complicated behavior than the simple logarithm. As the Menzerath-Altmann law corresponds to a simple pseudo-hyperbolic curve, the register hypothesis would prefer the simple logarithmic measure of information, which also displays a curve without a turning-point (of course inversely to the Menzerath-Altmann law), over the negentropy. If future studies confirm these findings, this could be interpreted in the following way: in case that the register hypothesis is true, the number of possible components which can be realized at a given position is significant for the human language processing system – not the probability of the individual alternatives. Moreover, the present results support a model which disregards the limitations which can be expressed as conditional probabilities. On the other hand, it seems still plausible that the (conditional) probabilities of the components at a given position play a role in the information processing mechanism. Only future theoretical and empirical investigations will give more evidence.

3.4.9 Dependency grammar and valency

The studies on syntactic structures and properties presented so far have in common that they are based on phrase structure grammars. The following analyses are examples of dependency-based or dependency-near approaches. Specifically, the concept of valency is a vantage point both for investigations that rely on traditional concepts of valency and for new approaches.

The traditional paradigm focuses on the verb[20] as the center of a sentence and starts with the assumption that the arguments of the verb are either complements or optional adjuncts (cf. Tesnière 1959; Comrie 1993; Heringer 1993; Čech, Pajas and Mačutek 2010). However, so far it has not been possible to give satisfactory criteria for this distinction – a problem which does not occur within a purely quantitative approach to valency (see Section 3.4.5).

Let us first show some studies on the basis of the traditional paradigm. The following examples use material extracted from a classical dictionary of verb valency, the one by Helbig and Schenkel (1991).

3.4.9.1 Distribution of the number of variants of verbs

The dictionary differentiates verb variants, which differ in valency and meaning. The German verb *achten* has two variants:

Variant 1: ("esteem")
    Subj. in nom., obj. in acc. ("so. esteems so.")
Variant 2: ("pay attention")
    1.1 Subj. in nom., prep.+obj. in acc. ("so. pays attention to sth.")
    1.2 Subj. in nom., subordinate clause with *dass*, *ob*, or *wer/was*
    1.3 Subj. in nom., infinitive ("so. cares for doing sth.")

20. Valency can be attributed not only to verbs but also to other parts-of-speech such as nouns and adjectives.

The number of variants a verb has can be considered as the result of a diversification process (Altmann 1991). We can imagine that a new verb has no variants immediately after coming into existence. Later, a certain probability arises for the emergence of a new variant if the verb was repeatedly used with a more or less deviant meaning. This probability should depend on the frequency of occurrence of the given verb. In the same way, another new variant may appear in dependence on the frequencies of the existing variants. For the sake of simplicity, only the frequencies of the neighboring classes are taken into account (cf. Altmann 1991). The assumption that the probability of a class x is a linear function of the probability of the class $x-1$ can be expressed as

$$P_x = \frac{a+bx}{x} P_{x-1}. \tag{3.18}$$

Substituting $a/b = k-1$ and $b = q$, the negative binomial distribution is obtained:

$$P_x = \binom{k+x-1}{x} p^k q^x, \quad x = 0, 1, \ldots \tag{3.19}$$

As every verb has at least one version, $P_0 = 0$ and $x = 1, 2, \ldots$, i.e. the mathematical formulation of our hypothesis on the distribution of the number of variants among the verbs of a language corresponds to the positive negative binomial distribution:

$$P_x = \frac{\binom{k+x-1}{x}}{1-p^k} p^k q^x, \quad x = 1, 2, \ldots \tag{3.20}$$

An empirical test of this hypothesis was conducted (Köhler 2005b) on data from a German verb valency dictionary (Helbig and Schenkel 1991). Table 3.20 shows the result of fitting this distribution to the data and the goodness-of-fit test. The first column of the table gives the number of variants, the second one the number of verbs with the given number of variants, and the third shows the theoretically expected number of verbs according to the positive negative binomial distribution. The probability $P = 0.91$ of the χ^2 value indicates that the observed data support the hypothesis in an excellent way.

Table 3.20: Fitting the positive negative binomial distribution to the German data

x_i	f_i	Np_i	x_i	f_i	Np_i
1	218	214.62	6	8	9.75
2	118	126.40	7	4	4.92
3	73	69.49	8	2	2.47
4	42	36.84	9	2	1.23
5	18	19.10	10	1	1.19

$k = 1.4992, p = 0.5287$
$\chi^2 = 2.67, DF = 7, P(\chi^2) = 0.91$

This result is illustrated by Figure 3.25.

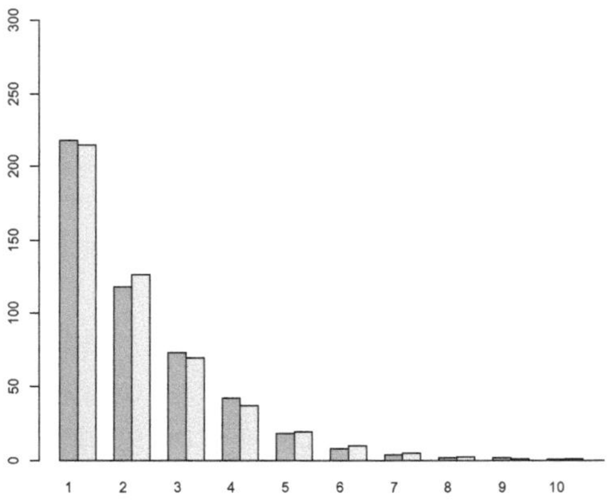

Figure 3.25: Distribution of the number of variants and expected values

3.4.9.2 Distribution of the number of sentence structures

In the present context, a sentence structure is defined as the specific pattern formed by the sequence of obligatory, optional, and alternative arguments. Let us mention a number of terminological conventions: if a verb variant provides a single way to form a sentence, viz. the sequence *subject in nominative case + object in accusative case*, the corresponding notation in Helbig and Schenkel (1991) is *SnSa*. If the object consisting of a noun in accusative case may be replaced by a subordinate clause with conjunction *dass* ("that"), the sentence pattern is recorded as $SnSa/NS\_dass$[21]. Optional arguments are indicated by parentheses: *SnSa(Sd)*. The code $Sn(pSa/Adj)Part/Inf$ describes a sentence pattern with a subject in nominative case facultatively followed by either a prepositional object in accusative case or an adjective, and an obligatory infinitive or a participle.

The material under investigation contains 205 different sentence structures; the most frequent one (*SnSa*) describes 286 verb variants. The next sentence structure is *SnSapS* with 78 variants. *SnpS* with 73 occurrences is not much less frequent followed by intransitive verbs (*Sa*) with 71 cases. The frequency distribution can be modelled using the Zipf-Mandelbrot distribution with an extremely good fitting result; the Chi-square test yields a probability that cannot be distinguished from 1.0. The result of the fitting is shown in Table 3.21.

Table 3.21: Frequencies of sentence structures of German verbs

x	f_x	Np_x	x	f_x	Np_x	x	f_x	Np_x
1	286	226.92	71	2	1.72	141	1	0.72
2	78	120.32	72	2	1.69	142	1	0.72
3	73	78.94	73	2	1.67	143	1	0.71
4	71	57.55	74	1	1.64	144	1	0.70
5	58	44.68	75	1	1.61	145	1	0.70
6	45	36.19	76	1	1.58	146	1	0.69
7	32	30.20	77	1	1.56	147	1	0.69
8	22	25.77	78	1	1.53	148	1	0.68
9	17	22.39	79	1	1.51	149	1	0.67
10	15	19.72	80	1	1.48	150	1	0.67
11	11	17.57	81	1	1.46	151	1	0.66
12	11	15.81	82	1	1.44	152	1	0.66
13	11	14.34	83	1	1.42	153	1	0.65
14	10	13.10	84	1	1.39	154	1	0.65
15	9	12.04	85	1	1.37	155	1	0.64
16	7	11.12	86	1	1.35	156	1	0.64

(continued on next page)

21. *S* and *NS* symbolize *Substantiv* (= noun) and *Nebensatz* (= subordinate clause).

Table 3.21 (continued from previous page)

x	f_x	Np_x	x	f_x	Np_x	x	f_x	Np_x
17	7	10.32	87	1	1.33	157	1	0.63
18	7	9.61	88	1	1.31	158	1	0.63
19	7	8.99	89	1	1.30	159	1	0.62
20	7	8.44	90	1	1.28	160	1	0.62
21	6	7.94	91	1	1.30	161	1	0.61
22	6	7.5	92	1	1.24	162	1	0.61
23	6	7.10	93	1	1.23	163	1	0.60
24	6	6.73	94	1	1.21	164	1	0.60
25	5	6.40	95	1	1.19	165	1	0.59
26	5	6.09	96	1	1.18	166	1	0.59
27	5	5.81	97	1	1.16	167	1	0.59
28	5	5.55	98	1	1.15	168	1	0.58
29	5	5.31	99	1	1.13	169	1	0.57
30	4	5.09	100	1	1.12	170	1	0.57
31	4	4.89	101	1	1.10	171	1	0.57
32	4	4.70	102	1	1.09	172	1	0.56
33	4	4.52	103	1	1.08	173	1	0.56
34	4	4.36	104	1	1.06	174	1	0.55
35	4	4.20	105	1	1.05	175	1	0.55
36	3	4.06	106	1	1.04	176	1	0.55
37	3	3.92	107	1	1.03	177	1	0.54
38	3	3.79	108	1	1.01	178	1	0.54
39	3	3.67	109	1	1.00	179	1	0.53
40	3	3.55	110	1	0.99	180	1	0.53
41	3	3.44	111	1	0.98	181	1	0.53
42	3	3.34	112	1	0.97	182	1	0.52
43	3	3.24	113	1	0.96	183	1	0.52
44	3	3.15	114	1	0.95	184	1	0.52
45	3	3.06	115	1	0.94	185	1	0.51
46	3	2.98	116	1	0.93	186	1	0.51
47	2	2.90	117	1	0.92	187	1	0.51
48	2	2.82	118	1	0.91	188	1	0.50
49	2	2.75	119	1	0.90	189	1	0.50
50	2	2.68	120	1	0.89	190	1	0.50
51	2	2.62	121	1	0.88	191	1	0.49
52	2	2.55	122	1	0.87	192	1	0.49

(continued on next page)

Table 3.21 (continued from previous page)

x	f_x	Np_x	x	f_x	Np_x	x	f_x	Np_x
53	2	2.49	123	1	0.86	193	1	0.49
54	2	2.44	124	1	0.85	194	1	0.48
55	2	2.38	125	1	0.84	195	1	0.48
56	2	2.33	126	1	0.83	196	1	0.48
57	2	2.27	127	1	0.83	197	1	0.47
58	2	2.23	128	1	0.82	198	1	0.47
59	2	2.12	129	1	0.81	199	1	0.47
60	2	2.13	130	1	0.80	200	1	0.47
61	2	2.09	131	1	0.79	201	1	0.46
62	2	2.05	132	1	0.79	202	1	0.46
63	2	2.01	133	1	0.78	203	1	0.46
64	2	1.97	134	1	0.77	204	1	0.45
65	2	1.93	135	1	0.76	205	1	0.45
66	2	1.89	136	1	0.76			
67	2	1.86	137	1	0.75			
68	2	1.82	138	1	0.74			
69	2	1.79	139	1	0.74			
70	2	1.76	140	1	0.73			

$$a = 1.2730, b = 0.5478, n = 205$$
$$\chi^2 = 86.49, DF = 150, P(\chi^2) \approx 1.00$$

Figures 3.26a and 3.26b present the results in graphic form; a logarithmic transformation of both axes (Figure 3.26b) is usually preferred for extremely steep distributions for the sake of clarity.

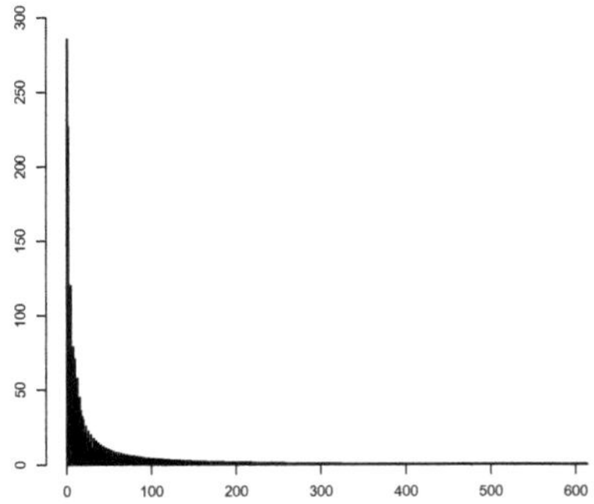

(a) No transformation

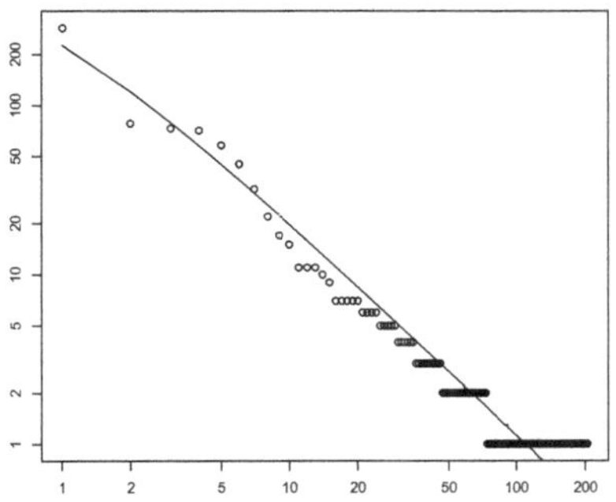

(b) Bi-logarithmic transformation

Figure 3.26: Zipf-Mandelbrot frequencies of the sentence structures

3.4.9.3 Distribution of semantic sub-categorisations

The German valency dictionary gives for each of the arguments, besides number and type of arguments, also a list of sub-categorisations which specify semantic features restricting the kind of lexical items which may be selected. The most important categories used here are "*Abstr*" (abstract), "*Abstr (als Hum)*" (collective human), "*Act*" (action), "*+Anim*" (creature) – possibly complemented by "*−Hum*" (except humans) – "*−Anim*" (inanimate), "*Hum*" (human), and "*−Ind*" (except individual). The complete description of the first variant of the verb *achten* has the form shown in Table 3.22.

Table 3.22: Valency of the first variant of the German verb "achten"

I.	achten 2 ($V1$ = hochschätzen)	
II.	achten → *Sn*, *Sa*	
III.	*Sn* →	1.*Hum* (Die Schüler achten den Lehrer.)
		2. *Abstr (als Hum)* (Die Universität achtet den Forscher.)
	Sa →	1. *Hum* (Wir achten den Lehrer.)
		2. *Abstr (als Hum)* (Wir achten die Regierung.)
		3. *Abstr* (Wir achten seine Meinung.)

achten in the sense "esteem" may be used with a human subject (the children) or with a collective name for institutions (university). The object (*Sa*) is open for three semantic categories: humans (the teacher), abstract humans (the government), and abstract designators (opinion). Thus, the first variant of this verb contributes two alternatives for the subject and three alternatives for the object. We set up the hypothesis that the distribution of the number of alternative semantic categories abides by a universal distribution law. Specifically, we will test the simple model (3.21), which expresses the assumption that the number of alternatives grows proportionally by a constant factor on the one hand and is decelerated (inversely accelerated) in proportion to the number of already existing alternatives. This model,

$$P_x = \frac{\lambda}{x} P_{x-1}\,, \tag{3.21}$$

yields the Poisson distribution

$$P_x = \frac{e^{-\lambda}\lambda^x}{x!}P_{x-1} \quad x = 0, 1, 2, \ldots \tag{3.22}$$

or rather – as the domain of the function begins with unity (every argument can be used with at least one semantic category – the positive Poisson distribution

$$P_x = \frac{\lambda^x}{x!(e^\lambda - 1)} \quad x = 1, 2, 3, \ldots \tag{3.23}$$

Fitting this distribution to the data yielded the results represented in Table 3.23; Figure 3.27 (p. 100) illustrates the results graphically.

Table 3.23: Observed and expected (positive Poisson distribution) frequencies of alternative semantic sub-categories of German verbs

x_i	f_i	Np_i
1	1796	1786.49
2	821	827.71
3	242	255.66
4	73	59.23
5	9	10.98
6	1	1.95

$\lambda = 0.9266$
$\chi^2 = 4.86$, $DF = 4$, $P(\chi^2) = 0.30$

3.4.9.4 *The functional dependency of the semantic sub-categories on the number of arguments*

The number of possible selections among the semantic sub-categories increases, of course, with the number of actants (obligatory, optional, and alternative complements) of a verb variant. However, the exact form of this dependence is not a priori obvious. The empirical relation between these two quantities can easily be extracted from the descriptions of the dictionary; it is shown in Table 3.24.

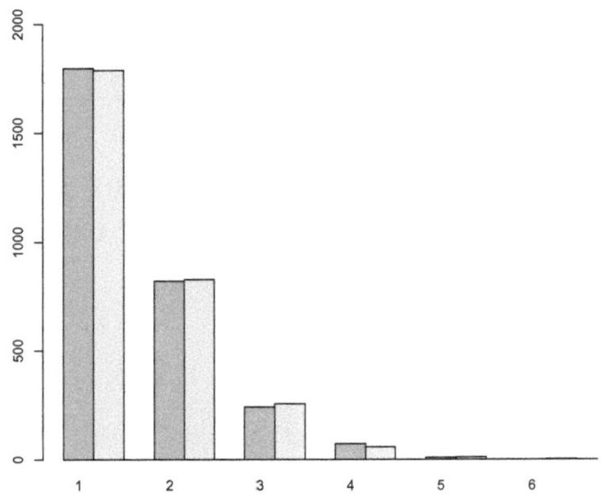

Figure 3.27: Fitting the positive Poisson distribution to the number of semantic subcategories of actants of German verbs

Table 3.24: The dependence of the number of alternatives on the number of actants

Number of actants	Mean number of alternatives
1	1.39
2	3.08
3	4.66
4	5.86
5	7.98
6	9.36
7	9.20
8	11.00
9	15.00
11	18.00

From Figure 3.28 it can be seen that the number of alternatives increases with the number of generally possible actants according to a linear function. A corresponding regression analysis yields the line $y = 1.5958x - 0.3833$ with a coefficient of determination $R^2 = 0.9696$.

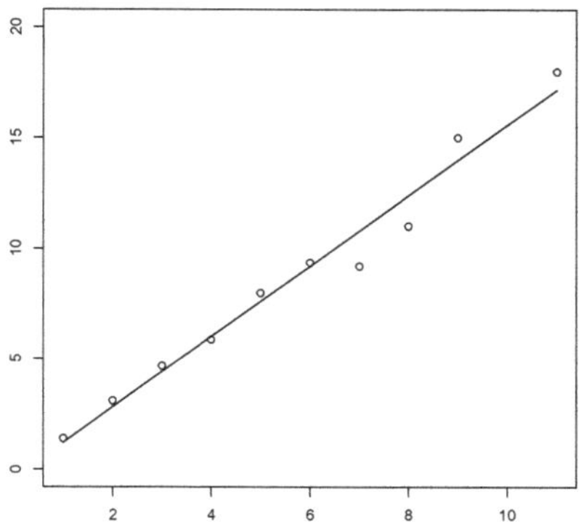

Figure 3.28: Regression line for the data in Table 3.28

3.4.9.5 Distribution of dependency types: a corpus-based approach

As opposed to a dictionary-based approach where valency is viewed as a constant property of words, another point of view is possible: We can for instance determine the arguments of the verbs in a corpus, i.e., observe the individual occurrences of verbs with their specific argument structure. In this way, the differentiation between complements and adjuncts can be considered as a gradual or quantitative criterion – or it can be abolished and replaced by a quantitative property, viz. valency as a tendency to bind other words.

Moreover, if valency is defined in a way such that not only the number of dependents or arguments is of interest but also the type, we can, after determining and annotating the dependency types of the individual dependents of a head, study the distribution of these link types, too. The Russian corpus we used above (cf. Section 3.4.4) provides this information: the links from the heads to the dependents are categorised; each link token in the corpus was assigned one of the types. The corpus differentiates the dependency types listed in Table 3.25 (p. 102).

We will not go into details, explicate, or discuss the syntactic analysis; we will rather use these tags as they are and study their quantitative behaviour. First, we present the distribution of the number of

Table 3.25: Dependency types as differentiated in the Russian Corpus SYNTAGRUS

1.	predicative	33.	approximative-quantitative
2.	dative-subjective	34.	quantitative-co-predicative
3.	agentive	35.	quantitative-delimitative
4.	quasi-agentive	36.	distributive
5.	non-intrinsic-agentive	37.	additive
6.	1-completive	38.	durative
7.	2-completive	39.	multiple-durative
8.	3-completive	40.	distantional
9.	4-completive	41.	circumstantial-tautological
10.	5-completive	42.	subjective-circumstantial
11.	copulative	43.	objective-circumstantial
12.	1-non-intrinsic-completive	44.	subjective-co-predicative
13.	2-non-intrinsic-completive	45.	objective-co-predicative
14.	3-non-intrinsic-completive	46.	delimitative
15.	non-actantial-completive	47.	parenthetic
16.	completive-appositive	48.	complement-clause
17.	prepositional	49.	expository
18.	subordinating-conjunctional	50.	adjunctive
19.	comparative	51.	précising
20.	comparative-conjunctional	52.	fictious
21.	elective	53.	sentential-coordinative
22.	(proper-)determinative	54.	conjunctional-coordinative
23.	descriptive-determinative	55.	communicative-coordinative
24.	approximative-ordinal	56.	multiple analytical
25.	relative	57.	passive-analytical
26.	(proper-)attributive	58.	auxiliary
27.	compound	59.	quantitative-auxiliary
28.	(proper-)appositive	60.	correlative
29.	dangling-appositive	61.	expletive
30.	nominative-appositive	62.	proleptic
31.	numerative-appositive	63.	elliptic
32.	(proper-)quantitative		

verbs with a given number of arguments (complements and adjuncts) within a text. We do not distinguish between complements (obligatory arguments governed by the verb) and adjuncts (optional arguments directly dependent on the predicate verb) because there is no absolutely convincing criterion for it. We rather leave the question open here; a future study will investigate whether such a distinction can be made on a significance criterion based on a degree of "obligatoriness" as determined by actual usage. Before this can be done the distribution of argument occurrence must be known. As a starting point, we study the number of verbs which occur with a given number of argument tokens (i.e. two or more arguments of the same type are counted individually) in contrast to the occurrence with x argument types (i.e., a verb with a subject and two complement clauses would count as verb with two argument types).

A first attempt at finding an appropriate mathematical model can be based on the assumption that the number of verb arguments is determined by a dynamic compromise between two effects. On the one hand, we assume that there is a more or less constant pressure towards addition of arguments caused by the requirement to express a thought as explicitly as possible. We will denote this quantity by a. On the other hand, an economy requirement, viz. the requirement of minimising coding effort, will try to limit this tendency and to decrease the effect of the first requirement. We assume further that the latter "force" will drastically grow with the number of arguments already present and introduce it into the formula as a parameter b with an exponent, which we expect, of course, to be greater than unity. Using Altmann's approach (cf. Altmann and Köhler 1996)

$$P_x = g(x)P_{x-1} \tag{3.24}$$

and specifying[22]

$$g(x) = \frac{a}{x^b}, \tag{3.25}$$

we set up the difference equation

$$P_x = \frac{a}{x^b}P_{x-1}\,. \tag{3.26}$$

The solution to the equation is the Conway-Maxwell-Poisson distribution[23] (Conway and Maxwell 1962) with parameters a and b:

$$P_x = \frac{a^x}{(x!)^b T}, \quad x = 0, 1, 2, \ldots \tag{3.27}$$

22. Note that this function is formally identical with one of the variants of the Menzerath-Altmann law.

23. In quantitative linguistics, this distribution has become known as an appropriate model in certain cases of word length distributions – cf. e.g., Nemcová and Altmann (1994), Wimmer et al. (1994).

with

$$T = \sum_{i=0}^{\infty} \frac{a^i}{(i!)^b}. \tag{3.28}$$

An empirical test on data from 16 arbitrarily selected texts from the Russian corpus yielded good and very good results for eleven and very bad results for the remaining five texts. Detailed information on fitting the Conway-Maxwell-Poisson (a,b) distribution to the number of verbs with x arguments in a single text – text no. 19 from the Russian corpus (“Что доктор прописал” [What the doctor prescribed]) with $N = 271$ – is shown in Table 3.26.

Table 3.26: Fitting the Conway-Maxwell-Poisson (a,b) distribution in text no. 19

x_i	f_i	Np_i
0	16	20.66
1	68	65.37
2	83	81.70
3	57	59.31
4	31	29.28
5	12	10.72
6	4	3.96
$a = 3.1641, b = 1.3400$		
$\chi^2 = 1.5210, DF = 4, P(\chi^2) = 0.82, C = 0.0056$		

Figure 3.29 illustrates the fitting results in graphical form.

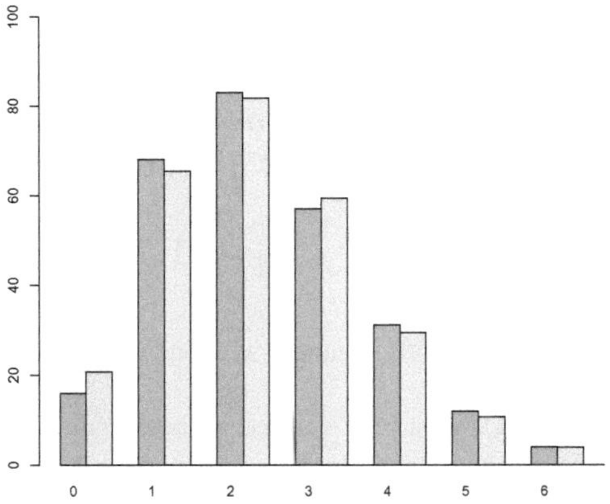

Figure 3.29: Result of fitting the Conway-Maxwell-Poisson (a,b) distribution

Table 3.27 offers the synopsis of fitting the Conway-Maxwell-Poisson (a,b) distribution to all 16 Russian texts: N is the text length, I and S are Ord's (1972) criteria – for details see p. 124.

Table 3.27: Fitting the Conway-Maxwell-Poisson (a,b) distribution to the number of verbs with x argument tokens

N	Parameter a	Parameter b	DF	$P(\chi^2)$	Np_1	I	S
249	9.3828	2.2691	3	0.74	4.96	1.9932	0.3559
119	8.3834	2.3757	3	0.72	3.46	2.0509	0.3533
271	3.1641	1.3400	4	0.82	20.66	1.3143	0.6809
218	2.5534	1.4222	3	0.02	27.60	1.4928	0.4302
210	4.1779	1.5452	4	0.97	11.04	1.4241	0.4973
317	3.5694	1.4826	4	0.11	22.00	1.4515	0.6260
163	1.7242	1.1554	3	0.00	32.56	1.1747	0.5588
100	4.8193	1.8231	3	0.79	5.32	1.5834	0.3229
93	5.2399	1.7862	3	0.33	3.94	1.6216	0.4920
142	1.0927	0.3041	4	0.00	26.96	1.1867	0.4886
174	1.0333	0.2852	3	0.00	36.51	1.3907	0.3791
122	4.5716	1.7409	3	0.03	6.64	1.6021	0.4184
87	5.3246	1.8086	3	0.43	3.65	1.5227	0.8248
102	1.1781	0.4048	4	0.00	19.40	1.2472	0.7874
196	5.6806	1.9438	3	0.67	8.34	1.7879	0.3462
93	1.7016	1.1151	3	0.00	18.46	1.2237	0.5132

Our second hypothesis concerns the distribution of texts with respect to the number of argument *types*. We do not assume a principally different mechanism but just different parameter values because the idea behind the model remains the same; we will have fewer classes, of course.

Table 3.28 shows the results of fitting the Conway-Maxwell-Poisson (a,b) distribution to the number of verbs with x argument types in all 16 Russian texts (N indicating text length, I and S Ord's criteria), which confirm these assumptions.

Table 3.28: Fitting the Conway-Maxwell-Poisson (a,b) distribution to the number of verbs with x argument types in 16 Russian texts

N	Parameter a	Parameter b	DF	$P(\chi^2)$	Np_1	I	S
249	11.2383	2.5241	3	0.54	4.45	2.2161	0.3100
119	9.7940	2.6264	2	0.74	3.19	2.3993	0.1436
271	4.2135	1.6528	4	0.92	15.95	1.4917	0.6100
218	3.2306	1.6813	3	0.19	22.25	1.6382	0.3718
210	4.8571	1.7676	3	0.82	10.32	1.6406	0.3020
317	4.2286	1.7366	4	0.12	20.26	1.6889	0.3869
163	1.8367	1.2495	3	0.00	31.37	1.2681	0.4203
100	4.4000	1.8459	2	0.88	6.56	1.7844	0.1383
93	6.1646	2.0683	2	0.31	3.79	2.0963	0.0555
142	1.0019	0.2471	3	0.00	29.86	1.3762	0.1743
174	1.0063	0.2714	3	0.00	37.89	1.5530	0.2809
122	5.4036	1.9690	3	0.05	5.93	1.7436	0.3580
87	5.6501	1.9192	3	0.90	3.64	1.6233	0.6917
102	1.0856	0.3549	3	0.00	21.51	1.5070	0.3980
196	6.7167	2.1827	3	0.82	7.49	1.9976	0.2723
93	1.9829	1.1897	3	0.07	15.20	1.2861	0.5096

As can be seen from the tables, those data files which fit worst[24] with the hypothesis have comparably small parameter values, both for a and b. Inspection of the data suggest that the deviations from the well-fitting texts consist of only single classes such that either random effects or influences from singular stylistic or other circumstances could be the reason. The deviating texts can be modelled applying related distributions such as the binomial, the Dacey-Poisson, Palm-Poisson and some of their variants. Figure 3.30 represents the values of the empirical distributions corresponding to the first hypothesis.

Ord's I (x axis) and S values (y axis) from Table 3.32 show that the frequency distributions which are not compatible with the Conway-Maxwell-Poisson distribution (triangles) occupy a separated area of the space. It can be seen that the distributions which do not fit with the Conway-Maxwell-Poisson distribution are separated from the others. Future studies will have to clarify the reason for the deviations.

24. The worst possible cases are those with $P(\chi^2) = 0.0$. The larger the value the better the fit; values of $P(\chi^2) \geq 0.5$ are considered to be indicators of good to very good fitting results.

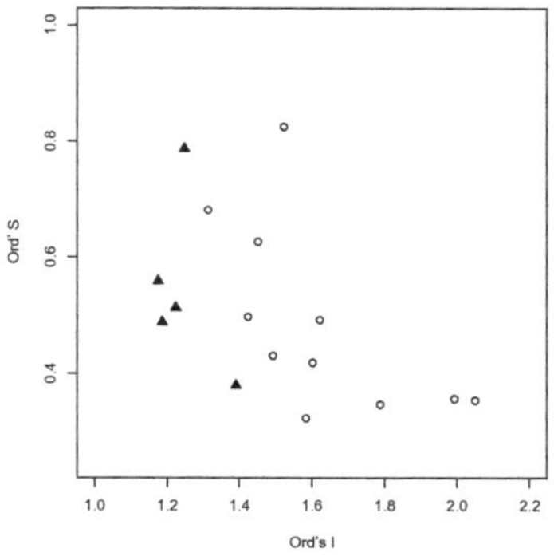

Figure 3.30: Ord's values for number of verbs with x argument tokens

Recently, Čech, Pajas and Mačutek (2010) published a study on the basis of the same principle. They call their approach "full valency", explicating the term as meaning "[...] that all arguments, without distinguishing complements and adjuncts are taken into account". The authors set up and test three hypotheses:

1. "Full valency" abides by a regular distribution. They consider the attribution of valency to verbs as a kind of classification; consequently, if this classification is a "theoretically prolific", one valency should follow a lawful distribution. They argue that the evolution of valency classes can be subsumed under the general principle of linguistic diversification processes (Altmann 1991) and thus should display a typical monotonously decreasing rank-frequency distribution.
2. The more frequent a verb, the more (full) valency frames can be observed. This hypothesis is set up by analogy with interrelations well-known from and consistent with synergetic linguistics: since frequent verbs occur in many different contexts, a considerable variation of valency frames can be expected.
3. The number of (full) valency frames depends inversely on the length of the verb.[25]

25. This effect is assumed as an indirect one: the dependence of length on frequency is known since Zipf (1935); hence, this hypothesis is a consequence of the second hypothesis. This hypothesis was already tested for the classical valency concept (Čech and Mačutek 2010).

Čech, Pajas and Mačutek tested these hypotheses on data from the Prague Dependency Treebank 2.0, a corpus with morphological, syntactic, and semantic annotations. As to the first hypothesis, they find in fact a monotonously decreasing rank-frequency distribution and succeed in fitting the Good distribution,

$$P_x = C\frac{p^x}{x^a},\ x = 1,2,\ldots \tag{3.29}$$

to the data with a probability of $P(\chi^2) = 0.8167$, which is a very good result. The second hypothesis, the dependence of the number of valency frames (or sentence structures) on verb frequency, is modelled by the authors using a function which is well-known from synergetic linguistics:

$$f(x) = cx^{\alpha}\,. \tag{3.30}$$

This simple formula is one of the special cases of the equation which Altmann (1980) derived for the Menzerath-Altmann law (cf. Cramer 2005) and also the result of a number of different approaches to various hypotheses. It seems to represent a ubiquitous principle (not only) in linguistics. In this case, it fits with the data from the Czech corpus with a coefficient of determination $R^2 = 0.9778$, i.e., it gives an excellent fit. The third hypothesis on the indirectly derivable dependence of the number of valency frames on verb length results in an acceptable coefficient of determination, too. The authors propose the function

$$f(x) = cx^{\alpha}e^{-bx} \tag{3.31}$$

which is also one of the special cases of the Menzerath-Altmann law and other interrelations and obtain $R^2 = 0.8806$, an acceptable but somewhat weaker result. They discuss some possible reasons for this comparably lower goodness-of-fit value but forget the fact that the assumption they test is an indirect relationship, a fact that is a good enough reason for more variance in the data and a weaker fit.

To sum up, the empirical findings presented by Čech, Pajas and Mačutek support their hypotheses and contribute considerably to this new field of research.

3.4.9.6 Distances in dependency structures

Liu (2007) applies a simple measure of distance between head (or governor) and dependent which was introduced in Heringer, Strecker, and Wimmer (1980: 187): "dependency distance" (*DD*) is defined as the number of words between head and dependent in the surface sequence +1. Thus, the DD of adjacent words is 1. In this way, a text can be represented as a sequence of DD values.

Liu uses this measure[26] for several studies on Chinese texts, using the data from the Chinese Dependency Treebank, a small annotated corpus of 711 sentences and 17809 word tokens. He investigates, amongst other things, the frequency distribution of the dependency distances in texts. He sets up the hypothesis that the *DD*'s in a text follow the right truncated Zeta distribution (which can be derived from a differential equation that has proved of value in quantitative and synergetic linguistics) and tests this assumption on six of the texts in the corpus. The goodness-of-fit tests (probability of χ^2) vary in the interval $0.115 \leq p \leq 0.641$, i.e. from acceptable to good. Figure 3.31 gives an example of the fitting results.

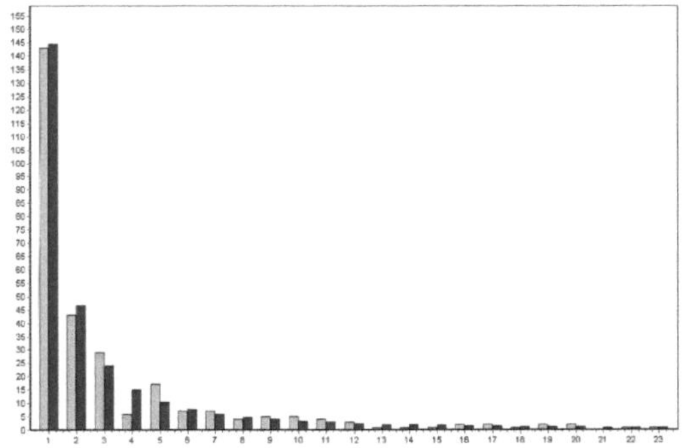

Figure 3.31: Fitting the right truncated Zeta distribution to the dependency distances to text 006 of the Chinese Dependency Treebank; the figure is taken from Liu (2007)

26. A related problem is scrutinised in Temperley (2008). The paper presents an investigation of dependency length, i.e. the lengths of the paths from the head over the vertices to the final dependents and the question as to how natural languages optimise the dependency structures and linearization to minimise these lengths.

In a follow-up study on data from the same six texts published in (Liu 2009), more distributional analyses are presented. Three variables were considered: dependency type[27], part of speech of the governor (head), and part of speech of the dependent. In all cases, the modified right truncated Zipf-Alekseev distribution (3.32) could be fitted to the data with good and very good results.

$$P_x = \begin{cases} \alpha & x = 1 \\ \dfrac{(1-\alpha)x^{-(a+b\ln x)}}{\sum\limits_{i=j}^{n} j^{-(a+b\ln j)}} & a,b \in \Re\,, 0 < \alpha < 1 \end{cases} \tag{3.32}$$

Figure 3.32, which is taken from Liu (2009), shows an example.

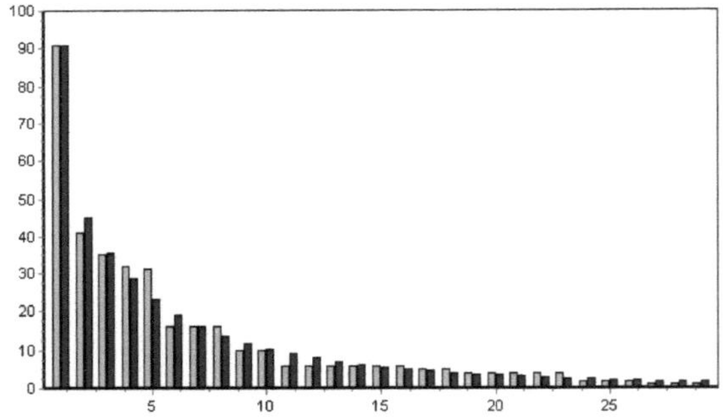

Figure 3.32: Fitting the modified right truncated Zipf-Alekseev distribution to dependency type data in text 001

The distribution of the three variables is then analysed individually for verbs and nouns as governors and dependents; the modified right truncated Zipf-Alekseev distribution could be successfully fitted in these cases, too.

27. Unfortunately, the types are not specified in the paper; just a hint is given that subject and object functions counted as dependency type. From a table with fitting results, which has 29 classes, the number of dependency types can be inferred.

3.4.9.7 Roles in Hungarian

There is another very interesting syntactically annotated corpus, which allows to study, among many other phenomena, valency-affine behaviour of verbs: the Hungarian "Szeged treebank"[28] of the Nyelvtechnológiai Csoport [Language Technology Group] of the Faculty for Informatics of the University of Szeged. This treebank with 1.2 million running words comes in XML notation and provides full morphological and syntactic annotation. The grammar used is a phrase structure grammar of Hungarian. Every phrase is tagged according to its grammatical type and constituent role. As opposed to English and many other languages where grammatical functions such as subject, object etc., and their cases do not indicate their semantic roles, Hungarian has a more overt coding technique. Most roles are expressed in form of suffixes with specialized meanings. Table 3.29 shows the suffixes which occurred in the corpus, the corresponding roles, their frequencies in one of the newspaper parts of the corpus, and examples of the corresponding suffixes.

As can be seen, the difference between the greatest and the lowest frequencies is very large; the rank-frequency distribution is rather skew. It has, on the other hand, a comparably short tail. As a consequence, regular probability distributions do not fit to the data although the rank-frequency distribution of roles/cases must be counted as a phenomenon within linguistic diversifications[29]. As an alternative, function (3.5) can be used. We repeat it here in the form

$$y = 1 + a_1 e^{b_1 x} + a_2 e^{b_2 x} + \dots \qquad (3.33)$$

which we will use as a model of the Hungarian frequency structure. Fitting this function with two terms yields a good result ($R^2 = 0.9548$). The estimated parameters are

$$\begin{aligned} a &= 346.5508 \\ b &= -0.0855 \\ c &= 8267.9798 \\ d &= -0.5818 \end{aligned}$$

28. http://www.inf.u-szeged.hu/projectdirs/hlt/; English version: http://www.inf.u-szeged.hu/projectdirs/hlt/index_en.html
29. Cf. Altmann (1991)

Table 3.29: Semantic roles in a newspaper part of the Hungarian "Szeged Treebank"

No.	Frequency	Role	Case Name	Example (suffix)
1	4685	NOM	alany (nominative)	∅
2	3761	ACC	tárgy (accusative)	-t
3	1081	INE	"belviszony" (inessive)	-ban/-ben
4	718	SUP	"rajtalevés" (superessive)	-n/-on/-en/-ön
5	717	SUB	"ráhelyezés" (sublative)	-ra/-re
6	583	INS	eszköz(határozó) (instrumental / comitative)	-val/-vel
7	350	DAT	részes(határozó) (dative)	-nak/-nek
8	317	ILL	"belso közelítő" (illative)	-ba/-be
9	311	DEL	"eltávolítás" (delative)	-ról/-ről
10	242	ELA	"távolító" (elative)	-ból/-bol
11	190	ALL	"külső közelítő" (allative)	-hoz/-hez/-höz
12	174	ABL	"távolító külviszony" (ablative)	-tól/-től
13	112	TO	hely: végpont	oda; a fa alá
14	108	TER	"határ" (terminative)	-ig
15	89	ADE	"közelében levés" (adessive)	-nál/-nél
16	87	CAU	causalis	-ért
17	81	GEN	birtokos (genitive)	∅, -nak/-nek
18	64	FAC	factive, translative	-vá/-vé
19	48	FOR	(essive-)formal	ként, -képp(en)
20	29	ESS	essive	-ul/-ül
21	19	TEM	temporalis	-kor
22	15	DIS	distributive	-nként
23	3	LOC	locativus	-tt

A plot of the data and the theoretical function is shown in Figure 3.34. The same function with only one term yielded a slightly worse result ($R^2 = 0.9487$, Figure 3.33), which might reflect the existence of two strata in the frequency structure. The x-axis represents the ranks of the roles as taken from Table 3.29, and the y-axis gives the corresponding frequencies.

A visual inspection of the plot underlines this difference between the two results. A plausible interpretation is based on the fact that there are cases and grammatical functions in Hungarian which are similarly ambiguous as subject and object in English, viz. the most frequent "roles" NOM and ACC and on the other hand all the almost unambiguous other ones.

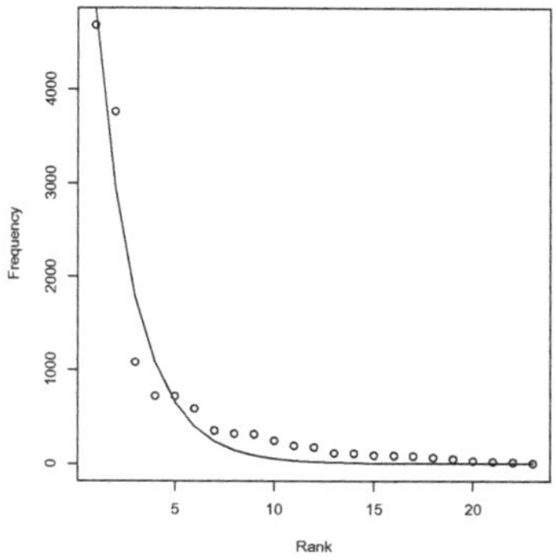

Figure 3.33: Graph of the function (3.33) with only the first term and the empirical role frequency data from the Hungarian corpus

In general, as well as in this special case, a classification or a category system (e.g. definitions) obtains important support if it yields distributions or functions which have a theoretical background and are confirmed as models also in other cases.

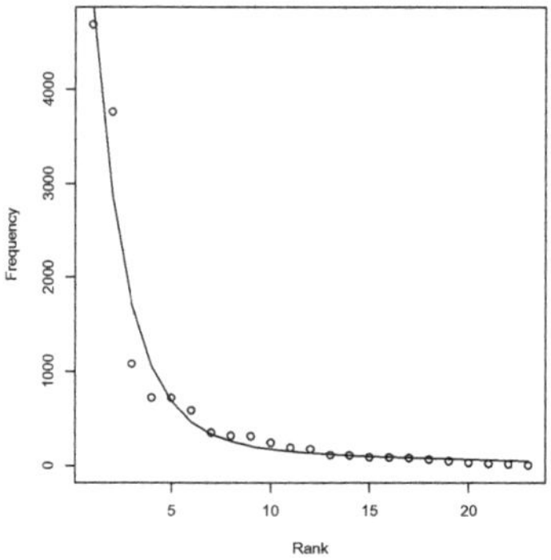

Figure 3.34: Graph of the function (3.33) with both terms and the empirical role frequency data from the Hungarian corpus. The x-axis represents the ranks of the roles as taken from Table 3.29 and the y-axis gives the corresponding frequencies

3.4.9.8 Roles in Finnish

A similar study can be performed on role ("case") data from Finnish, which were published in Väyrynen, Noponen and Seppänen (2008) on the basis of Pajunen and Palomäki (1982). Unfortunately, absolute numbers were not given, but it is possible to reconstruct them approximately using the sample size of 20 000. As we do not use a distribution anyway, we can calculate parameter estimations and goodness-of-fit, although on the basis of the given proportions. Table 3.30 shows the rank-frequency data of the Finnish cases.

Table 3.30: Percentages of occurrences of Finnish cases

Case	Percentage	Case	Percentage
Nominative	29.5	Essive	2.6
Genitive	20.3	Allative	2.3
Partitive	13.7	Translative	2.2
Inessive	7.1	Instructive	1.9
Illative	6.3	Abessive	0.2
Elative	4.4	Comitative	0.1
Adessive	4.4	Ablative	1.0
Accusative	3.1		

Figure 3.35 displays the data together with the graph of the theoretical function according to formula (3.33); the x-axis represents the ranks of the roles and the y-axis gives the corresponding percentages. The estimated parameters are: $a_1 = 42.0786$ and $b_1 = -0.3703$; the coefficient of determination indicates a very good fit ($R^2 = 0.9830$).

3.4.10 Motifs

Over the last decade, growing interest in methods for the analysis of the syntagmatic dimension of linguistic material can be observed in areas which traditionally employ methods that ignore the linear, sequential arrangement of linguistic units. Thus, the study of distributions of frequency and other properties as well as the study of relations between two or more properties is based on a "bag-of-words" model, as

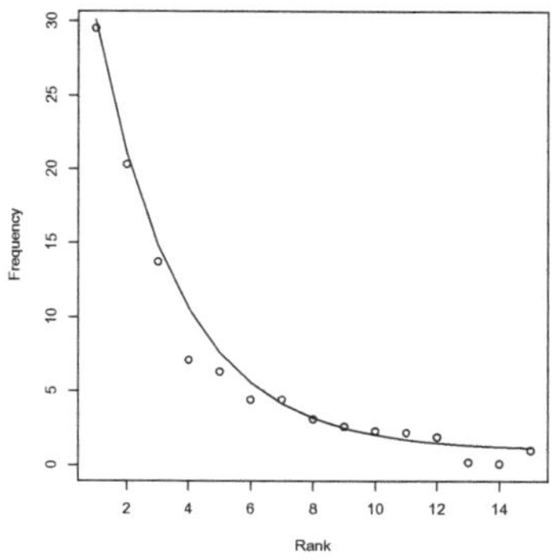

Figure 3.35: Graph of the function (3.33) with one term only and the empirical role frequency data from Finnish

it is called in corpus linguistics and information retrieval, or "language in the mass"[30] as Herdan (1966: 432) put it in a more general way. When periodicity, e.g. a periodic or quasi-periodic rhythm in poetry is expected, methods well-known in other disciplines are often applied. One of them is Fourier analysis, established in technical fields and in phonetics (cf. Uhlířová 2007), another one is time series analysis (cf. Pawłowski 2001)[31]. All these methods may work but some of them have in common that, in most cases, important preconditions for their use are not met by language (or text). An example is time series analysis:

1. The method assumes that the data are cyclic. As a consequence, the successor of the last unit of a text or corpus (which does, of course, not exist) is identified with the first unit as if the text under analysis were cyclic.
2. There is no natural mapping of symbolic or categorical data to numerical values, which are needed for time series analysis; researchers who nevertheless apply this method choose arbitrary values. We will not discuss this problem here.

30. In contrast to "language in the line".
31. Still another way to study such phenomena is the evaluation of the fractal dimension of properties of units in a sequence (cf. Section 3.4.11.2).

Other approaches avoid such shortcomings and can also be applied if periodicity does not play a major role or no role at all. Thus, Anderson (2005) tested uniformity of the syntagmatic structure of a text with respect to word length in two ways: (1) by dividing the text in portions and comparing their word length characteristics and (2) by comparing the lengths of word-chains of varying numbers of components. Uhlířová (2007, 2009) studied word frequency with respect to position in a syntagmatic frame. In particular, she associated word frequency with position in sentences, i.e., she set up a table where the frequency values of the word types of a text (the number of their occurrences in the given text) were related to the positions in which the respective words occurred in the sentences. To overcome problems caused by the length differences among the sentences, she defined relative position by introducing an artificial scale on which the real positions could be mapped, and found rhythmic patterns of frequencies, especially of hapax legomena. Other attempts she made based on absolute positions and average frequencies in sentence-initial and -final positions. She tested also variations of Fourier analysis, time series, and motif methods and found her general hypothesis supported: rhythmic patterns of frequency values of words within texts can be found in the syntagmatic structure of texts.

A method recently introduced into linguistics (cf. Köhler 2006a, 2008a,b; Köhler and Naumann 2008, 2009) can be applied to any linguistic unit and any ordinal or metric property and used with respect to any larger frame unit. There are, in principle, several ways to define units which could be used to detect syntagmatic patterns based on numerical properties. Units which are defined in terms of linguistic structures such as words, clauses, or phrases suffer, however, from two fundamental disadvantages:

1. They provide an appropriate granularity only for a very limited scope; e.g. clauses seem to be too big and words too small units to unveil syntagmatic properties with quantitative methods.
2. Linguistic units are inherently connected to specific models (e.g., grammars) – apart from the general disadvantage of leading inevitably to some kind of "language in the mass" approach.

Therefore, a new unit was established that is based on the rhythm of the property under study itself: the motif. A motif is defined as a maximal sequence of monotonically increasing numbers, where these numbers represent the numerical values of properties of adjacent units in the frame unit under study. Using this definition, we segment, for instance, a given text in a left to right fashion starting with the first unit, like word. In this way, a text or other frame unit can be represented as an uninterrupted sequence of motifs. Let us illustrate the procedure by way of Example (2):

(2) In this way, a text or other frame unit can be represented as an uninterrupted sequence of motifs.

If words are chosen as units and length (measured in terms of the number of syllables) as the property to be studied, the following series of motifs would represent this sentence:

$$(1\ 1\ 1\ 1\ 1\ 1\ 2)(1\ 2)(1\ 1\ 4)(1\ 1\ 5)(2)(1\ 2).$$

This kind of segmentation is similar to Boroda's F-motif for musical "texts". Boroda (1982) defined his F-motif in an analogous way but with respect to the duration of the notes of a musical piece. The advantage of such a definition is obvious: any text or other frame unit can be segmented in an (1) objective, (2) unambiguous and (3) exhaustive way.

If length is chosen as the property to investigate syntagmatic patterns in a higher unit, we call the corresponding variants[32] of motifs L-motifs. Analogously, F- and T-motifs are formed by monotonically increasing sequences of frequency and polytextuality[33] values. Other units than words can be used as basic units, such as morphs, syllables, phrases, clauses, sentences, and other properties such as polysemy,

32. In most cases, several variants can be defined depending on the operationalisation of the individual property and unit. Thus, word length can be measured in terms of the number of syllables, sounds, morphs, letters etc., the word consists of.
33. Polytextuality is a specific operationalisation of the concept of context specificity. It was introduced in Köhler (1986) and is measured in terms of the number of texts in a corpus in which the given linguistic entity occurs at least once. In corpus linguistics and document retrieval, if the given unit is a word ("term"), this measure is called "document frequency", which is, by the way, a funny misnomer.

synonymy, age etc., can be used for analogous definitions. In the same way, any appropriate frame unit can be chosen: texts, sentences, paragraphs or sections, verses etc. – even discourses and hypertexts could be investigated with respect to properties of texts or other components they are formed of if some kind of linearity can be found, such as the axis of time of formation of the components.

The definition given above has yet another advantage: the unit motif is highly scalable. Thus, it is possible to form *LL*-motifs from a series of *L*-motifs; Example (2) given above would yield the *LL*-motifs

$$(7)(2\ 3\ 3)(1\ 2).$$

Similarly, *FF*-motifs (representing the frequency of frequency motifs) etc. are possible; even *FL*-, *LF*-, *LLL*-, *LFT*-, etc., motifs have been successfully applied (cf. Köhler and Naumann 2010). Here, some illustrations of the use of motifs for various studies will be presented. One of the first questions concerning motifs is whether they follow lawful patterns in a text. We will show here in a simple experiment that *L*-motifs based on word length measured in syllables (which is known to abide by certain distributional laws) display such a lawful behaviour. Specifically, the hypothesis is set up that any appropriate segmentation of a text will display a monotonously decreasing frequency distribution. Furthermore, it is assumed that the balance between the repetition of (length-based) rhythmical segments and the introduction of new ones in the course of the text will resemble the well-known type-token relation of words.

To test these hypotheses, the first part (the first 23 434 words) of Dostoevsky's *Crime and Punishment* [Преступление и наказание][34] in its Russian original is analysed with respect to its word length. Then, the text is segmented into *L*-motifs according to the definition given above (cf. p. 117) and a frequency analysis is conducted. Table 3.31 shows the twenty most frequent *L*-segments in this text.

Here, neither the motifs themselves are considered nor their individual frequencies or ranks, but their rank-frequency distribution as a whole. For this purpose, the Altmann-Fitter was used to find an appro-

34. I thank Peter Grzybek for providing the length data of this text fragment, based on the Slavic Text Data Base at Graz University http://quanta-textdata.uni-graz.at/.

Table 3.31: The 20 most frequent *L*-motifs in the analysed text

Rank	*L*-motif	Frequency	Rank	*L*-motif	Frequency
1	2	825	11	1 1 2	207
2	1 3	781	12	1 5	177
3	1 2	737	13	2 4	164
4	1 4	457	14	1 3 3	135
5	3	389	15	1 1 4	132
6	1 2 3	274	16	1 2 4	122
7	2 3	269	17	1 3 4	98
8	1 1 3	247	18	4	93
9	2 2	245	19	1 2 2 3	87
10	1 2 2	235	20	1 1 2 3	77

priate probability distribution for these data and conduct a goodness-of-fit test. It could be expected that the Zipf-Mandelbrot, the Waring or a similar frequency distribution would fit the data. To test the second hypothesis, the type-token function of the text is calculated with respect to the *L*-motifs, and function (3.9) $y = Ax^b$ is fitted to the data. The best results can be obtained from fitting the right truncated modified Zipf-Alekseev distribution and the Zipf-Mandelbrot distribution to the rank-frequency data of the *L*-motifs (cf. Figures 3.36a and 3.36b).

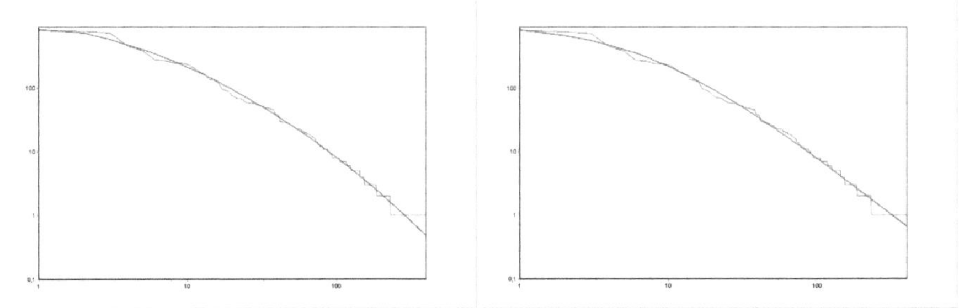

(a) Zipf-Alekseev distribution *(b)* Zipf-Mandelbrot distribution

Figure 3.36: Fitting results for right truncated modified distributions

Figure 3.36a shows the results of fitting the right truncated modified Zipf-Alekseev distribution (3.32); the parameters are $a = 0.2741$ and $b = 0.1655$; $n = 401$; $\alpha = 0.0967$; $\chi^2 = 133.24$ with $DF = 338$; $P(\chi^2) \approx 1.0$. Figure 3.36b shows the results of fitting the right truncated modified Zipf-Mandelbrot distribution (both axes logarithmic); in this case, the parameters are $a = 1.8412$ and $b = 7.449$; $n = 401$; $\chi^2 = 158.87$ with $DF = 356$; $P(\chi^2) \approx 1.0$.

The second one of these first hypotheses is also confirmed: *L*-motifs have a TTR according to the theoretical model. Figure 3.37 shows the results of fitting function (3.9) $y = Ax^b$ with parameters values $A = 10.2977$ and $b = 0.4079$; the determination coefficient is $R^2 = 0.9948$.

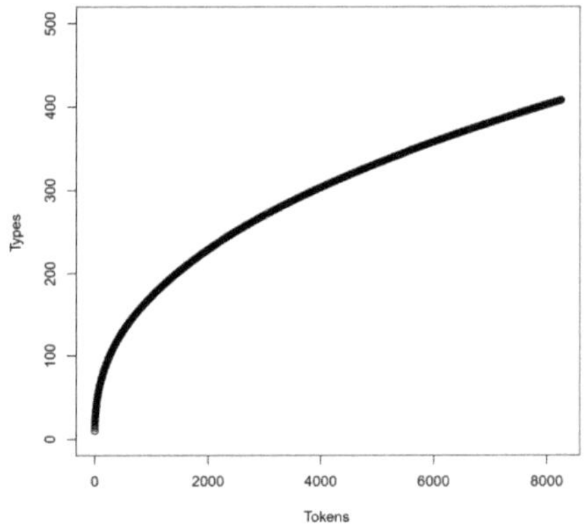

Figure 3.37: Fit of the function (3.9): $y = Ax^b$

The theoretical curve cannot be seen in the diagram because of the perfect match between the theoretical line and the more than 8000 empirical values. The extraordinarily good fit is also reflected by the very high value of the determination coefficient $R^2 = 0.9948$. As opposed to word-based TTR studies, where the parameter *A* in the formula is always 1 as long as both, i.e. types and tokens, are measured in terms of words (or word-forms), the present analysis yields a value of slightly more than 10. As types and tokens have been counted in the same way, this fact is probably due to the influence of a still unknown factor, which has an effect on the *L*-segment repetition structure.

Similar results were obtained on data from 66 German texts (prose and poetry by Brentano, Goethe, Rilke, and Schnitzler (cf. Köhler and Naumann 2008) – not only with *L*-motifs, but also with *F*- and *T*-motifs (based on frequency and polytextuality of words).

Let us now look at another property of motifs: instead of their frequency, their own length will be considered. But this time we will set up a more specific and detailed hypothesis; we will form a theoretical model on the basis of three plausible assumptions:

1. There is a tendency in natural language to form compact expressions. This can be achieved at the cost of more complex constituents on the next level. An example is the following: the phrase "as a consequence" consists of 3 words, where the word "consequence" has three syllables. The same idea can, more or less, be expressed using the shorter phrase "consequently", which consists of only one word of four syllables. Hence, more compact (i.e., less complex) expressions on one level (here on the phrase level) go along with more complex expressions on the next level (here the morphological structure of the words). Here, the consequence of the formation of longer words is relevant. The variable K will represent this tendency.
2. There is an opposed tendency, viz. word length minimisation. It is a result of the same tendency of effort minimisation which is responsible for the first tendency but now considered on the word level. We will denote this requirement by M.
3. The mean word length in a language can be considered as constant, at least for a certain period of time. This constant will be represented by q.

According to a general approach proposed by Altmann – cf. Altmann and Köhler (1996) – and substituting $k = K - 1$ and $m = M - 1$, the following equation can be set up:

$$P_x = \frac{k+x-1}{m+x-1} q P_{x-1}, \tag{3.34}$$

which yields the hyper-Pascal distribution (cf. Wimmer and Altmann 1999):

$$P_x = \frac{\binom{k+x-1}{x}}{\binom{m+x-1}{x}} q^x P_0, \quad x = 0, 1, 2, \ldots \tag{3.35}$$

with $P_0^{-1} = {}_2F_1(k,1;m;q)$ – the hypergeometric function – as normalising constant. As *L*-motifs of length 0 are impossible (*L*-motifs with 0 words logically do not exist) the distribution will be used in a 1-displaced form. The empirical tests on the data from the 66 texts support this hypothesis with good and very good results. Figure 3.38 shows a typical example of a narrative text. Another example is sen-

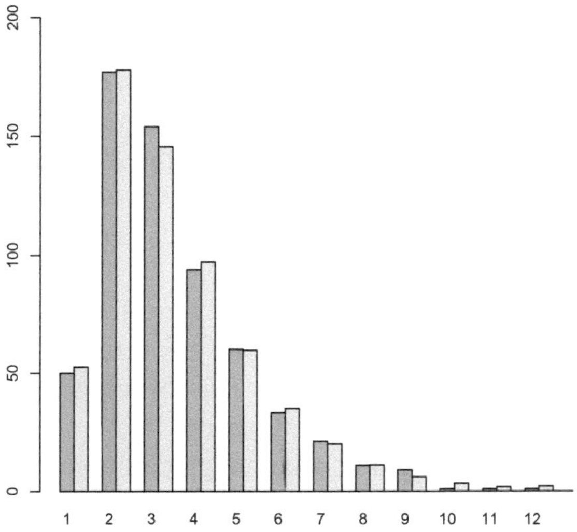

Figure 3.38: Theoretical and empirical distributions of the lengths of *L*-motifs in a German short story

tence length. Sentence length studies are usually conducted in terms of the number of words a sentence consists of – although this kind of investigation suffers from several shortcomings; among them the following are the most severe ones:

1. Words are not the immediate constituents of sentences and, therefore, do not form units of appropriate granularity.
2. It is very unlikely to get enough data for each length class as the range of sentence lengths in terms of s varies between unity and several dozen; for this reason, the data are usually pooled but do not form smooth distributions nevertheless.

Therefore, we will measure sentence length in terms of the number of clauses. The *L*-motif types obtained in this way are also best represented by the Zipf-Mandelbrot distribution with very good χ^2 values ($P(\chi^2)$ close to unity, cf. Figure 3.39).

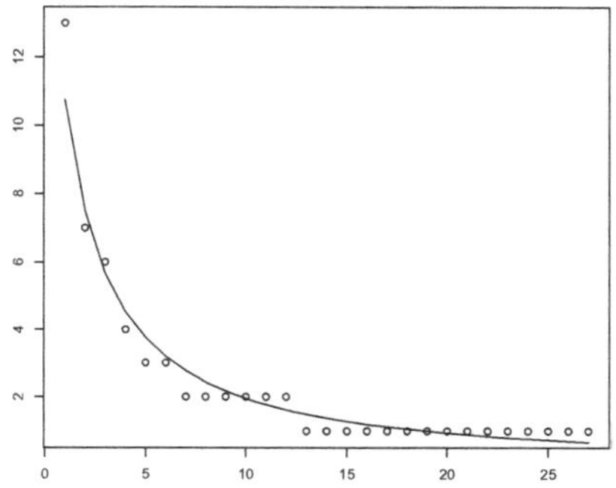

Figure 3.39: Zipf-Mandelbrot distribution of *L*-motif types formed on the basis of sentence lengths in the number of clauses

We will now set up a theoretical model of the length distribution of sentence *L*-motifs in analogy to the study above where word *L*-motifs were investigated with respect to their lengths. We find a similar but slightly different situation in the case of sentences:

1. In a given text, the mean sentence length, the estimation of the mathematical expectation of sentence length, can be interpreted as the sentence length intended by the text expedient (speaker / writer).
2. Shorter sentences are formed in order to decrease decoding / processing effort (the requirement *minD* in synergetic linguistics) within the sentence. This tendency will be represented by the quantity *D*.
3. Longer sentences are formed where they help to compactify what otherwise would be expressed by two or more sentences and where the more compact form decreases processing effort with respect to the next higher (inter-sentence) level; this will be represented by *H*.

(1) and (3) are the causes of deviations from the mean length value while they, at the same time, compete with each other. We express this interdependence in form of Altmann's approach (Altmann and Köhler 1986): The probability of sentence length x is proportional to the probability of sentence length $x-1$, where the proportionality is a linear function:

$$P_x = \frac{D}{x+H-1} P_{x-1}\,. \tag{3.36}$$

D has an increasing influence on this relation whereas H has a decreasing one. The probability class x itself has also a decreasing influence, which reflects the fact that the probability of long sentences decreases with the length. This equation leads to the hyper-Poisson distribution (Wimmer and Altmann 1999: 281):

$$P_x = \frac{a^x}{{}_1F_1(1;b;a)b^{(x)}},\ x = 0,1,2,\dots\ a \geq 0, b > 0, \tag{3.37}$$

where ${}_1F_1(a;b;t)$ is the confluent hypergeometric function

$${}_1F_1(a;b;t)b^{(x)} = \sum_{j=0}^{\infty} \frac{a^{(j)}t^j}{j!b^{(j)}}\,. \tag{3.38}$$

Here, $a^{(j)}$ stands for the ascending factorial function, i.e. $a(a+1)(a+2)\dots(a+j-1)$, $x \in \mathbb{R}$, $n \in \mathbb{N}$. According to this derivation, the hyper-Poisson distribution, which plays a basic role with word length distributions (Best 1997), should therefore also be a good model of L-motif length on the sentence level although motifs on the word level, regardless of the property considered (length, polytextuality, frequency), follow the hyper-Pascal distribution(3.35). In fact, many texts from the German corpus follow this distribution (cf. Figure 3.40).

Others, however, are best modelled by other distributions such as the hyper-Pascal or the extended logarithmic distributions. Nevertheless, all the texts seem to be oriented along a straight line in the I/S plane of Ord's criterion (cf. Figure 3.41). This criterion consists of the two indices I and S, which are defined as

$$I = \frac{m_1}{m_2},$$

$$S = \frac{m_3}{m_2},$$

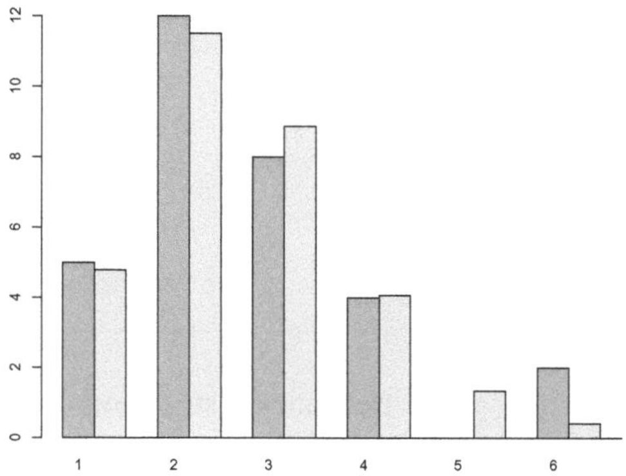

Figure 3.40: Fitting the hyper-Poisson distribution to the frequency distribution of the lengths of *L*-motifs on the sentence level

where m_1 is the first non-zero moment, and m_2 and m_3 are the second and third central moments, i.e. variance and skewness, respectively. These two indices show characteristic relations to each other depending on the individual distribution. On a two-dimensional plane spanned by the I/S dimensions, every distribution is associated with a specific geometric object (the Poisson distribution corresponds to a single point, which is determined by its parameter λ, others correspond to lines, rectangles or other partitions of the plane). The data marks in Figure 3.41 are roughly scattered along the expected line $S = 2I - 1$.

Obviously, these few studies presented here form not more than a first look at the behaviour of motifs in texts. Innumerable variations are possible and should be scrutinised in the future: the length distribution of the frequency motifs of polytextuality measures of morphs, the dependency of the frequency of length motifs of words on the lengths of their polytextuality etc. In particular, the potential of such studies for text characterisation and text classification could be evaluated – cf. the first, encouraging results in Köhler and Naumann (2010).

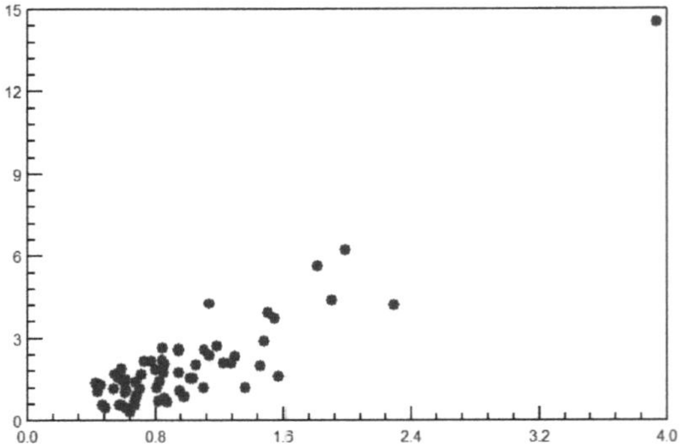

Figure 3.41: Ord's criterion of the frequency distribution of the lengths of the *L*-motifs

3.4.11 Gödel Numbering

3.4.11.1 Altmann's binary code

Gödel numbers are natural numbers which are used to encode sequences of symbols. A function

$$y : M \to \mathbb{N} \tag{3.39}$$

is called Gödel numbering if y is injective and computable, $y(M)$ is decidable, and the inverse function of $y(M)$ is computable. Kurt Gödel (Gödel 1931) used the encoding technique for his famous proof of his incompleteness theorem. His method is based on the numbering of the symbols and assigning the positions prime numbers which are then raised to the power of the corresponding symbol's number. The number which results from multiplying all the powers is the Gödel code of the sequence (e.g. a formula or even a text), from which the complete information which was encoded into a single (albeit extremely large) number can unambiguously be reconstructed. Gödel's specific technique is not the only possible Gödel numbering function.

In Altmann and Altmann (2008), another method was introduced and exemplified; it was applied and its usefulness was demonstrated on a considerable number of texts in various languages in (Popescu et al. 2010).

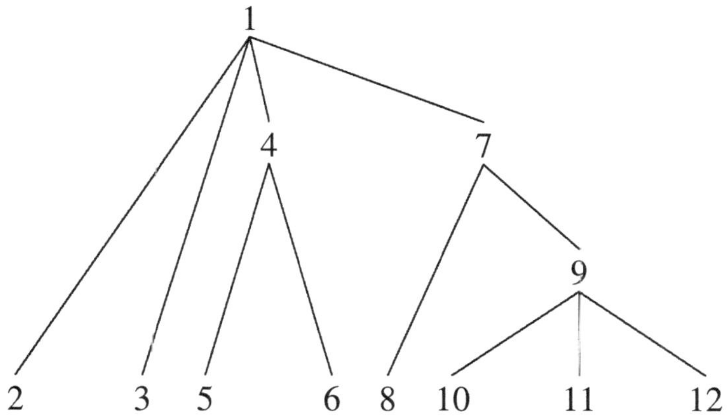

Figure 3.42: Tree with numbered nodes

We will present here only the application to syntactic structures. Altmann's method takes into account only part of the syntactic information because the node types are ignored. The advantage of this simplification is clear: The only information to be encoded is the adjacency information.

Therefore, binary Gödel numbers suffice to represent and reconstruct the complete information. If node symbols such as '*S*', '*NP*', '$\bar{\bar{N}}$' etc. have to be included, a larger set of natural numbers must be used. Such a tree can be transformed into (or better: represented as) an adjacency matrix if the nodes are numbered in a consistent way, e.g. recursively depth-first, top down, left to right. Then, an adjacency function (3.40) is defined

$$a_{i,j} = \begin{cases} 0 & \text{if the vertices } i \text{ and } j \text{ are not adjacent,} \\ 1 & \text{if the vertices } i \text{ and } j \text{ are adjacent.} \end{cases} \quad (3.40)$$

Next, a triangular adjacency matrix is set up, as it is represented in Table 3.32.

Table 3.32: Upper triangular adjacency matrix of the graph in Figure 3.32

v	1	2	3	4	5	6	7	8	9	10	11	12
1	–	1	1		1	0	0	1	0	0	0	0
2		–	0	0	0	0	0	0	0	0	0	0
3			–	0	0	0	0	0	0	0	0	0
4				–	1	1	0	0	0	0	0	0
5					–	0	0	0	0	0	0	0
6						–	0	0	0	0	0	0
7							–	1	1	0	0	0
8								–	0	0	0	0
9									–	1	1	1
10										–	0	0
11											–	0
12												–

Altmann's specific Gödel numbering function, which he calls "Binary Code", calculates the sum

$$\begin{aligned}BC =& a_{12}2^0 + a_{13}2^1 + \ldots + a_{1n}2^{n-2} + a_{23}2^{n-1} + \ldots + a_{2n}2^{2n-3} + \ldots \\ & + \ldots + a_{n-1,n}2^{k-1}\end{aligned} \tag{3.41}$$

from the values in the matrix. Altmann and Altmann's (2008) example yields

$$\begin{aligned}BC =& 1(2^0) + 1(2^1) + 1(2^2) + 1(2^5) + 1(2^{30}) + 1(2^{31}) + \\ & + 1(2^{51}) + 1(2^{52}) + 1(2^{60}) + 1(2^{61}) + 1(2^{62}) \\ & = 8077205934910210087.\end{aligned}$$

As a normalisation, i.e. the transformation of a number into the interval [0..1] is advisable for many purposes, Altmann divides every *BC* by the maximum *BC* of the given structure, i.e.

$$BC_{\max} = \sum_{i=0}^{\frac{n(n-1)}{2}-1} 2^i = 2^{\frac{n(n-1)}{2}} - 1\,, \tag{3.42}$$

and uses the resulting BC_{rel} value. Thus, Goethe's famous *Erlkönig* can be represented, with respect to the sentence structures, by the following BC_{rel} sequence:

0.1095; 0.3779; 0.3779; 0.0147; 0.0147; 0.4286; 0.3751; 0.0469; 1.0000; 0.1095; 0.4286; 0.3752; 0.3783; 1.0000; 0.3783; 0.3750; 0.3799; 0.3779; 0.4286; 0.4286; 0.0009; 0.4286; 0.4286; 0.4286; 0.3750; 0.0469; 0.4286; 0.0000001; 0.4286; 0.4286; 0.3779; 0.4286; 0.0147; 0.3751; 0.1111; 0.0146; 0.4286; 0.4286; 0.0009; 0.0469; 0.09557; 0.1111; 0.1095; 0.0029.

Popescu et al. (2010) show a wealth of applications of BC_{rel} measurements, e.g. for finding text segments by determining significant changes in the course of the corresponding sequence, for text comparison, for the characterisation of texts with respect to various criteria etc.

3.4.11.2 Fractal dimension

Figure 3.43 visualises the sequence of BC_{rel} values representing the sentence structures (according to the dependency grammar that was used by the Russian linguists) of one of the texts of the Russian treebank (cf. Section 3.4.4). We will now determine the fractal dimension of this number series as its shape very much reminds of fractal and self-similar objects. To our knowledge, Hřebíček was the first to propose the measurement of fractal structures in language – cf., e.g., Hřebíček (1994), Andres (2010).

The dimension of regular geometric objects is well defined and its calculation is straightforward. The measurement of the dimension of an object which is irregular (either because it is of a stochastic nature or because of its empirical origin) is more complicated. Several methods have been developed to estimate the dimension of such objects: Lyapunov exponents, which we, however, exclude from our considerations because they are too hard to calculate; the compass dimension, which is applicable only to time series; and three remaining measures called (1) correlation dimension, (2) hull dimension, and (3) capacity dimension.

Hull and capacity dimension measures can be calculated in two variants each: using block city or Euclid geometry. The four dimension measures were tested on BC_{rel} data describing sentence structures. The most stable and promising results were obtained with the capacity dimension.

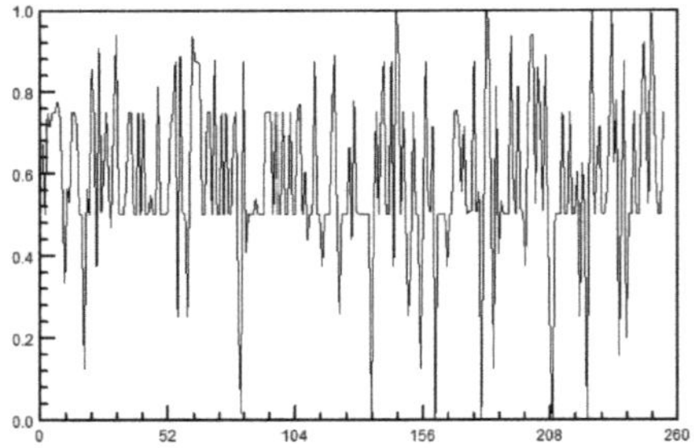

Figure 3.43: Visualisation of the sequence of BC_{rel} values representing the sentence structures of a Russian text

The capacity dimension[35] can be iteratively calculated:

$$d_i = \frac{\ln \dfrac{N_{i-1}}{N}}{\ln \partial} \tag{3.43}$$

where N denotes the number of rectangles containing at least one dot of the object, ∂ symbolizes the contraction factor, and i is the running number of iterations.

Let us demonstrate the principle of the procedure with the help of a concrete example. To make it illustrative we will scatter a number of points in a one-dimensional space (Figure 3.44) and place a mesh over them. We choose arbitrarily a mesh of three intervals for the first step.

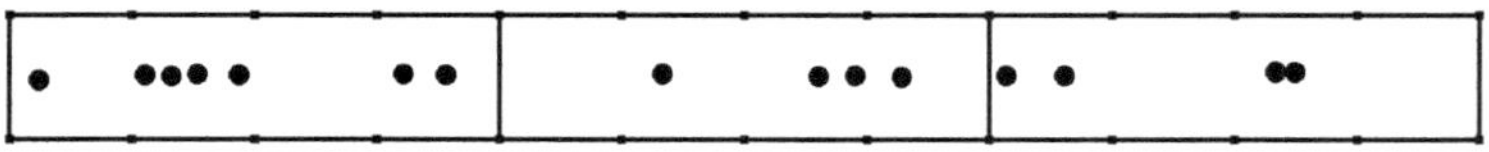

Figure 3.44: One-dimensional space with points and a mesh of three boxes

35. Cf. Hunt and Sullivan (1986)

Now we count the boxes which contain at least a minimal part (e.g., one pixel) of the object under study. All three boxes meet the criterion, whence $N = 3$. In the next step, we reduce the mesh aperture by the factor ∂, for which we choose, say 0.5. We obtain the situation shown in Figure 3.45 with six intervals (boxes).

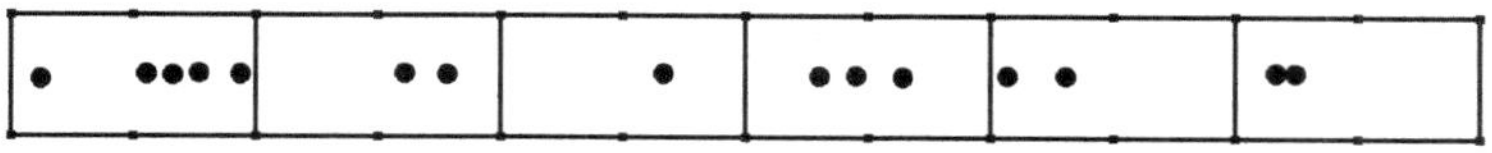

Figure 3.45: One-dimensional space with points and a mesh of six boxes

Counting yields $N = 6$ non-empty boxes. Applying the contraction factor $\partial = 0.5$ to the interval length again yields the mesh in Figure 3.46 with twelve boxes, of which 8 contain at least a tiny part of the structure and four empty boxes.

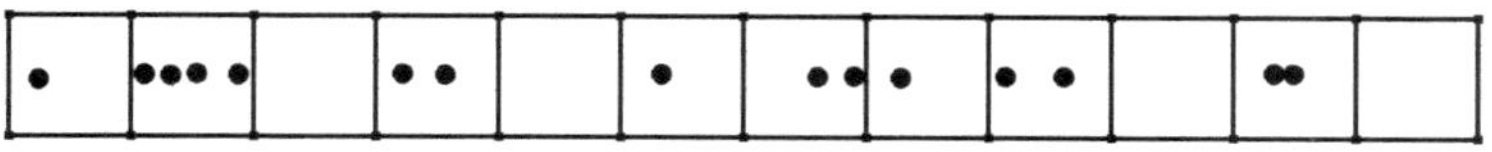

Figure 3.46: One-dimensional space with points and a mesh of 12 boxes

With the resulting values of N and the contraction parameter $\partial = 0.5$ the first two iteration cycles of the approximation procedure with formula (3.43) are as follows:

$$d_1 = \frac{\ln \frac{3}{6}}{\ln 0.5} = \frac{-0.69314718}{-0.69314718} = 1.0,$$

$$d_2 = \frac{\ln \frac{6}{8}}{\ln 0.5} = \frac{-0.28768207}{-0.69314718} = 0.415037.$$

More iteration cycles approximate stepwise the fractal dimension of the object. Experience shows that the approximation process is not a smooth convergence but displays abrupt jumps. Therefore, it is advisable to conduct a non-linear regression accompanying the procedure.

We set up the hypothesis that sequences of BC_{rel} values of texts have a fractal dimension. Diagrams such as Figure 3.43 suggest – because of the straight lines from one data point to the next one – a dimensionality of one or more. We should, therefore, keep in mind that data of this kind form a set of points, i.e. one-dimensional objects. Hence, the dimension of the sets should be somewhere between 0 and 1.

Table 3.33 presents the BC_{rel} sequences of three short Russian texts, and Table 3.34 the results of the dimensional analysis of the 20 first texts of the Russian corpus (SYNTAGRUS, see Section 3.4.4). For each text, the BC_{rel} values of all its sentences were calculated. The twenty sequences were then analysed with respect to their capacity dimension. For this computationally costly procedure an accelerated version of the algorithm was chosen.

Table 3.33: sentence lengths and BC_{rel} sequences of three short Russian texts

Text # 11			Text # 12			Text # 13		
1	4	0.59	1	4	0.59	1	2	1.00
2	9	0.75	2	13	0.81	2	10	0.76
3	25	0.50	3	22	0.75	3	17	0.75
4	17	0.16	4	27	0.50	4	10	0.75
5	12	0.50	5	10	0.50	5	15	0.50
6	17	0.75	6	8	0.75	6	17	0.53
7	13	0.50	7	2	1.00	7	13	0.75
8	17	0.50	8	10	0.63	8	9	0.75
9	16	0.50	9	32	0.50	9	18	0.50
10	5	0.35	10	29	0.50	10	9	0.50
11	10	0.50	11	10	0.50	11	12	0.75
12	6	0.52	12	13	0.75	12	9	0.50
13	5	0.51	13	13	0.75	13	9	0.56
14	7	0.75	14	19	0.50	14	17	0.50
15	22	0.50	15	15	0.75	15	14	0.50
16	15	0.75	16	18	0.50	16	9	0.50
17	13	0.50	17	4	0.65	17	24	0.56
18	11	0.88	18	12	0.50	18	8	0.50
19	14	0.75	19	24	0.50	19	9	0.75
20	6	0.52	20	13	0.50	20	23	0.75
21	12	0.50	21	16	0.50	21	19	0.50
22	17	0.75	22	23	0.50	22	18	0.50
23	14	0.50	23	9	0.75	23	15	0.75
24	23	0.50	24	15	0.75	24	7	0.51
25	27	0.63	25	24	0.75	25	17	0.50
26	5	0.63	26	5	0.76	26	15	0.50
27	9	0.63	27	17	0.88	27	2	1.00
28	4	0.78	28	21	0.75	28	20	0.59
29	6	0.51	29	10	0.75	29	6	0.75
30	13	0.75	30	24	0.75	30	26	0.88
31	11	0.50	31	3	0.86	31	6	0.75
32	8	0.53	32	17	0.50	32	16	0.50
33	3	0.43	33	24	0.50	33	24	0.50

(continued on next page)

Table 3.33 (continued from previous page)

Text # 11			Text # 12			Text # 13		
34	10	0.50	34	34	0.75	34	7	0.07
35	8	0.75	35	7	0.51	35	30	0.75
36	10	0.50	36	12	0.75	36	13	0.63
37	11	0.88	37	10	0.52	37	7	0.75
38	28	0.75	38	43	0.50	38	4	0.78
39	28	0.13	39	21	0.50	39	14	0.50
40	18	0.50	40	16	0.50	40	15	0.50
41	6	0.53	41	31	0.50	41	6	0.52
42	4	0.59	42	22	0.69	42	13	0.75
43	9	0.50	43	15	0.75	43	19	0.56
44	7	0.51	44	14	0.75	44	17	0.50
45	11	0.50	45	13	0.75	45	18	0.84
46	11	0.88	46	12	0.75	46	30	0.20
47	13	0.50	47	17	0.75	47	31	0.53
48	11	0.50	48	14	0.50	48	11	0.81
49	8	0.53				49	14	0.55
50	18	0.75						
51	3	0.86						
52	9	0.50						
53	9	0.63						
54	6	0.52						
55	5	0.76						
56	18	0.88						
57	12	0.75						
58	12	0.75						

The general hypothesis that we will find fractal dimensions in the specified interval was corroborated.

Another observation is that the texts differ considerably in length, as can be seen from the second and fifth columns of the table above, where text length in terms of the number of sentences is given. As can also be seen, the fractal dimensions of the texts (with respect to their BC_{rel} values) seem to correlate roughly with text length. However, such an interpretation of the data is not plausible. We would rather assume a dependence of the fractal dimension on the variety of syntactic complexity. If all the sentences in a text have the same complexity, their BC_{rel} values would display a more or less monotonous shape:

Table 3.34: Capacity dimensions of the BC_{rel} values of 20 Russian texts

Text no.	length (sentences)	Capacity dimension (accelerated)	Text no.	length (sentences)	Capacity dimension (accelerated)
Text 1	254	0.96	Text 11	58	0.79
Text 2	229	0.99	Text 12	48	0.70
Text 3	492	1.00	Text 13	49	0.73
Text 4	480	0.99	Text 14	42	0.82
Text 5	489	0.99	Text 15	26	0.63
Text 6	481	0.99	Text 16	64	0.90
Text 7	50	0.73	Text 17	49	0.63
Text 8	86	0.85	Text 18	38	0.77
Text 9	57	0.78	Text 19	100	0.88
Text 10	47	0.79	Text 20	36	0.77

low values for simple and short structures, large values for complex sentences with deeply embedded and highly branched structures. Both would not result in much fractality; only a ragged surface makes an object more or less fractal: the more fissured it is, the higher the fractal dimension[36]. This means in our case that a high value of the fractal dimension indicates a text with vivid changes of syntactic complexity from sentence to sentence. Hence, the measured fractal dimension might contribute to the criteria by means of which automatic text classification, author identification etc. could be improved. Only further theoretical and empirical research will shed light on this question.

36. Remember the example of Norway's coastline: the finer the scale of measurement the longer the coast.

4 Hypotheses, laws, and theory

4.1 Towards a theory of syntax

As stated above in Chapter 2, there is not yet any elaborated linguistic theory in the sense of the philosophy of science. We will put some emphasis on the fact that only laws and systems of laws, i.e. theories provide means to explain and to predict. Descriptive tools such as grammars or dictionaries do not have any explanatory power, although linguists in some sub-disciplines insist on calling grammar types and even formalisms or notations "theories". Chomsky has always been aware of this fact and, consequently, avoided claiming that his approach would be able to explain anything. Instead, he classified the grammars which are possible within this approach into two kinds: those with descriptive adequacy, and those with explanatory adequacy (without claiming that the latter ones can explain anything). Most of his followers and also most of the exponents of "post-Chomskyan mainstream" linguistics are less informed or interested in the concepts of the philosophy of science and make no effort to reflect the status of their statements.

Another aspect we should make clear is that syntax comprises only one of many linguistic sub-systems, all of which are in multiple and complex interrelations with one another. Hence, a theory of syntax must remain drastically incomplete; it cannot be formulated as a stand-alone system. Nevertheless, due to the overwhelming complexity of the aim to describe and explain language, a subdivision into levels and fields of linguistic analysis were introduced very early. In the same way, we have to try and set up sub-theories of language. In this sense, we will present some tesserae of a first sub-theory for the field of syntax – keeping in mind that it will depend on countless interfaces to other sub-theories.

A number of linguistic laws has been found in the framework of QL, and there are first attempts at combining them into a system of interconnected universal statements, thus forming an (even if embryonic) theory of language: the first one was synergetic linguistics (cf.

Köhler 1986, 1987, 1993, 1999), the second one Wimmer's and Altmann's unified theory (2005). The aspects that have been modelled within these approaches are spread over all levels of linguistic analysis. We will here, of course, present only that part of the corresponding work that is devoted to syntax.

We will begin with individual hypotheses and proceed to more and more integrative models. Here, we will concentrate on those hypotheses which were set up by logical deduction and claim universal validity. Such assumptions have the status of "plausible hypotheses", which have the potential to become laws if they find strong enough empirically support.

4.1.1 Yngve's depth hypothesis

Victor Yngve (1960) brought forth the hypothesis that right-branching structures are preferred over left-branching ones in English. Specifically, he claimed that there is a fixed length maximum of about seven for path lengths from roots to terminal nodes in left-branching structures. It is reported that empirical findings do not support the hypothesis on the basis of Yngve's depths definitions using his way of determining depth (Sampson 1997); of quite a number of alternative counting methods only a single one led to a result which could be considered as compatible with Yngve's assumption.

Although Yngve's attempt at explaining the postulated phenomenon was based on the general idea that avoiding left-branching structures facilitate language processing by reducing memory effort, his hypothesis is limited in its scope (English language usage). Consequently, it is not a candidate for a universal language law. Nevertheless, there is a simple way of modifying and generalising this idea and transforming it into a universal law hypothesis: If in fact right-branching structures are preferred due to memory efficiency in language processing, all constituents should show, on the average, an increasing depth of embedding with increasing position in all languages.

We will now formulate the hypothesis in form of the differential equation (4.1), which has been used as a good model also of other interrelations in quantitative and synergetic linguistics (cf. Sections 4.2.6

and 4.2.7). The reason why we think that it is an appropriate approach of the dependence of depth on constituent position is that Yngve's depths saving principle cannot be the only factor governing the linguistic behaviour. We rather assume a second requirement with an opposite effect: If limitation of depth were the only one, a tendency towards constructions with zero depth should be expected and – over the long run – languages should end in non-embedding structures (or avoid embedding from the very beginning). Therefore, another principle must exist which results in the tendency to form embedded structures. In fact, we find such a requirement in the preference of compact expressions, which can be achieved by structure embedding. Hence, we will set up a differential equation describing a process in which two competing requirements have to form an ever-changing compromise, which may differ from time to time (observed over centuries or longer) and from language to language, depending on varying external needs such as the language's environment (cf. Section 4.2.6).

We assume further that the dependence of depth on position is not constant but that the effect of the latter varies with increasing position, i.e. the pressure of position on depth grows the more right-positioned a constituent is. The corresponding differential equation is given by

$$\frac{T'}{T} = \frac{R}{P} - B, \tag{4.1}$$

where T represents the current depth of a constituent, T' its first derivative, i.e. its change, R stands for the current power of forming more compact expressions by embedding, P for the position of the given constituent, and B for Yngve's depth saving principle. The solution to this equation is the function

$$T = AP^R e^{-BP}. \tag{4.2}$$

The parameter A is a constant which is obtained from integration; its linguistic interpretation is that of a function of the depths of nodes at position 1. The background is the following: if $B = 0$ and hence $e^0 = 1$, equation (4.2) simplifies to (4.3):

$$T = AP^R. \tag{4.3}$$

Inserting $P = 1$, i.e. the depth at position 1 into (4.3) yields $T(1) = A$. Remember: all this is true only if $B = 0$. As parameter R represents the effect toward more complex and therefore deeper embedded structures, we would expect that with growing R, also the limiting effect of B increases. Evidence for this interdependence was in fact provided by empirical studies already on parameters of analogous relations, e.g. on the Menzerath-Altmann law (cf. below, Section 4.1.3). As a matter of principle, the statement that parameter A stands for the depth at position 1 is not correct if $B \neq 0$; it will nevertheless approximately prove true because of the compensatory effect of the two parameters. However, the actual value of A depends on the fitting procedure as well. We have to treat it preliminary as an empirical parameter whose value must be estimated from data.

In order to test this hypothesis, depth (depth value 1 was assigned at sentence level) and absolute position (in the mother constituent and, separately, from the beginning of the sentence) were evaluated in (Köhler 1999) on data from the Susanne corpus[1]. The empirical interrelation is shown in Figures 4.1 and 4.2: Figure 4.1 shows the empirical dependence of depth of embedding on constituent position (measured in running words from the beginning of the sentence) for the four text types included in the Susanne corpus; positions above 50 are not represented in the graph because of their small frequencies.

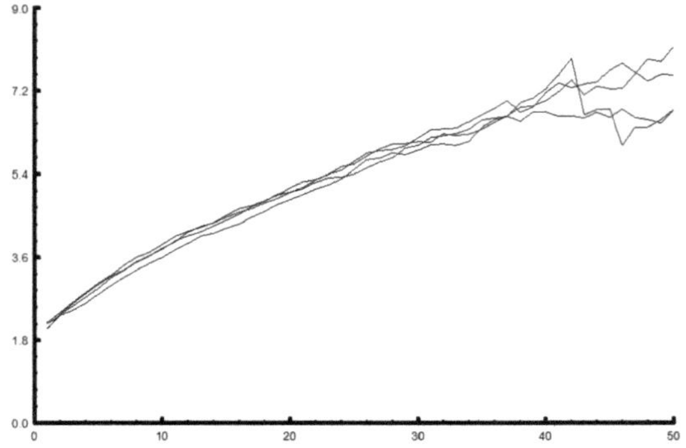

Figure 4.1: The empirical dependence of depth of embedding on constituent position for the four text types included in the Susanne corpus

1. Cf. Section 4.1.3

Figure 4.2 shows the empirical dependence of depth of embedding on constituent position (measured in running words from the beginning of the sentence) for the entire Susanne corpus (dots); positions above 40 are not represented in the graph because of their small frequencies. In addition to the empirically observed data, Figure 4.2 also represents the theoretical data obtained from fitting function (4.2) to the data: fitting the function $T = 1.8188P^{3.51}e^{0.00423P}$ yielded a coefficient of determination $R^2 = 0.996$, i.e. an extremely good fit.

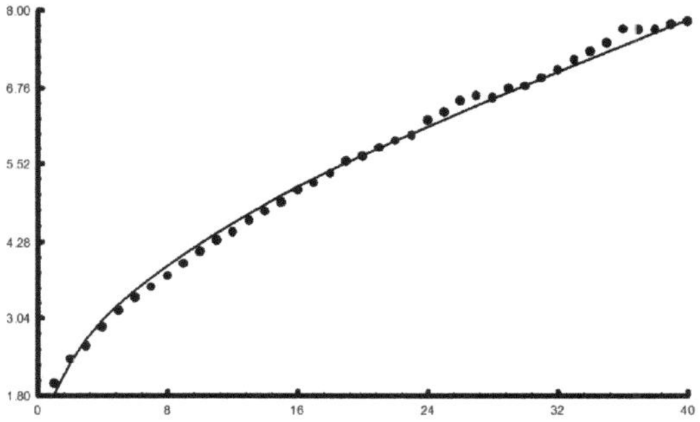

Figure 4.2: The empirical dependence of depth of embedding on constituent position for the entire Susanne corpus (dots) and results of fitting function (4.2) to the data

We consider the hypothesis in the modified and extended form as preliminary supported by the test on data from English. Further research will have to perform more tests on other corpora and languages.

4.1.2 Constituent order

Languages differ in the degree of 'word order' rigidity. English is known as a language with relatively fixed order of the syntactic components; its basic word order is SVO (the subject is followed by the verb, which is followed by the object). Other languages have different but similarly fixed word order patterns, again others, e.g. Russian, display a relatively free order. But all languages seem to have some flexibility, though. English allows, e.g. two different orders of the direct and the indirect object as in Examples (1-a) and (1-b):

(1) a. She gave him the box.
b. She gave the box to him.

We will not discuss here matters of emphasis, theme-rheme division and topicalisation as a function of syntactic coding by means of word order, or Givón's discourse pragmatic "the most important first" principle etc.; there is another, quite interesting quantitative interrelation, viz. the preference of one of the possible orders of components in dependency on their lengths.

The first to notice this dependency was Otto Behaghel, a German philologist. In his publication of 1930 (Behaghel 1930), he reported his observation of an overwhelming preference of a word order 'long after short' for all kinds of pairs of components with equal status. He called the phenomenon "das Gesetz der wachsenden Glieder"[2] and presented empirical evidence from German, Latin and classical Greek. He interpreted it as a reflex of semantic importance, which over time became a rigid pattern and resulted finally in an unconscious rhythmic feeling.

After several decades of word order discussions in the disciplines of linguistic typology and language universals research, a new aspect was introduced by Hawkins. He replaced the dichotomous criterion which classifies languages either as VO or as OV types by a pattern of "cross-categorial harmony" (CCH), using adpositions as indicators (cf. Hawkins 1990, 1992, and especially 1994). Later, he develops a cognitive-functional principle which motivates the observed preferences on the basis of assumptions on parsing mechanisms of the human language processing device. He calls his hypothesis the "early immediate constituent" (EIC) principle and gives a detailed description of the processes and elements of this device. The basic idea is that the 'long after short' order enables the (human) parser to get the earliest overview of the syntactic structure of an expression. The sentences (2-a) and (2-b), taken from Hawkins (1994), illustrate this idea quite plausibly:

(2) a. I [$_{VP}$ gave [$_{PP}$ to Mary] [$_{NP}$ the valuable book that was extremely difficult to find]].
b. I [$_{VP}$ gave] [$_{NP}$ the valuable book that was extremely difficult to find] [$_{PP}$ to Mary]

2. Approximately: Law of growing parts

In Example (2-a), the complete structure of the VP is available already at the position of "the", i.e. after the third word of the VP whereas in (2-b), this information can be induced only with the beginning of the PP "to Mary", i.e. after the 10th word. The details of the approach and a discussion of the characteristics of the assumed mechanism in the case of left-branching languages such as Japanese can be found in the cited literature. We will here concentrate on possible operationalisations of constituent order and length/complexity and on corresponding measures and tests.

There is, in particular, good reason to be unsatisfied with the empirical evaluation of the hypothesis as performed by Hawkins. Although he and his group collected relevant data from nine typologically different languages the methodology used to verify the EIC principle are not acceptable. The authors relied on intuitive assessments of the frequencies observed instead applying the methodology of statistical test procedures, which are based on test theory in the framework of mathematical statistics. This important shortcoming is criticised also by Hoffmann (2002). She collects data from an English corpus and counts the number of extrapositions of 'heavy' subjects. Table 4.1 and Figure 4.3, both taken from Hoffmann (2002), show the dependency of the ratio (*RFRQ*) of performed extrapositions (*PFRQ*) and possible extrapositions (*AFRQ*) on the lengths of the subjects.

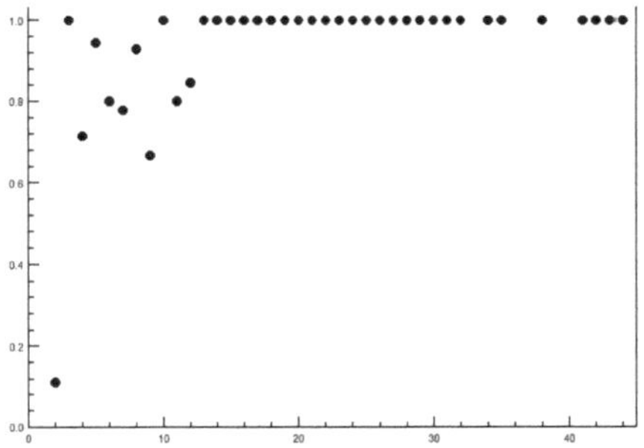

Figure 4.3: Dependency of the number of extrapositions (y-axis) on the length of the subjects.

Table 4.1: Dependency of the number of extrapositions on the length of the subjects

length	*PFRQ*	*AFRQ*	*RFRQ*	length	*PFRQ*	*AFRQ*	*RFRQ*
2	4	36	0.111111	21	4	4	1.000000
3	4	4	1.000000	22	4	4	1.000000
4	5	7	0.714286	23	1	1	1.000000
5	17	18	0.944444	24	4	4	1.000000
6	12	15	0.800000	25	5	5	1.000000
7	14	18	0.777778	26	5	5	1.000000
8	13	14	0.928571	27	2	2	1.000000
9	12	18	0.666667	28	3	3	1.000000
10	12	12	1.000000	29	7	7	1.000000
11	12	15	0.800000	30	3	3	1.000000
12	11	13	0.846154	31	4	4	1.000000
13	7	7	1.000000	32	2	2	1.000000
14	8	8	1.000000	34	4	4	1.000000
15	13	13	1.000000	35	1	1	1.000000
16	14	14	1.000000	38	1	1	1.000000
17	7	7	1.000000	41	2	2	1.000000
18	9	9	1.000000	42	1	1	1.000000
19	9	9	1.000000	43	1	1	1.000000
20	6	6	1.000000	44	1	1	1.000000

As the amount of available data is not large enough for a statistical test, Hoffmann conducts another study and collects data on the order of syntactically equal PP's in VP's from the Penn Treebank. Here, she tests the hypothesis that the number of cases with the longer PP after the shorter one is significantly greater than vice versa. The number of appropriate VP's in the sample is 1657. In this case, as two PP's are studied with respect to both their relative position and their lengths, the difference of the lengths was taken as the independent variable. Specifically, she shows that the probability of a long constituent being placed after a shorter one is a monotonous function of the difference of their lengths. Figure 4.4, also taken from Hoffmann (2008), shows the number of realisations of 'long after short' order. Hoffmann fitted two variants of growth functions to the data. The first variant was

$$y = 1 - \frac{1}{ae^{bx}}. \tag{4.4}$$

For the second variant Hoffmann (2008) chose the function

$$y = 1 - \frac{1}{ax^b}. \tag{4.5}$$

Variant (4.4) yields a good result ($R^2 = 0.9197$; cf. Figure 4.4, dashed line), as compared to the acceptable result for (4.5), with $R^2 = 0.8602$ (dotted line).

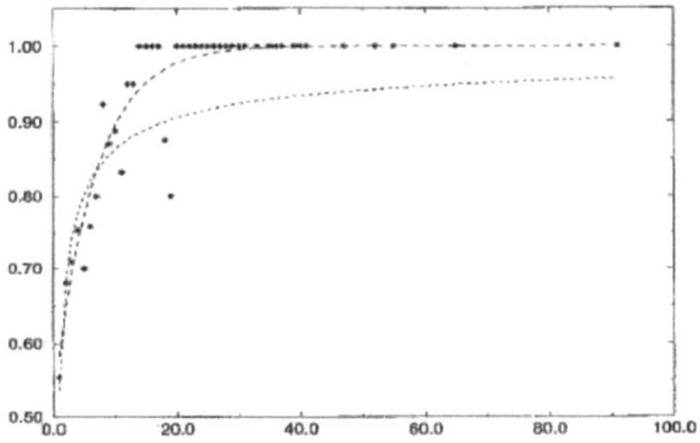

Figure 4.4: Relative number of 'long after short' order pairs of *PP*'s; the figure is taken from Hoffmann (1999)

Another empirical study on the relation between position and length of words can be found in Uhlířová (1997a,b). Köhler (1999) sets up a modified hypothesis, which is based, instead of length, on complexity of syntactic structures. Complexity of a syntactic structure is defined in this context as the number of its immediate constituents. The restriction concerning 'equality' of constituents is dropped; the hypothesis can be generalised as follows:

Hypothesis 1
The position of a constituent in the mother constituent is a monotonously increasing function of its complexity.

Given the fact that the phenomenon is also observable when word length is considered instead of the number of immediate constituents, we assume that we are concerned with an indirect effect. The modified hypothesis is tested on data from the Susanne corpus. Whereas the previously described investigations took into account only constituent pairs of 'equal status', in the cited study length, complexity, and absolute position data were collected and evaluated for all constituents in the corpus in two ways: on the sentence level and recursively on all levels. Figure 4.5 shows an example of the empirically observed interrelations; values of positions greater than 9 have not been taken into account because of their small frequency.

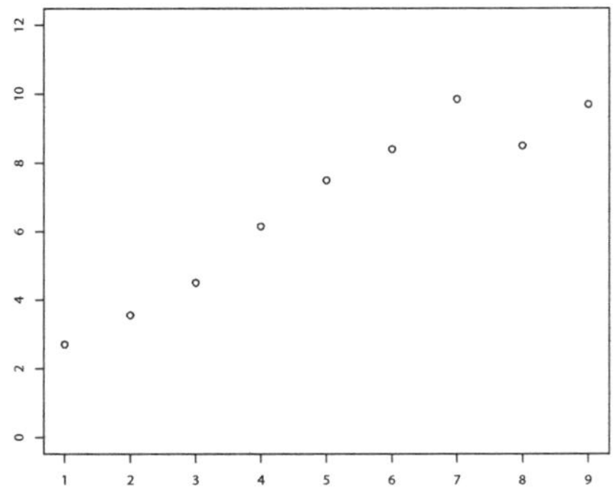

Figure 4.5: The empirical dependence of the average constituent length (in number of words) on position in the mother constituent

A theoretically derived hypothesis about the exact form of the dependence was not given in Köhler (1999); we will deliver one in section 4.2.6.

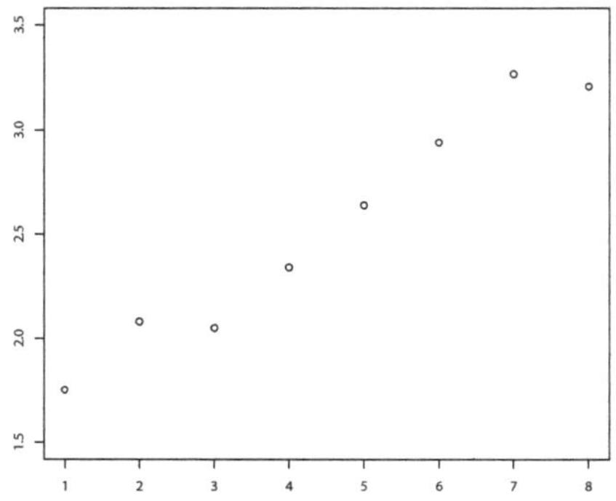

Figure 4.6: The empirical dependence of the average constituent complexity (in number of immediate constituents) on position in the mother constituent. The values of positions greater than 8 have not been taken into account because of their small frequency (< 10)

4.1.3 The Menzerath-Altmann law

The first observations of corresponding phonetic phenomena were published in the early 20th century – cf. the historical remarks in Cramer (2005). They described a 'compression effect', the fact that vowels tend to be pronounced in less time if they occur in long syllables. These studies remained on a purely descriptive level; the authors did not find a way to interpret or explain their findings.

The German phonetician and psychologist Paul Menzerath was the first to detect that the phenomenon is not limited to sound duration but can also be observed in form of the dependence of syllable length on word length: The longer a word (measured in terms of the number of syllables it consists of) the shorter (on average) the syllables of the given word. Menzerath interpreted his empirical results as an effect of a psychological principle, a 'rule of economy'economy. He assumed that this rule kept linguistic expressions manageable and summarised it in the statement "The larger the whole the smaller the parts" (Menzerath 1954: 100).

In 1980, Altmann hit upon Menzerath's works and published a paper generalising the hypothesis with respect to all levels of linguistic analysis (Altmann 1980). He formulated: "The longer a language construct the shorter its components (constituents)" (l.c.). He gave a theoretical derivation and the corresponding differential equation (4.6):

$$\frac{y'}{y} = -c + \frac{b}{x}. \tag{4.6}$$

The solution to this differential equation is the function

$$y = ax^{b}e^{-cx}, \tag{4.7}$$

where y is the (mean) size of the immediate constituents, x is the size of the construct, and a, b and c are parameters which seem to depend mainly on the level of the units under investigation – much more than on language, the kind of text, or author as previously expected. This law has been tested on data from many languages and on various levels of linguistic investigation. On the sentence level, however, not too many studies have been done for obvious reasons. Moreover, the existing results are not always comparable because there are no accepted standards, and researchers often apply ad-hoc criteria. We will, therefore, present here the results of the few existing studies and some additional new ones.

As far as we know, Köhler (1982) conducted the first empirical test of the Menzerath-Altmann law on the sentence level, analyzing German and English short stories and philosophical texts. The operationalisation of the concepts of construct and component was applied as follows: the highest constructs are sentences, their length being measured in the number of their constituents (i.e. clauses). Since it is not necessary to determine the lengths of the individual clauses, the mean length of the clauses of a sentence was calculated as the number of words of the given sentence divided by the number of clauses. The number of clauses is determined by counting the number of finite verbs in a sentence. The tests on the data confirmed the validity of the law with high significance. Table 4.2 shows an example (Köhler 1982) of the dependence of mean clause length on sentence length. Figure 4.7 illustrates the results, with a power function as fitted to the data.

Table 4.2: Empirical data: testing the Menzerath-Altmann law on the sentence level

sentence length (in clauses)	Mean clause length (in words)
1	9.7357
2	8.3773
3	7.3511
4	6.7656
5	6.1467
6	6.2424

There is strong empirical evidence for the assumption that, depending on the level of linguistic analysis, one of the two factors of the function – the exponential one or the power function – can be neglected. Consequently one of the parameters, b or c, can be set to 0. We obtain in a simplified form, either $y = ae^{-cx}$ or $y = ax^{b}$.

It is obvious from a large number of observations that the investigation of lower levels such as the phonetic or phonologic level yield a constellation of parameters where parameter b is close to zero whereas

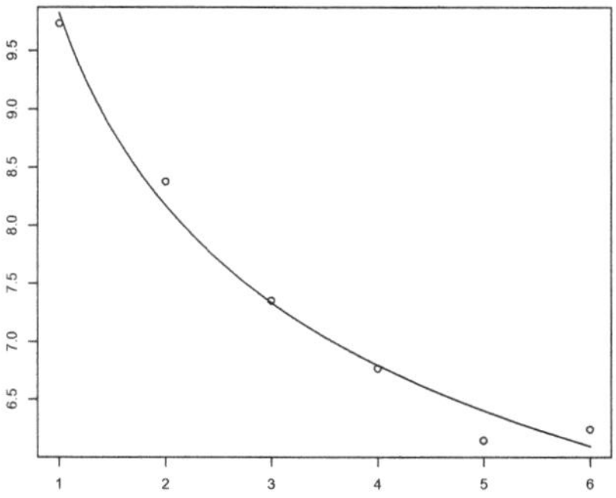

Figure 4.7: The Menzerath-Altmann law on the sentence/clause/word levels

higher levels lead to very small values of parameter *c*; only on intermediate levels, such as word length in morphs and morph length in syllables, the full formula is needed, i.e. with the exponential and the power law factor. This is why we estimate only *a* and *b* when the sentence level is under study.[3] Fitting the power function to the data from above yields $a = 9.8252$, $b = -0.2662$ and a determination coefficient $R^2 = 0.9858$.

Another study (Heups 1983) evaluates 10668 sentences from 13 texts (juridical publications, scientific and journalistic texts, novels, and letters) separated with respect to text genre. Her results confirm the Menzerath-Altmann law also with high significance.

Finally, we present four new tests, which were performed on data from four of the texts of the small corpus of literary language we used in Section 3.4.10; Table 4.3 gives the results of the fits.

Table 4.3: The Menzerath-Altmann law on the sentence level

	Text 1	**Text 2**	**Text 3**	**Text 4**
Parameter *a*	11.2475	10.7388	10.6450	12.5914
Parameter *b*	−0.3150	−0.2385	−0.2894	−0.3415
R^2	0.9457	0.7768	0.9355	0.9807

3. This has the advantage that the model has only two parameters, cf. above, p. 52.

Figures 4.8a–4.8d (p. 150) display the corresponding plots. As can

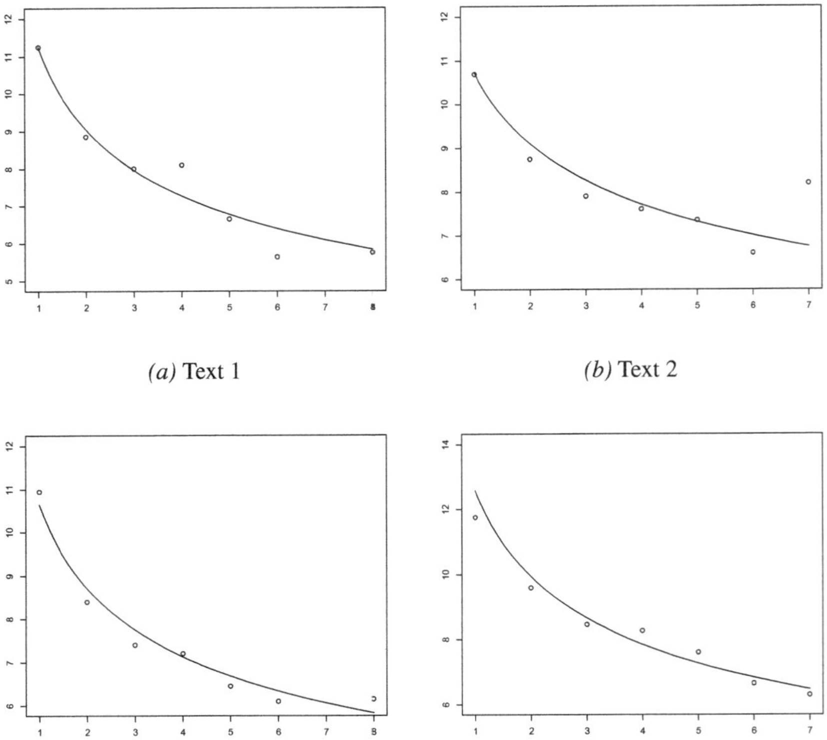

(a) Text 1 *(b)* Text 2

(c) Text 3 *(d)* Text 4

Figure 4.8: Plots of the Menzerath-Altmann law as fitted to the data from the four texts (cf. Table 4.3)

be seen, our studies confirm the validity of the Menzerath-Altmann law as do all the other investigations performed by many researchers on large amounts of data from dozens of languages. This is why this law is considered one of the most frequently corroborated laws in linguistics.

4.1.4 Distributions of syntactic properties

In Section 3.4.5 we presented the frequency distribution of syntactic construction types, i.e. the distribution of the frequency of specific units. Here, we will deal with distributions of properties of syntactic constructions. In Köhler (1999) a number of properties were defined and operationalised, in Altmann and Köhler (2000) the distributions of these properties were scrutinized on data from the Susanne and the Negra corpora[4]. We will present here these properties and show how they are measured. To illustrate the procedures we give a full graphical representation of the first sentence of the text A01 of the Susanne corpus (which was shown in its original column form in Section 4.1.3); the tags and the presentation differ from that in the corpus in order to make the analysis clearer.

4. Cf. Section 3.3.5

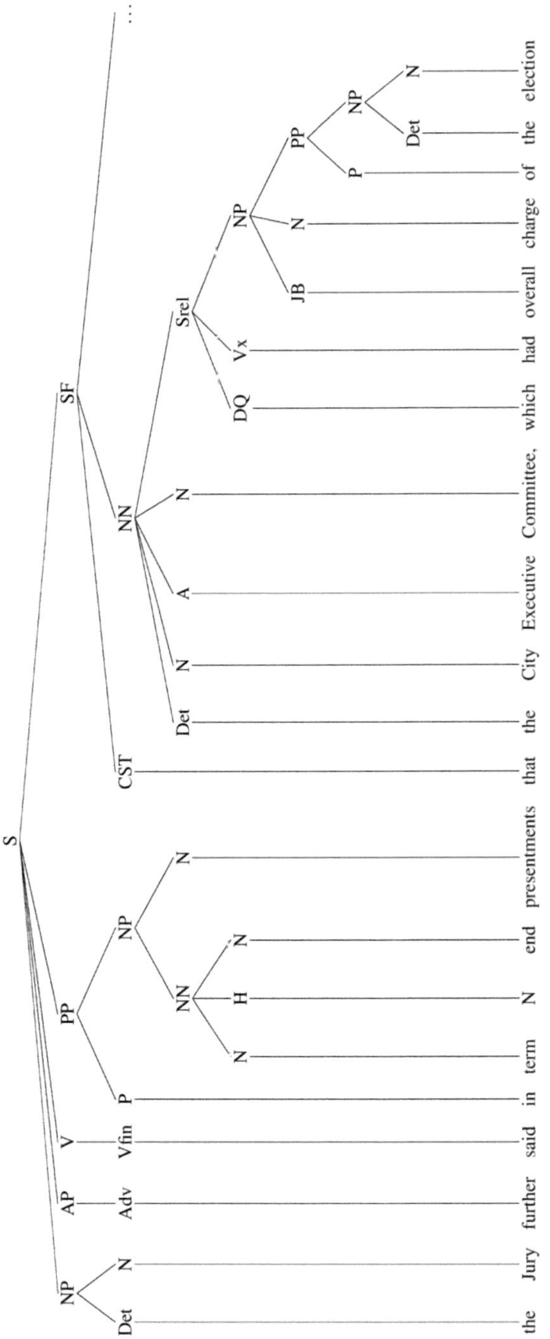
S
NP
AP
V
PP
SF
Det
N
Adv
Vfin
P
NP
CST
NN
NN
N
H
N
N
Det
N
A
N
Srel
DQ
Vx
NP
JB
N
PP
P
NP
Det
N
...
the
Jury
further
said
in
term
N
end
presentments
that
the
City
Executive
Committee,
which
had
overall
charge
of
the
election

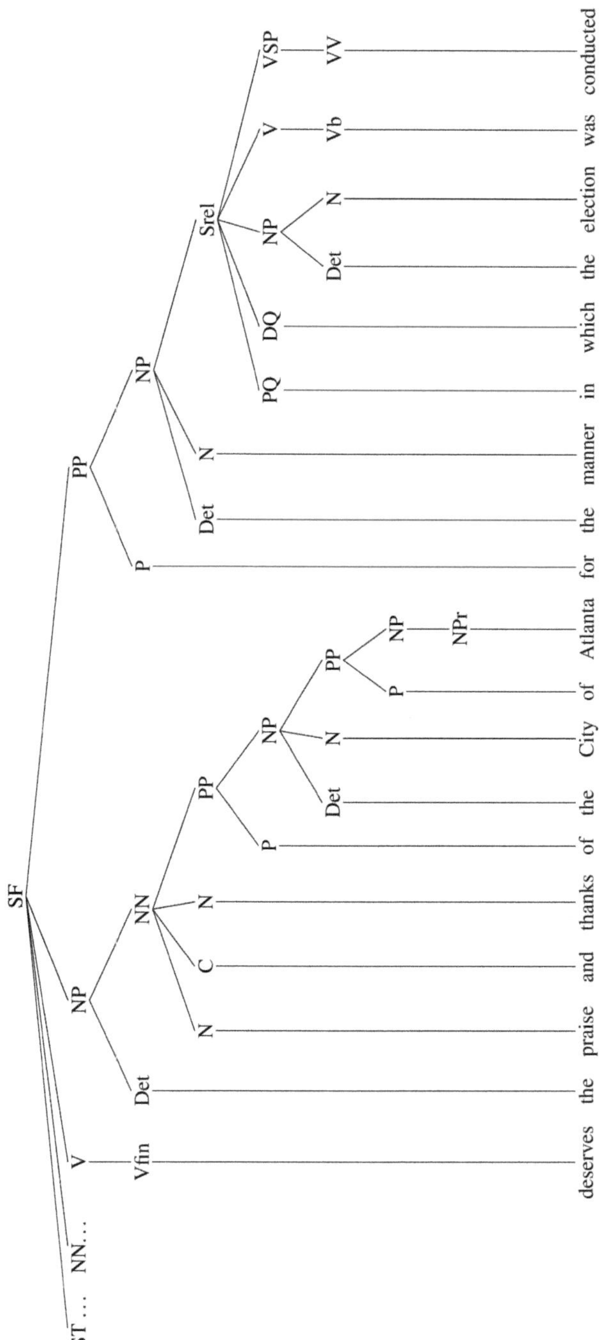

Figure 4.9: The structure of a sentence from text A01 in the Susanne corpus

4.1.4.1 Complexity

We define the complexity of a syntactic construction in terms of the number of its immediate constituents. In the sentence in Figure 4.9, *S* has a complexity of 5, the first *NP* has 2, and the *AP* and *V* have 1; the last clause of the sentence, a relative clause (tagged as *SRel*), has complexity 5. In this way, the complexities of all syntactic constructions in the corpora were measured. Then, the number of constructions with a given complexity was considered as a random variable.

First, we will show how we arrive at a mathematical model of a probability distribution, which then can be tested on empirical frequency distributions. We assume the following quantities to exert effects on the distribution:

1. A requirement of maximizing compactness. This enables diminishing the complexity on a given syntactic level by embedding constituents, which displace a part of the complexity to the next level. Thus, the sentence "The professors were not prepared and had to..." can be transformed into "The unprepared professors had to...", which is less complex (by one constituent) while the subject *NP* becomes more complex (by one constituent). Therefore, *minX* on level *m* corresponds to the requirement *maxH* on level $m+1$. We introduced this kind of compactness need above where we discussed the dependence of complexity on position (cf. Section 4.1.2). We will denote this quantity by *maxH*;
2. The requirement for minimization of the complexity of a syntactic construction in order to decrease memory effort in processing the construction. It will be symbolised by *minX*;
3. A quantity *E* representing the average degree of elaborateness, the default value of complexity. This quantity is variable in dependence on speaker/writer, situation etc., but it can be considered constant within a given text;
4. $I(K)$ – the size of the inventory of constructions. The more different types of constructions are available in the inventory, the less complexity is necessary on the average.

To set up a model of the frequency distribution of complexity, we assume that the number of constructions with complexity x depends on the number of constructions with complexity $x-1$. The idea behind this is that more complex constructions are formed on the basis of less complex ones by adding one (or more) constituents. The requirement *maxH* has an increasing effect on the probability of a higher complexity whereas *minX* has a decreasing effect. Furthermore, it seems plausible to assume that the probability of an increase of a given complexity $x-1$ by 1 depends on $x-1$, i.e. on the complexity already reached. The quantities E and $I(K)$ have opposite effect on complexity: the greater the inventory, the less complexity must be introduced. According to a general approach proposed by Altmann (cf. Altmann and Köhler 1996), the following equation can be set up:

$$P_x = \frac{maxH + x}{minX + x} \frac{E}{I(K)} P_{x-1} \, . \tag{4.8}$$

With $maxH = k-1$, $minX = m-1$, and $E/I(K) = q$, (4.8) can be written in the well-known form

$$P_x = \frac{k+x-1}{m+x-1} q P_{x-1} \, , \tag{4.9}$$

which yields the hyper-Pascal distribution (cf. Wimmer and Altmann 1999):

$$P_x = \frac{\binom{k+x-1}{x}}{\binom{m+x-1}{x}} q^x P_0 \tag{4.10}$$

with $P_0^{-1} = {}_2F_1(k,1;m;q)$ – the hypergeometric function – as normalising constant. Here, (4.10) is used in a 1-displaced form because complexity 0 is not defined.

An empirical test of the corresponding hypothesis was conducted using the complete Susanne corpus with its 101138 constituents, whose complexities and their frequency distribution were determined. Another test was conducted on the corresponding data from the Negra-Korpus with a sample size of 71494 constructions. Fitting the hyper-Pascal distribution to these data yielded the results shown in Tables 4.4 (cf. Figure 4.10) and Table 4.5 (cf. Figure 4.11).

Table 4.4: Complexity data from the Susanne corpus

x_i	f_i	Np_i	x_i	f_i	Np_i
1	29723	29003.27	7	225	572.41
2	40653	41471.76	8	51	242.79
3	16423	17645.46	9	5	102.97
4	9338	7493.70	10	2	43.67
5	3681	3180.43	11	3	18.52
6	1033	1349.40	12	1	13.63
$k = 0.0054, m = 0.0016, q = 0.4239$					
$\chi^2 = 1245.63, DF = 8, C = 0.0123$					

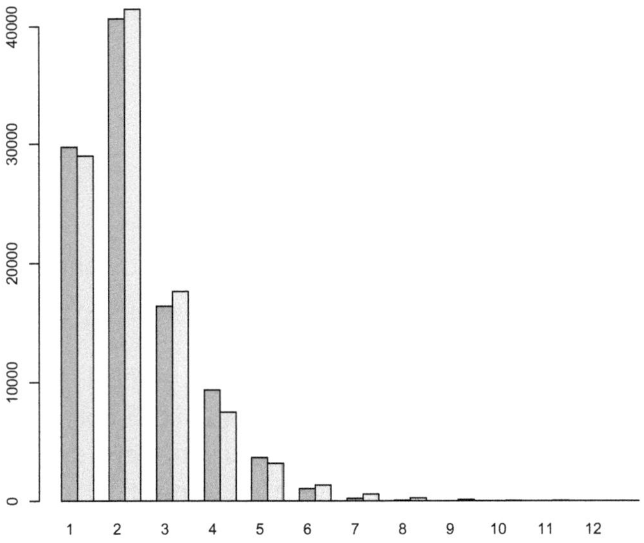

Figure 4.10: Complexity data from the Susanne corpus

Table 4.5: Complexity data from the Negra corpus

x_i	f_i	Np_i	x_i	f_i	Np_i
1	1565	2488.46	9	18	58.39
2	27993	28350.87	10	5	17.38
3	23734	22107.40	11	3	5.03
4	11723	11264.09	12	3	1.43
5	4605	4689.75	13	1	0.40
6	1425	1731.26	14	0	0.11
7	353	589.76	15	1	0.04
8	65	189.64			

$k = 2.6447, m = 0.0523, q = 0.2251$
$\chi^2 = 760.50, DF = 8, C = 0.0106$

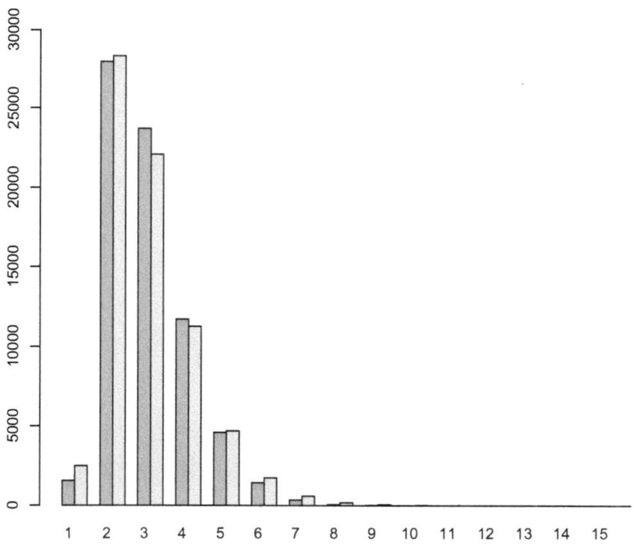

Figure 4.11: Complexity data from the Negra-Korpus

The samples are rather large and therefore the χ^2 test must fail. Instead, the coefficient $C = \chi^2/N$ is calculated. When $C \leq 0.02$, the fit is acceptable. Hence, both hypotheses are considered as compatible with the data. Consequently, the assumptions which led to the model may be maintained until counter-evidence is provided.

4.1.4.2 Depth

As depth in the sense of Section 4.1.1 varies from construction to construction in a text and in a corpus, we consider it as a random variable and determine its frequency distribution. Again, to set up a mathematical model we have to reflect which quantities play a role in the variability of depth. As in (4.1), the requirement of maximization of compactness (*maxH*) has an increasing effect on the tendency towards great depths (because it is depth, which makes compactness possible without loss of information). And the opposing "force", the requirement of limiting the depth of embedding (*minT*), which represents, in analogy to Yngve's depth saving principle, the limitations of the language processing memory. To arrive at a probability distribution we proceed in a similar way as above with the complexity variable. Starting with equation (4.11)

$$P_x = \frac{maxH + x}{minT + x} E P_{x-1}, \tag{4.11}$$

we substitute $maxH = k - 1$, $minT = n - 1$, and $E = q$ and obtain

$$P_x = \frac{k + x - 1}{m + x - 1} q P_{x-1}. \tag{4.12}$$

In spite of the fact that (4.11) contains only three parameters whereas (4.8) had four of them, we obtain again the hyper-Pascal distribution (4.10). The reason is simple: $I(K)$, which is not present in (4.11) is constant (in a language and also within the stylistic and grammatical repertoires of an author), whence the only formal difference between the two models is the value of a parameter.

The results of fitting the hyper-Pascal distribution, to the depth data of the two corpora is shown in Table 4.6 (cf. Figure 4.12) and Table 4.7 (cf. Figure 4.13), from which we conclude that the present hypothesis is compatible with the data.

Table 4.6: Fitting the hyper-Pascal distribution to depth data (Susanne corpus)

x_i	f_i	Np_i	x_i	f_i	Np_i
0	6699	6637.72	11	284	385.04
1	26632	27015.06	12	164	232.88
2	21501	22474.77	14	42	84.38
3	16443	15976.09	15	22	50.59
4	11300	10679.13	16	7	30.27
5	7484	6907.69	17	5	18.08
6	4684	4377.71	18	3	10.78
7	2789	2735.89	19	2	6.42
8	1601	1692.58	20	2	3.82
9	899	1039.09	21	1	5.56
10	481	634.07			

$k = 0.5449, m = 0.0777, q = 0.5803$
$\chi^2 = 370.20, DF = 18, C = 0.0037$

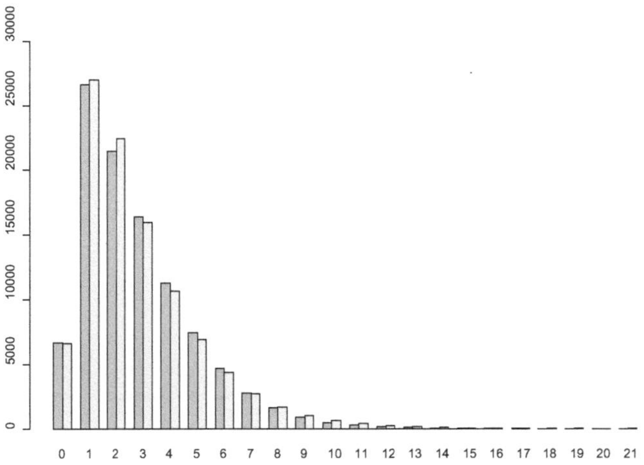

Figure 4.12: Fitting the hyper-Pascal distribution to depth data (Susanne corpus)

Table 4.7: Fitting the hyper-Pascal distribution to depth data (Negra-Korpus)

x_i	f_i	Np_i	x_i	f_i	Np_i
1	9954	10988.90	7	1050	1409.45
2	20254	20795.84	8	372	635.07
3	18648	17293.82	9	155	276.65
4	11913	10924.60	10	47	117.36
5	6333	5978.07	11	12	48.73
6	2752	2992.45	12	4	33.07

$k = 0.5449, m = 0.0777, q = 0.5803$
$\chi^2 = 370.20, DF = 18, C = 0.0037$

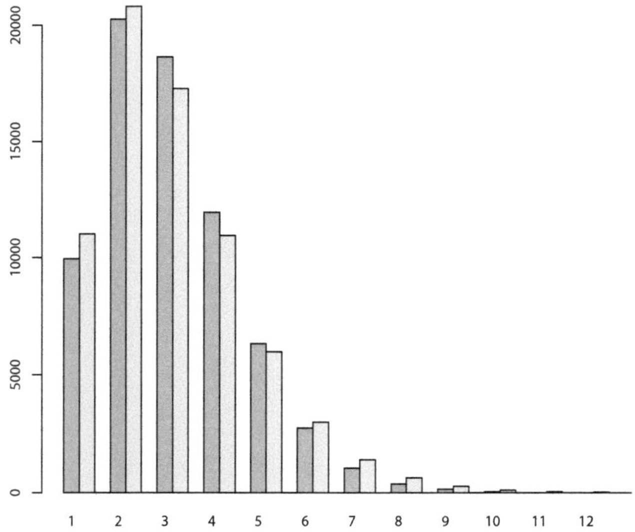

Figure 4.13: Fitting the hyper-Pascal distribution to depth data (Negra-Korpus)

4.1.4.3 Length

As mentioned in Section 4.1.2, Hawkins (1990, 1992, 1994) collected data on constituent length in terms of the number of words as a measure of the variable he took for relevant for the effect on constituent order, whereas we used complexity in terms of the number of immediate constituents. Now, it seems quite obvious that constituent length in the number of words is a (stochastic) function of complexity in our sense: the more daughter nodes, the longer the terminal projection (we assume that type 0 grammars can be excluded from our considerations). The function is not deterministic because we do not have the full trees in our focus and cannot know to how many daughter nodes the immediate constituents we look at are expanded.

Now, as length is a function of complexity, the requirement *minX* is given implicitly and must not be represented in the model of length distribution again. Hence, we set $minX = 0$ in (4.8) and obtain

$$P_x = \frac{maxH + x}{x} \frac{E}{I(K)} P_{x-1} \,. \tag{4.13}$$

Substituting $maxH = k-1$, $E/I(K) = q (0 < q < 1)$ and, since length 0 is not defined here, solving for $x = 2, 3, \ldots$, we obtain the positive negative binomial distribution

$$P_x = \frac{\binom{k+x-1}{x} p^k q^x}{1-p^k} \,. \tag{4.14}$$

For the special case when $maxH = -1$ we obtain from (4.14) the logarithmic distribution

$$P_x = \frac{q^x}{-x \ln(1-q)} \,. \tag{4.15}$$

The complexity distribution (4.10) is unimodal whereas the logarithmic distribution decreases monotonously. In (4.8), Complexity 2 is the most frequent, which means that length 1 must be less frequent than length 2. Therefore, (4.15) is displaced by one unity to the right and the missing probability at $x = 1$ is estimated *ad hoc* as $1 - \alpha$, with

$\hat{\alpha} = 1 - f_1/N$. Thus, we obtain from (4.14) the extended positive negative binomial distribution (4.16)

$$P_x = \begin{cases} 1-\alpha & x = 1 \\ \dfrac{\alpha \binom{k+x-2}{x-1} p^k q^{x-1}}{1-p^k} & x = 2,3,\ldots \end{cases} \tag{4.16}$$

and from (4.15) the extended logarithmic distribution (4.17)

$$P_x = \begin{cases} 1-\alpha & x = 1 \\ \dfrac{aq^x}{-(x-1)\ln(1-q)} & x = 2,3,\ldots \end{cases} \tag{4.17}$$

The empirical test of the hypothesis that length is distributed according to the extended logarithmic distribution, conducted on the Susanne data is shown in Table 4.8.

Table 4.8: Fitting the extended logarithmic distribution to the data of the Susanne corpus

x	f_x	Np_x	x	f_x	Np_x	x	f_x	Np_x
1	28557	28557.00	63	2	13.11	125	0	0.21
2	21903	23480.24	64	5	12.21	126	0	0.20
3	12863	11110.29	65	2	11.37	127	0	0.19
4	6706	7009.50	66	4	10.60	128	0	0.18
5	4809	4975.09	67	0	9.88	129	0	0.17
6	3742	3766.55	68	3	9.21	130	0	0.16
7	2903	2970.41	69	2	8.59	131	1	0.15
8	2342	2409.47	70	1	8.01	132	0	0.14
9	1959	1995.18	71	1	7.47	133	0	0.13
10	1709	1678.35	72	1	6.97	134	0	0.12
11	1430	1429.48	73	2	6.50	135	1	0.11
12	1297	1229.81	74	2	6.07	136	1	0.11
13	1109	1066.85	75	1	5.67	137	0	0.10
14	989	931.95	76	2	5.29	138	0	0.09

(continued on next page)

Table 4.8 (continued from previous page)

x	f_x	Np_x	x	f_x	Np_x	x	f_x	Np_x
15	845	818.96	77	1	4.94	139	0	0.09
16	808	723.36	78	1	4.62	140	0	0.08
17	691	641.77	79	0	4.31	141	0	0.08
18	644	571.61	80	4	4.03	142	0	0.07
19	606	510.89	81	1	3.77	143	0	0.07
20	540	458.04	82	2	3.52	144	0	0.07
21	437	411.79	83	0	3.29	145	0	0.06
22	417	371.14	84	0	3.08	146	0	0.06
23	400	335.27	85	2	2.88	147	0	0.05
24	351	303.49	86	1	2.69	148	0	0.05
25	291	275.24	87	0	2.52	149	0	0.05
26	281	250.05	88	0	2.35	150	0	0.05
27	264	227.54	89	1	2.20	151	0	0.04
28	233	207.36	90	0	2.06	152	0	0.04
29	205	189.22	91	1	1.93	153	0	0.04
30	193	172.90	92	2	1.80	154	0	0.04
31	173	158.17	93	1	1.69	155	0	0.03
32	171	144.85	94	0	1.58	156	0	0.03
33	133	132.80	95	1	1.48	157	0	0.03
34	122	121.87	96	2	1.39	158	0	0.03
35	98	111.94	97	1	1.30	159	0	0.03
36	102	102.90	98	0	1.22	160	0	0.02
37	103	94.68	99	1	1.14	161	0	0.02
38	70	87.18	100	0	1.07	162	0	0.02
39	78	80.33	101	0	1.00	163	0	0.02
40	47	74.07	102	0	0.94	164	0	0.02
41	47	68.34	103	0	0.88	165	0	0.02
42	54	63.10	104	1	0.82	166	0	0.02
43	46	58.29	105	1	0.77	167	0	0.02
44	37	53.88	106	0	0.72	168	0	0.01
45	26	49.83	107	1	0.68	169	0	0.01
46	30	46.11	108	0	0.64	170	0	0.01
47	27	42.69	109	0	0.60	171	0	0.01
48	24	39.54	110	0	0.56	172	0	0.01
49	17	36.64	111	0	0.52	173	0	0.01
50	13	33.97	112	0	0.49	174	0	0.01

(continued on next page)

Table 4.8 (continued from previous page)

x	f_x	Np_x	x	f_x	Np_x	x	f_x	Np_x
51	19	31.50	113	0	0.46	175	1	0.01
52	21	29.23	114	0	0.43	176	0	0.01
53	7	27.13	115	1	0.41	177	0	0.01
54	12	25.19	116	1	0.38	178	0	0.01
55	14	23.39	117	0	0.36	179	0	0.01
56	7	21.74	118	0	0.33	180	0	0.01
57	9	20.20	119	1	0.31	181	0	0.01
58	7	18.78	120	0	0.29	182	0	0.01
59	11	17.47	121	2	0.28	183	0	0.01
60	7	16.25	122	1	0.26	184	0	0.01
61	12	15.12	123	0	0.24	185	0	0.01
62	5	14.08	124	1	0.23	186	1	0.09

$\alpha = 0.9464$, $\theta = 0.7176$
$\chi^2 = 795.00$, $DF = 109$, $C = 0079$

Figure 4.14 illustrates the results of fitting these data to the extended logarithmic distribution.

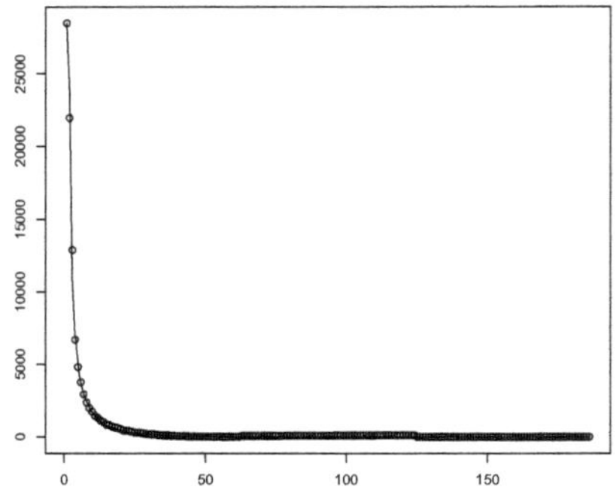

Figure 4.14: Fitting the extended logarithmic distribution to the data of the Susanne corpus

Again, the large sample sizes cause the χ^2 test to fail, but the C values are quite good ($C = 0.0079$ for the Susanne data and $C = 0.0091$ in the case of the Negra data) and we may consider the hypotheses as supported by the data.

4.1.4.4 Position

In Section 4.2.7, the functional dependences between complexity and position and between position and depth will be analysed. It may be counter-intuitive but we will show that position too can be treated as a random variable with its corresponding distribution. Every constituent is located at a definite position in its mother constituent. In the example sentence in Figure 4.9 (p. 153f.), the first *NP* has position 1 in the sentence, *AP* has position 2, *V* has 3, *PP* has 4, and so forth. In the *PP*, *P* has the first position, and *NP* the second. In this *NP*, *NN* has position 1, and *N* has 2. We will now consider the probability of finding a constituent at a given position x in its mother constituent. This probability depends on the complexity of the mother constituent (which is, as we know, distributed according to the hyper-Pascal distribution), because there is no position in a constituent which exceeds the number of its daughter constituents. We will now consider the distribution of the number of constituents in a corpus which are located at a given position (there are f_1 constituents at position 1 in their mother constituent, f_2 constituents at position 2, and so forth).

For a theoretical derivation of a probability distribution for this variable we have to take into account that complexity is given implicitly (the complexity of a constituent is its maximum position); the requirement does not play any role here. Using the same approach as before we can set $minX = 0$ in (4.8), thus leaving x in the denominator. Compactness, resulting from the requirement of minimization of complexity on the level of the mother constituent, is a constant for every given constituent, where position is regarded as the random variable, and is therefore set to $n+1$ (where n is the maximum position). Substituting p/q for $E/I(K)$, we obtain

$$P_x = \frac{n-x+1}{x}\frac{p}{q}P_{x-1}\,,\ x = 1,2,\ldots,n, \tag{4.18}$$

which solves to the binomial distribution

$$P_x = \binom{n}{x} p^x q^{n-x}\,,\ x = 0,1,\ldots,n. \tag{4.19}$$

Since position 0 is not defined, the distribution must be displaced to the right by one. As was observed in Altmann and Köhler (2000), and as can be seen from Figures 4.15a and 4.15b, the empirical data from the two corpora are quite different. The Negra-Korpus has even a non-monotonous shape which may be due to the grammatical analysis used for this corpus, which is flat and attaches the finite verb directly to the *S* node.

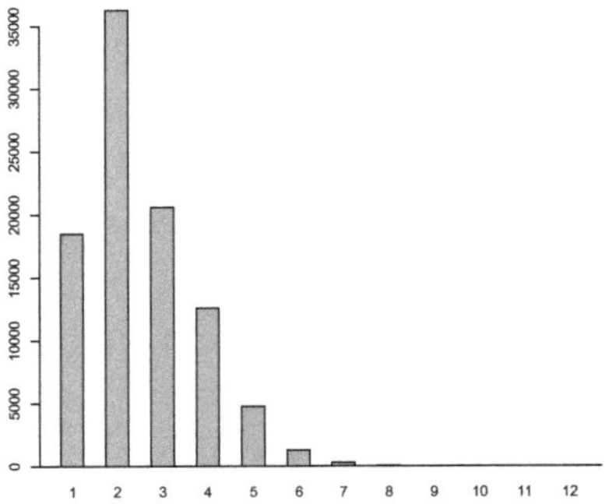

(a) Susanne corpus

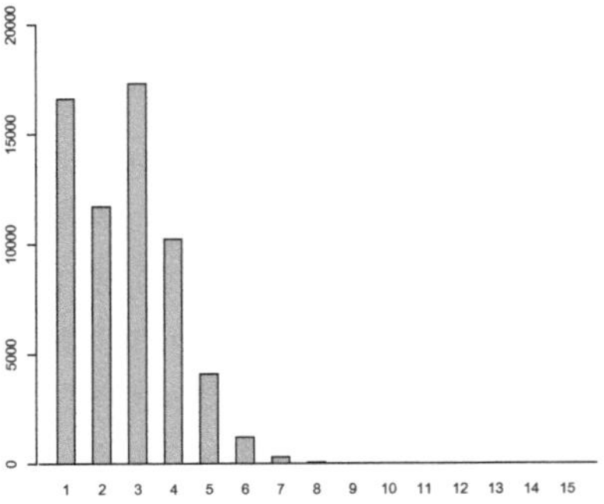

(b) Negra-Korpus

Figure 4.15: Empirical distribution of the position variable

A mathematical model which can take account of such distortions can be set up by modifying the original distribution accordingly in the following way ($P'x$ is the resulting distribution):

$$P'_x = \begin{cases} P_0 + \alpha P_1 & x = 1 \\ P_1(1-\alpha) & x = 2 \\ P_{x-1} & x = 3, 4, \ldots, n+1 \end{cases} \tag{4.20}$$

i.e., a part of the probability is shifted from P_1 to P_0, which yields the so-called 1-displaced Cohen-binomial distribution (cf. Cohen 1960; Wimmer, Witkowský, and Altmann 1999), explicitly:

$$P'_x = \begin{cases} q^n(1 + \alpha np/q) & x = 1 \\ npq^{n-1}(1-\alpha) & x = 2 \\ \binom{n}{x-1} p^{x-1} q^{n-x+1} & x = 3, 4, \ldots, n+1 \end{cases} \tag{4.21}$$

For modifications of this kind, which are common in empirical sciences when measurement errors or influences by the design of the analysis must be taken into account – see Wimmer and Altmann (1999).

The results of fitting (4.21) to the Susanne corpus can be seen in Tables 4.9 and in Figure 4.16; the C values are rather good; therefore, we consider the hypotheses as supported by the data.

Table 4.9: Fitting the Cohen-binomial distribution to the position data from the Susanne corpus

x_i	f_i	Np_i	x_i	f_i	Np_i
1	18492	20200.81	7	281	297.12
2	36277	31639.56	8	61	57.78
3	20621	24324.79	9	9	9.58
4	12599	12170.34	10	5	1.37
5	4790	4460.65	11	4	0.17
6	1299	1276.79	12	1	0.02
$p = 0.0337$, $\alpha = 0.0011$					
$\chi^2 = 1474.41, DF = 6, C = 0.0015$					

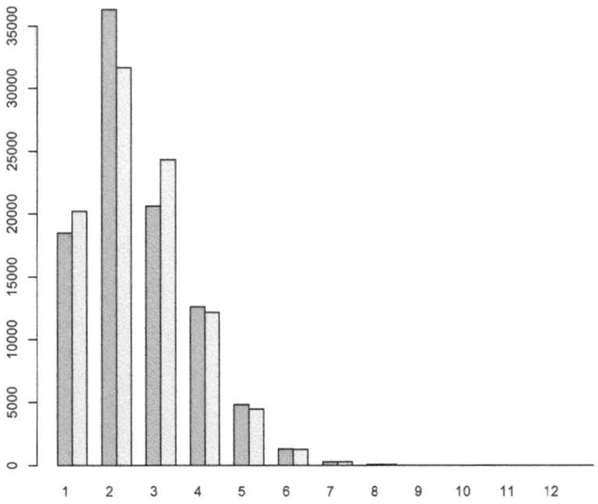

Figure 4.16: Fitting the Cohen-binomial distribution to the position data from the Susanne corpus

Fitting the data from the Negra corpus to (4.21), yields the results in Table 4.10; the results from Table 4.10 are graphically presented in Figure 4.17 (p. 168). As can be seen, the C values are rather good in both cases; we therefore consider the hypothesis as supported by the data.

Table 4.10: Fitting the Cohen-binomial distribution to the position data from the Negra corpus

x_i	f_i	Np_i	x_i	f_i	Np_i
1	16600	16865.62	9	19	5.38
2	11704	11184.08	10	8	0.52
3	17308	17682.06	11	3	0.04
4	10229	10242.64	12	4	0
5	4093	4079.10	13	2	0
6	1212	1181.44	14	1	0
7	297	256.64	15	1	0
8	59	42.48			

$p = 0.1265$, $\alpha = 0.4046$, $n = 14$
$\chi^2 = 63.06$, $DF = 3$, $C = 0.0010$

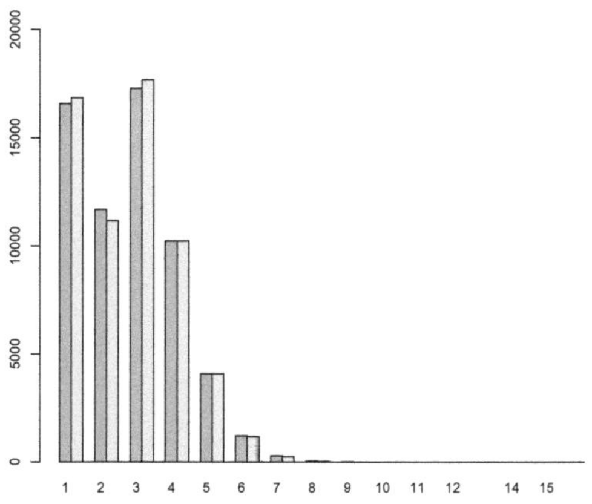

Figure 4.17: Fitting the Cohen-binomial distribution to the position data from the Negra corpus

4.2 Structure, function, and processes

4.2.1 The synergetic approach to linguistics

Theories consist of systems of universal laws, without which explanation is not possible. The main concern of synergetic linguistics, an approach that was presented in Köhler (1986), is to provide a framework for linguistic theory building. This is a modelling approach which can be used to set up universal hypotheses by deduction from theoretical considerations, to test them, to combine them into a network of laws and law-like statements, and to explain the phenomena observed. Another concern is to re-establish a view on language that has been lost during the last decades: the view of language as a psycho-social and as a biological-cognitive phenomenon at the same time (the emphasis that the cognitive paradigm has put on the latter aspect has almost completely displaced the former one in linguistics.)

As linguistic explanation is not likely to be possible by means of causal relations, synergetic linguistics aims at functional explanation (similar to biology). This type of explanation, however, is logically sound only under certain circumstances. A central axiom of synergetic linguistics is, therefore, that language is a self-organising and self-regulating system (similar to an organism, a view which may remind of 19th century concepts) – a special kind of dynamic system with particular properties. It is a happy coincidence that the theoretical results of linguistic research that self-organisation is an essential property of linguistic and some other semiotic systems, together with its empirical corroboration, has come at the same time as the emergence of a new sub-discipline of systems theory: synergetics.

The synergetic approach is a specific branch of systems theory (von Bertalanffy 1968) and can be characterised as an interdisciplinary approach to modelling certain dynamic aspects of systems which occur in different disciplines at different objects of investigation in an analogous way. Its particularity which separates it from other systems theoretical approaches is that it focuses on the spontaneous rise and the development of structures. Some emphasis should be put on the fact that considering an object as a system does not describe in any way a property of that object but rather says that the researcher wants to analyse the object with regard to certain aspects and by means of certain methods. Specifically, synergetic research concentrates on self-organising systems, which have been investigated since 30 years in several sciences. Outstanding exponents of this research are Manfred Eigen (1971) with his seminal work on the emergence of biological systems (macromolecules) by self-organisation of ordinary matter, Ilya Prigogine (Prigogine 1979; Prigogine and Stengers 1988) who works on self-regulating chemical processes, and Hermann Haken who founded – starting from his research on the laser effect – synergetics as a comprehensive theory of cooperative processes in systems far from equilibrium (cf. Haken and Graham 1971; Haken 1978).

Stable systems irreversibly evolve towards a stable state and increase in this process their entropy (second principle of thermodynamics); i.e. their degree of order decreases over time (the particles of an ink drop in a glass of water distribute more and more and will never find together again to form a drop. Only systems far from equilibrium have, under certain conditions, the ability to spontaneously form new structures by transformation from old structures or even out of chaos. Frequently mentioned examples of spontaneously built structures are cloud patterns, patterns in liquids being heated, oscillating chemical reactions, the coherent light of a laser, the emergence of life out of inanimate matter and its evolution towards higher and higher levels of organisation. The synergetic approach offers concepts and models which are suitable to explain such phenomena as results of a combination of the vagaries of chance and necessity. A characteristic property of self-organising systems is the existence of cooperative (and competing) processes, which constitute, together with external factors, the dynamics of the system. Other crucial elements of synergetics are the enslaving principle and the order parameters: if a process *A* follows dynamically another process *B*, it is called enslaved by *B*; order parameters are macroscopic entities which determine the behaviour of the microscopic mechanisms without being represented on their level themselves.

The explanatory power of synergetic models is based on the process-oriented approach of synergetics. The modelling procedure starts from known or assumed mechanisms and processes of the object under study and formulates them by means of appropriate mathematical expressions (e.g. differential equations). The system's behaviour can then be derived from the relations between the processes and the controlling order parameters. The possibility to form new structures is essentially connected with the existence of fluctuations, which make up the motor of evolution. The possible system states ("modes") which can occur (driven by the fluctuations) on the basis of the relations described by the equations are limited by the boundary conditions and order parameters. Only those modes can prevail in their competition with other ones which fit with these limitations. In self-organising systems, the prevailing modes are those which contribute in some way or other to the function of the system.

There is an indispensable pre-condition for the application of synergetic models: a view of language – or more generally of semiotic systems – that goes beyond the structural relations between the elements (i.e., the structuralist view, which is still present in the current formalisms of mainstream linguistics), viz. a concept that integrates also the function and thus the usage of the signs. An explanation of existence, properties, and changes of semiotic systems is not possible without the aspect of the (dynamic) interdependence of structure and function. Genesis and evolution of these systems must be attributed to repercussions of communication upon structure – cf. Bunge (1998), as opposed to Köhler and Martináková (1998). To outline the essential features of synergetic-linguistic modelling, a rough sketch of an application of the corresponding method to a linguistic (or semiotic) problem will be given without going into mathematical detail. Starting point is the question why semiotic systems change. We know that in the use (realisation) of semiotic systems and signs, in every particular communicative situation, fluctuations occur: every time new variants appear in different degrees of variation. The survival probability of the resulting configurations of features (modes), i.e. the extent to which they are recognised as realisations and exponents of the intended sign, depends on how well they confirm to certain conditions – in the first place the order parameters, which mediate between the needs of the language users (macro-level) and the microscopic mechanisms of sign production and perception. An example of such a need is the requirement of minimisation of production effort (symbolised in synergetic linguistics by *minP*), which was introduced already by G.K. Zipf (1949) as "principle of least effort"effort. This need corresponds to the speakers' (unconscious) strategy to, e.g. neglect phonetic or graphematic distinctions in order to diminish the efforts of muscle movement and coordination. One of the unintended side-effects of this behaviour is the increase of the overall similarity of the sounds (or letters) in the system. Another order parameter, viz. the requirement of minimisation of memory effort (*minM*), supports economising distinctive features, and promotes therefore a process, which co-operates with the previously considered one. According to what has been said up to now, a phoneme system which would optimally meet the needs of its users should consist of sounds with maximum similarity (absolute similarity would produce a system of identical sounds, i.e. of just one single sound). This hypothetical impossibility of differentiation between sounds has an effect on another variable of the sound system – the size of inventory: The more the possibility of differentiation decreases, the smaller becomes the number of sounds which can be used effectively. This effect on the inventory size is, by the way, favourable as far as *minM* is concerned – the economisation of memory. On the other hand, reduction in distinctiveness always diminishes intelligibility on the side of the hearer, whose need for reduction of decoding effort has also to be met. This need (*minD*) leads to changes which are opposite in effect to the former ones: it produces a tendency towards a lower similarity of sounds and (indirectly) towards a larger inventory. A change of inventory size, however, has a direct effect on the average length of the words. The more sounds (phonemes) are available for the formation of lexical units, the shorter becomes the mean length of the resulting words. The needs *minP* and *minM*, however, call for the smallest possible value of the variable word length.

Thus, we can see that a concept which considers the development and change of languages as a dynamic characteristic of organism-like systems may help to understand the processes which are responsible for the origin of the structures observed by linguistics. So far, the example has shown in which way the requirements of the language environment are used as instances for a functional explanation (see below).

The elements under consideration have become a part of the language system, because they possess certain properties and have certain functions within the system. We will show that the same principle holds also for the field of syntax.

The role of mutation and selection in the process of language change can be compared to those in biology. The inevitable deviations and variations in syntactic structures e.g., by unifying word order patterns *per analogiam* in the speech process can be regarded as a source of mutations, whereas the feed-back provided by the hearer takes care for the necessary selection. Neglecting the local micro-processes associated with the human individuals, the common effect of the processes represents an adaptation mechanism influencing the equilibrium on the competitive needs of speaker and hearer – without ever being able to reach a stable state, since the language environment changes itself and since the approximation to a potential stable state in one subsystem may have opposite effects in other subsystems.

4.2.2 Language Evolution

If the motor of evolution consist merely of mutation and selection, then how can complicated systems such as language develop? Obviously the huge space of possible values of parameters could not successfully be handled by these two mechanisms alone in order that optimal solutions be found. Another objection is the existence of local maxima, which act as traps for development based on optimisation by mutation and selection. Finally, a process of development towards structures of increasing complexity seems to contradict basic laws of nature. At this point the problem cannot be treated in detail; yet, an idea of how these questions might be answered can be given as follows:

1. We must not consider a variable and its dynamics in isolation. Adaptation proceeds in all elements of the system simultaneously. Therefore, a variable which is trapped at a local optimum for a certain time will be drawn away from it by the other variables to which it is connected via functional dependencies.
2. Development is not restricted to the lowest (or any single) level of the system. A system such as language consists of a large num-

ber of hierarchically structured levels. Thus, if a subsystem on a given level is subject to change, all its parts, i.e. subsystems on lower levels will also be affected. The same is true of other parts of the system which are not parts of the given one but are functionally connected to it. In this way, a small step of one subsystem or on one level may cause a series of large leaps in other subsystems or on other levels.

3. The more complicated a system appears from one point of view the less it may do so from another. The objection formulated above only makes sense if we regard the simplest system as a completely unstructured one. This means that the elements of the system are unconnected to each other or connected in an unpredictable way. Under those criteria the situation is in fact the most complex one – its description must contain at least as many items as there are elements among them in the system. Thus, an introduction of structure (clusters, patterns, hierarchies) reduces complexity. So, in the case of evolutionary self-organisation, more ordered structures appear, whenever a reduction in complexity meets the requirements of the environment. In the case of language, systems have to evolve along with the biological and cultural evolution of humankind. Human language and human physiological equipment are results of and reflect the co-evolution of these systems.

4.2.3 The logics of explanation

According to the results of the philosophy of science, there is one widely accepted type of explanation: the deductive-nomologic one, which can be illustrated by the scheme

$$\frac{\left.\begin{array}{l} L_1, L_2, L_3, \ldots, L_n \\ C_1, C_2, C_3, \ldots, C_m \end{array}\right\} \text{Explanans}}{E \qquad\qquad \text{Explanandum}}$$

from Hempel and Oppenheim (cf. Hempel 1965), where the L_i are laws, the C_i boundary conditions, and E is the proposition to be explained. The scheme shows that E is explained if it can be logically deduced from laws and boundary conditions.

As an example of linguistic explanation in the field of syntax let us consider one of the empirical findings we presented earlier in this book (cf. section 4.1.2): the more complex a syntactic construction the greater the probability that it will be placed after less complex sister constructions. The reason why constructions have this property can be found if we know the corresponding law. Behaghel's "Gesetz der wachsenden Glieder" was an inductively found hypothesis; it was induced by observation. Therefore, it has the status of an empirical generalisation, which prevents it from being a law hypothesis or – after sufficient corroboration on data – a law. With the advance of Hawkins' Early Immediate Constituent principle, we have the chance to formulate a law hypothesis on the basis of a plausible mechanism and even to connect it to other hypotheses and laws. If this succeeds (we will show that this is the case) and enough evidence is provided to support it, we may call it a law and subsume individual observations under it so that we can arrive at a scientific explanation.

It is important to differentiate between two kinds of law. It is sufficient to find just one single case where a phenomenon diverges from the prediction in order to reject a deterministic law. Most language and text laws, however, are stochastic. Such laws include in their predictions the deviations which are to be expected as a consequence of the stochastic nature of the language mechanism concerned. Therefore, a stochastic law is rejected if the degree of disagreement between the theoretical ideal and empirical results becomes greater than a certain value, determined by mathematical methods according to a chosen significance level. Only after a number of well-confirmed laws have been established in a discipline, can the construction of a theory begin. The first step is the combination of single laws into a system of laws, which is then enriched with interpretations, conventions and so on.

From classical physics and chemistry we are used to trying to answer why-questions by means of causal relationships.[5] In the case of language, however, there are no known causal laws which can connect

5. Modern physics, e.g. particle physics and quantum mechanics, have long dropped the idea to explain their findings by causal relations and employ instead probability statements and symmetry principles.

e.g. human needs for communication and a particular property of a linguistic unit or subsystem. Moreover, it does not seem at all reasonable to postulate such kinds of laws. On the other hand, there are good reasons for the assumption that we ought to use functional explanation in linguistics (cf. Altmann 1981). This type of explanation is a special case of the deductive-nomological explanation. It brings with it, however, several logical problems, the most important of which is the problem of functional equivalents. It has been shown (cf. Köhler 1986: 25ff.) that a logically perfect explanation scheme can be formulated for those systems, for which self-organisation can be introduced as structural axiom. A functional explanation of a linguistic phenomenon E_f can then be pursued according to the following scheme:

---

1. The system S is self-organising, i.e. it possesses mechanisms to alter its state and structure according to external requirements.
2. The requirements $N_1..N_k$ have to be met by the system.
3. The requirement N can be met by the functional equivalents $E_1..E_f..E_n$.
4. The interrelation between those functional equivalents which are able to meet the requirement N is given by the relation $R_N(E_{N_1}..E_{N_n})$.
5. The structure of the system S can be expressed by means of the relation $Q(s_1..s_m)$ among the elements s_i of the system

---

E_f is an element of the system S with load R_{N_f}.

This explanation holds if all the alternative solutions are excluded or are not as good as E_f. In order to complete a functional analysis it would be necessary to obtain the functions $R_i(E_{i_1}..E_{i_n})$ which determine the loads of the functional equivalents for each requirement N_i in such a way that they are optimally met. Functions of this kind can only be derived theoretically.

An example will illustrate what is meant by functional equivalent: The particular requirement for a device enabling specification or differentiation of the meaning of an expression requires the existence of elements in the system which have a corresponding function. Languages possess several ways to develop specification subsystems. The lexical way to specify (to make more specific than a given meaning) merely consists of the creation of new lexemes with the specific meanings required for the particular purpose in question. The syntactic method consists in adding attributes (or restrictions) to an expression which was too unspecific in a given situation, and the morphological one in compounding, derivation, and inflection. Methods which use prosody also exist but have less power than the others on the discussed level. These possible methods have differing influence on other elements of the system. The lexical method, for example, increases lexicon size, the syntactic one phrase length, and the morphological one word length. The actual existing languages make use of these three possibilities to different extents; some of them restrict themselves to the use of only one or two of these functional equivalents. A functional analysis of the specification subsystems requires the construction of a model representing the relation between these equivalents and their influence on the rest of the system (cf. Köhler 1988).

4.2.4 Modelling technique

Modelling in the framework of synergetic linguistics proceeds iteratively in refining phases, where each phase consists of six individual steps. In the first step, axioms are set up for the subsystem under consideration. There is one structural axiom which belongs to the synergetic approach itself: the axiom that language is a self-organising and self-regulating system. Other axioms take the form of system requirements, such as those given in the first column of Table 4.11. In synergetic terminology, these requirements are order parameters. They are not part of the system under consideration but are linked to it and have some influence on the behaviour of the system. In the terminology of the philosophy of science, they play the role of boundary conditions. These requirements can be subdivided into three kinds (cf. Köhler 1990b: 181f.):

1. language-constituting requirements (among them the fundamental coding requirement, representing the necessity to provide expressions for given meanings, the application requirement, i.e.

the need to use a given expression in order to express one of its meanings, the specification requirement, representing the need to form more specific expressions than the ones which are available at a given time, and the de-specification requirement for the cases where the available expressions are too specific for the current communicative purpose);
2. language-forming requirements (such as the economy requirement in its various manifestations);
3. control-level requirements (the adaptation requirement, i.e. the need for a language to adapt itself to varying circumstances, and the opposite stability requirement). Table 4.11 provides a short summary of some of the requirements, processes, and variables which have already been studied. Requirements specific of syntax have not been included in this list but will be introduced in the following sections.

The second step is the determination of system levels, units, and variables which are of interest to the current investigation. Examples of levels and units on the one hand and variables in connection with them are: morphs (with the variables frequency, length, combinability, polysemy/homonymy etc.), words (with variables frequency, length, combinability, polysemy/homonymy, polytextuality, motivation or transparency etc.), syntactic structures (with frequency, length, complexity, compactness, depth of embedding, information, position in mother constituent etc.), inventory sizes (phonological, morphological, lexical, syntactic, semantic, pragmatic, . . .).

In step three, relevant consequences, effects, and interrelations are determined. Here, the researcher sets up or systematises hypotheses about dependences of variables on other variables, e.g. with increasing polytextuality of a lexical item its polysemy increases monotonically, or, the higher the position of a syntactic construction (i.e. the more to the right hand side of its mother constituent) the less its information, etc.

The forth step consists of the search for functional equivalents and multi-functionalities. In language, there are not only 1 : 1 correspondences – many relations are of the 1 : n or m : n type. This fact plays an important role in the logics of functional explanation. Therefore,

Table 4.11: Requirements (taken from Köhler 2005c)

Requirement	Symbol	Influence on
coding	*Cod*	Size of inventories
Specification	*Spc*	Polysemy
De-specification	*Dsp*	Polysemy
Application	*Usg*	Frequency
Transmission security	*Red*	length of units
Economy	*Ec*	Sub-requirements
Minimisation of production effort	*minP*	length, complexity
Minimisation of encoding effort	*minC*	Size of inventories, polysemy
Minimisation of decoding effort	*minD*	Size of inventories, polysemy
Minimisation of inventories	*minI*	Size of inventories
Minimisation of memory effort	*minM*	Size of inventories
Context economy	*CE*	Polytextuality
Context specifity	*CS*	Polytextuality
Invariance of the expression-meaning-relation	*Inv*	Synonymy
Flexibility of the expression-meaning-relation	*Var*	Synonymy
efficiency of coding	*OC*	Sub-requirements
Maximisation of complexity	*maxC*	Syntactic complexity
Preference of right-branching	*RB*	Position
Limitation of embedding depth	*LD*	Depth of embedding
Minimisation of structural information	*minS*	Syntactic patterns
Adaptation	*Adp*	Degree of adaptation readiness
Stability	*Stb*	Degree of adaptation readiness

for each requirement set up in step 1, one has to look for all possible linguistic means to meet it in any way, and, the other way around, for each means or method applied by a language to meet a requirement or to serve a certain purpose, all other requirements and purposes must be determined that could be met or served by the given method. The extent to which a language uses a functional equivalent has effects on some of the system variables, which, in turn, influence others. A simple scheme, such as given in Figure 4.18, can serve as an illustration of this type of interrelation.[6] The diagram shows a small part of the

6. It goes without saying that only a part of the structure of such a model can be displayed here; e.g. the consequences of the extent to which a language uses prosodic means to

lexical subsystem with the requirements coding (*Cod*), Redundancy for securing information transmission (*Red*) and minimising inventory sizes (*minI*) and their effects on some variables.

Step five is the mathematical formulation of the hypotheses set up so far – a precondition for any rigorous test – and step 6 is the empirical test of these mathematically formulated hypotheses.

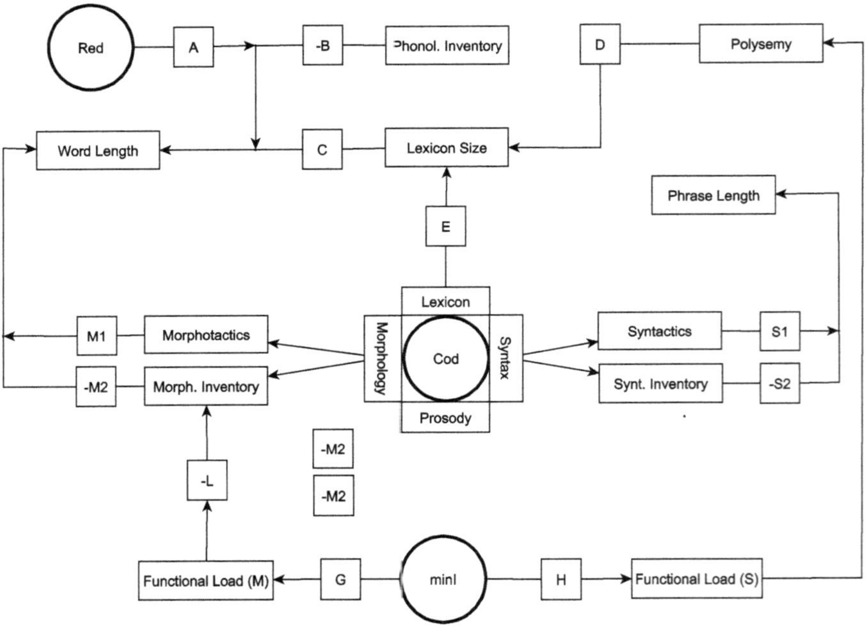

Figure 4.18: Part of the lexical subsystem with three requirements

4.2.5 Notation

A straightforward way for taking down linguistic hypotheses in a mathematical form is, of course, the use of formulae as done throughout this book and elsewhere in quantitative linguistics. However, complex networks of interrelations as set up in synergetic linguistics become unclear and unmanageable rather soon. Therefore, another kind of notation is used whenever a more illustrative or intuitive alternative seems

code meanings, and many other interrelations have been omitted in the diagram.

to be in order: graphical diagrams. Since mathematical rigor must not be lost, a combination of graph theory and operator algebra forms the basis of this notation (cf. Köhler 1986).

In the framework of synergetic linguistics, the elements used for graphical notations are

- rectangles representing quantities, i.e. system variables (state and control variables),
- circles symbolise requirements (order parameters in the terminology of synergetics),
- squares correspond to operators (operator types, of which proportional operators are the most frequently used ones; these are either numbers[7] or variable symbols, mostly letters),
- arrows specifying the links between variables and the directions of the dynamic effects they stand for. The conventions for representing linguistic hypotheses are, according to the rules of linear operator algebra and graph theory, the following ones:
- quantities which are arranged on a common edge are multiplied,
- a junction is interpreted as numerical addition.

The following graph illustrates the interpretation of a simple structure given as a graph by means of a function:

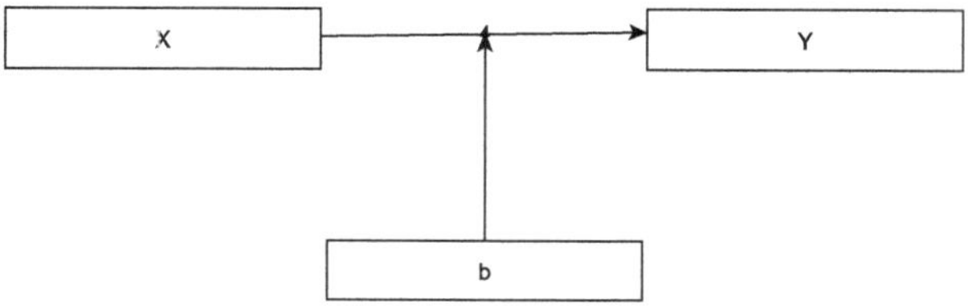

This structure contains three interconnected elements and corresponds to a function with two variables and one constant:

$$y = x + b$$

The roles of the elements as variables and constants are, of course, a matter of previous definition. Similarly, the structure

7. In some introductory texts the numbers or variable symbols are, for the sake of simplicity, replaced by the signs ('+' or '−') of their values.

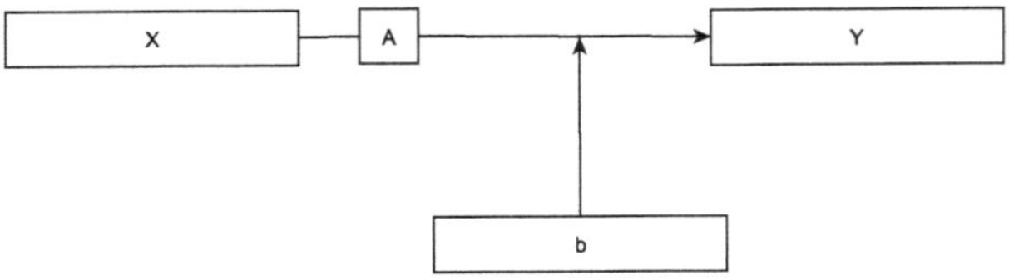

with a fourth element A, previously defined as an operator, will be interpreted as corresponding to the function

$$y = ax + b.$$

In this example, the coefficient a corresponds to the value of the proportional operator A in the structure. The identity operator 1 will never be displayed in our diagrams. Some of the operator types commonly used in systems theory are, besides the proportional operator, the difference operator Δ, the differential operator d, the lag operator E^{-1} for time-relative dependences and their inverses.

The two simple rules for multiplication and addition suffice to calculate the function of a feedback structure, too. Thus, from the structure

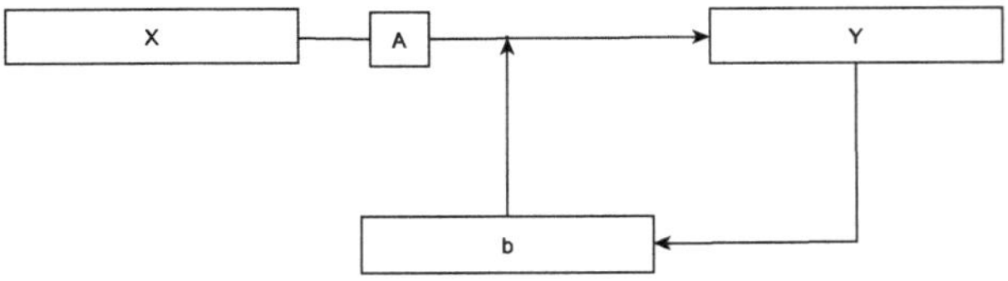

the function can be calculated in the following way:

$$y = ax$$
$$z = ax + by$$

where z is an auxiliary variable representing the junction of the paths from b and x. Therefore

$$y = ax + by$$
$$y - bx = x$$

and finally

$$y = \frac{a}{1-ab}x.$$

More complex structures can easily be simplified by considering them step by step. The structure

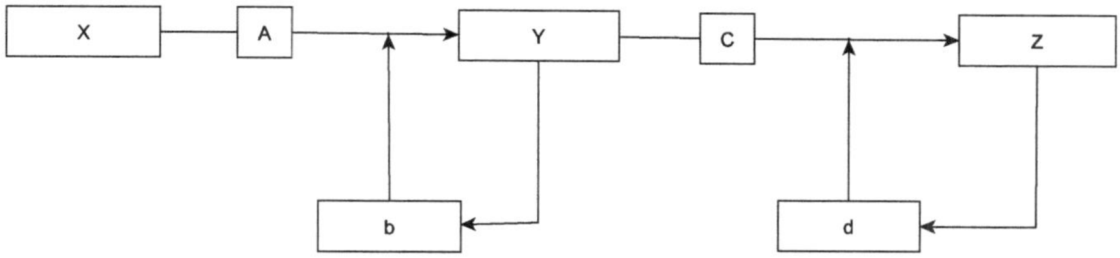

consists of two feedback loops, of which the left one is identical with the previous example and has therefore the same function. The right feedback loop has the same structure and thus the function

$$z = \frac{c}{1-cd}y.$$

If we call these two functions F and G, we obtain the total function by applying the first rule to the corresponding structure

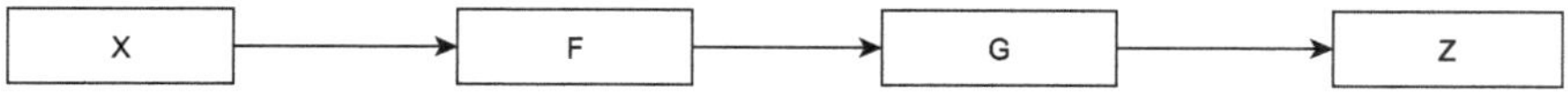

and by inserting the full formulae for f and g

$$z = \frac{ac}{(1-ab)(1-cd)}x.$$

In the same way, the functions of even very complicated structures with several input and output variables can be calculated.

4.2.6 Synergetic modelling in linguistics

Research in quantitative linguistics has shown that linguistic data are neither distributed according to the normal distribution nor are the dependences among linguistic variables linear functions. Some examples of typical interrelations in the lexical subsystem can be taken from (Köhler 1986):

1. $LS = COD^{V} PS^{-L}$
   Lexicon size is a function of the influence of the coding requirement (in this case the number of meanings to be coded) and of the mean polysemy. The quantity V is a function of the requirements Spc, Var, and Inv.
2. $PN = minD^{Y_1} minK^{-Y_2}$
   Phoneme number is a result of a compromise reflecting the requirements of minimisation of coding and decoding efforts.
3. $L = LG^{A} Red^{Z} PH^{-P} F^{-N}$
   word length is a function of lexicon size (the more words are needed the longer they have to be on the average – on condition of a constant number of phonemes/tonemes), of redundancy (on the level of usage of phonological combinations), of the phonological inventory size, and of frequency.
4. $PL = minK^{Q_2} minD^{-Q_1} L^{-T}$
   Polysemy results from a compromise between the effects of the requirements *minC* and mind on the one hand and word length on the other (the longer a word the less its polysemy).
5. $PT = CE^{S_2} CS^{-S_1} PL^{G}$
   Polytextuality (the number of possible contexts) is a function of a compromise between the effects of the context-globalising and context-centralising processes and of polysemy.
6. $F = Usg^{R} PT^{K}$
   The frequency of a lexical item depends on the communicative relevance of its meanings (represented in the model by the application requirement) and on its polytextuality.
7. $SN = Cod^{VW} PL^{M}$
   Synonymy is a function of polysemy and of the coding requirement to the extent VW, which is the result of a compromise between the requirements of flexibility and those of constant form-meaning relation.

As can be seen from these examples, the typical dependency between two or more linguistic quantities takes the form of a power law. Models on the basis of linear operator algebra, however, cannot directly map power law functions. This is why we have to linearize the original formulae using a logarithmic transformation. Let us, for the sake of illustration, consider example (5). The hypothesis is $PT = CE^{S_2} Cs^{-S_1} PL^G$. The logarithm of this equation is

$$\ln PT = G \ln PL + S_2 \ln CE - S_1 \ln CS.$$

The corresponding structure is given by

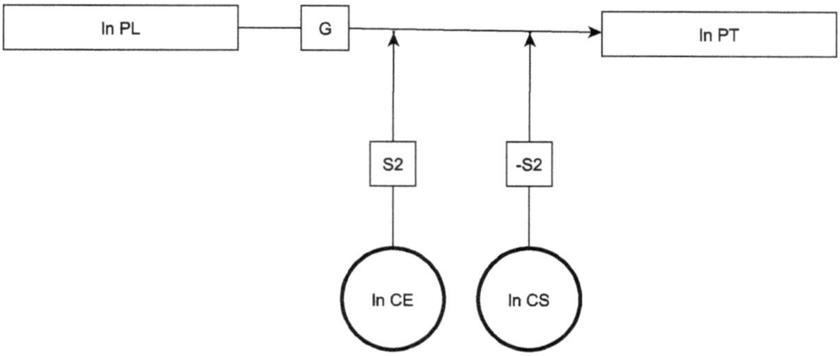

Figure 4.19: Structure that corresponds to a power law function representing the dependence of polytextuality on polysemy

where the circles represent system requirements, i.e. quantities outside of the semiotic system which have an effect on the self-organising processes.

Another type of function frequently found in linguistics is the product of a power law and an exponential function. We have presented such a case with the Menzerath-Altmann law. The exponential function makes a logarithmic transformation impossible; instead, we introduce[8] an additional operator "EXP" for the exponential function. In this way, we can visualize the structure which corresponds to the function $y = ax^b e^{-cx}$ as:

We will need this technique for a model of some of the syntactic interrelations in the next section.

8. Cf. Köhler (2006b)

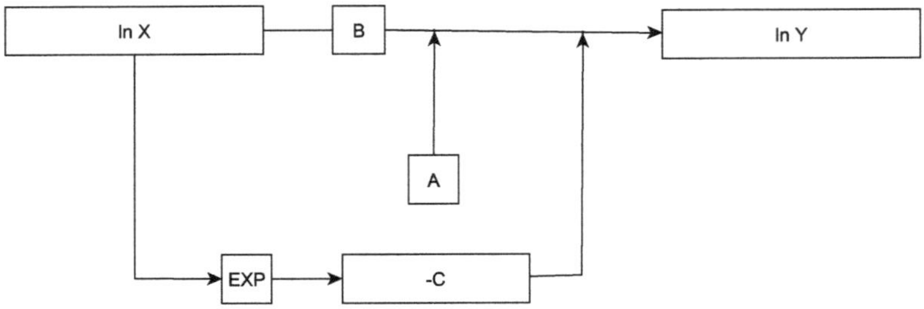

Figure 4.20: Introducing the EXP operator

4.2.7 Synergetic modelling in syntax

The first attempt at applying synergetic modelling to a syntactic subsystem was made in Köhler (1999). Before, studies on networks of lexical and morphological units and properties had been conducted – cf. the references in Köhler (1999). We will present here the overall model, some of the basic hypotheses and findings from this study and some new (or more specific) hypotheses and tests.

The units chosen for the syntactic level were syntactic constructions on the basis of a phrase structure grammar, i.e. of the constituency relation. For this pilot study, the following eight properties of syntactic constructions and four inventories were selected:

- *Frequency* (of occurrence in the text corpus),
- *length* (the number of the terminal nodes [= words] which belong to the given constituent),
- *Complexity* (the number of immediate constituents of a given constituent),
- *Position* (in the mother constituent or in the sentence, counted from left to right),
- *Depth of embedding* (the number of production steps from the start symbol),
- *information* (in the sense of information theory, corresponding to the memory space needed for the temporary storage of the grammatical relations of the constituent)
- *Polyfunctionality* (the number of different functions of the construction under consideration),

- *Synfunctionality* (the number of different functions with which a given function shares a syntactic representation)
- the inventory of *syntactic constructions* (constituent types),
- the inventory of *syntactic functions*,
- the inventory of *syntactic categories*,
- the inventory of *functional equivalents* (i.e., of constructions with a similar function to the one under consideration).

For the empirical aspect of the investigation, the afore-mentioned Susanne and NEGRA corpora were used.

The first step on the way to a model in the framework of the synergetic approach consists in setting up axioms. From earlier works (e.g., Köhler 1986, 1990a; Hoffmann and Krott 1998) we take, together with the general and central axiom of self-organisation and self-regulation of language systems, the communication requirement (*Com*) with its two aspects of the coding (*Cod*) and the application requirement (Usg). Further language-external requirements that the system must meet are introduced below.

The next step includes the search for functional equivalents which can meet the requirements, and the determination on their effects on other system variables. The influences of *Cod*, of which we consider here only that part which is connected with syntactic coding means as a functional equivalent, directly affect the inventory size of syntactic constructions (in perfect analogy to the lexical subsystem where lexicon size is affected by *Cod*). In a similar analogy to the situation in the lexicon, Usg represents the communicative relevance of an expression in the inventory and results in a corresponding frequency of application of the given construction (cf. Figure 4.21 for the corresponding linearized system structure).

Before entering the next phase – the empirical testing of the hypotheses set up – we introduce another axiom, viz. the requirement of optimal coding (*OC*), as known from earlier models, with two of its aspects: the requirement of minimising production effort (*minP*), and the requirement of maximisation of compactness (*maxC*). "Production effort"effort refers to the physical effort which is associated with the articulation while uttering an expression. In the case of syntactic constructions, this effort is determined by the number of terminal nodes

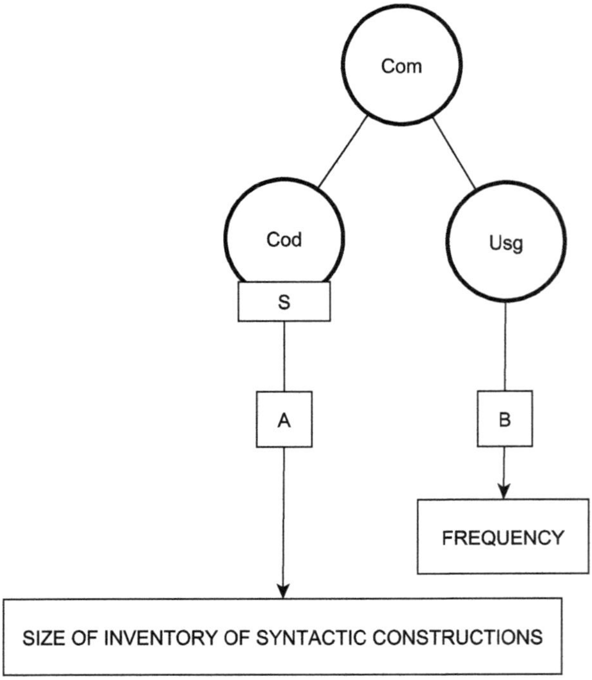

Figure 4.21: Linearized structure consisting of the language-constituting requirement *Cod* (only syntactic coding means are considered) and the language-forming requirement *Usg* with two of their depending variables

(words) – even if the words are of different lengths[9] – and here is called length of a syntactic construction. As in the case of lexical units, *minP* affects the relation between frequency and length, in that maximal economisation is realised when the most frequent constructions are the shortest ones (cf. Figure 4.22).

9. The actual mean effort connected with the utterance of a syntactic construction is indirectly given by the number of its words and on the basis of the word length distribution (in syllables) and the syllable length distribution (in sounds). One has also to keep in mind, however, the influence of the Menzerath-Altmann law, which is, for the sake of simplicity, neglected here.

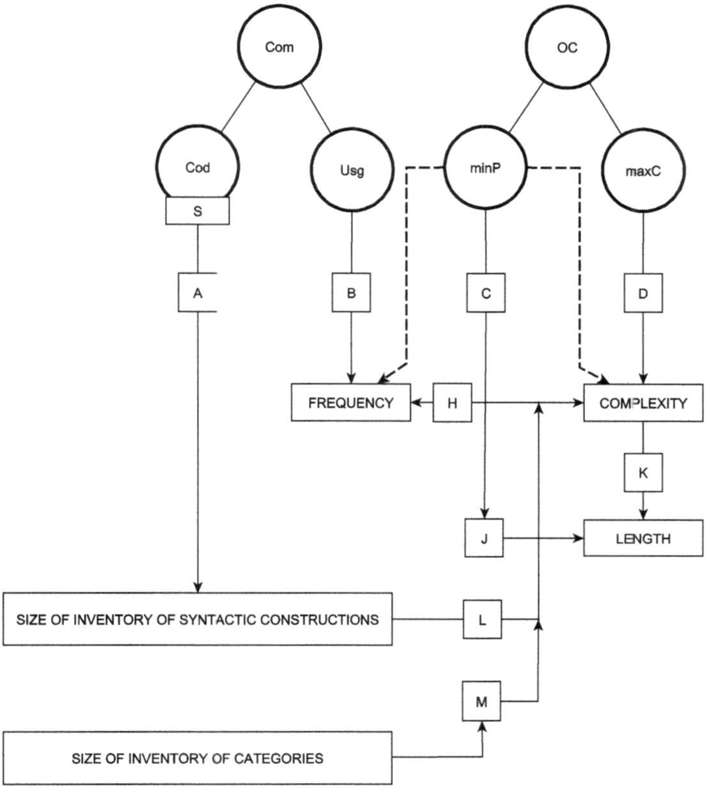

Figure 4.22: The interrelation of complexity/length and frequency

As a consequence, an optimised distribution of the observed frequencies and a corresponding rank-frequency distribution can be expected, in a form similar – though probably not identical – to Zipf-Mandelbrot's law. There is, undoubtedly, an effect of shortening syntactic constructions in dependence on their frequency; however, this interrelation should be explained in the first place by the preferential application of shorter constructions over longer ones.

According to the data from the Susanne corpus, these distributions display, in fact, the expected forms (cf. Figure 4.23). The well-known Waring distribution could be fitted to the empirical frequency spectrum (fitting with the Altmann Fitter 2.0 (1997) yielding the parameter estimations $b = 0.6699$ and $n = 0.4717$; the result of the Chi-square test was $\chi^2 = 81.01$ with 85 degrees of freedom and a probability of $P(\chi^2) = 0.6024$), which is very good.

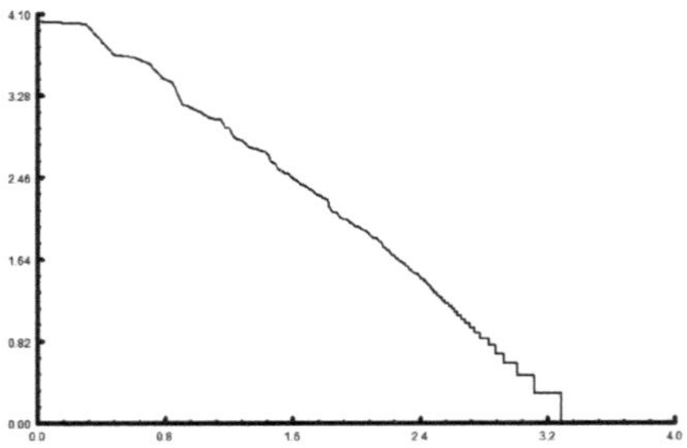

Figure 4.23: The rank-frequency distribution of the constituent type frequencies in the Susanne corpus (logarithmic axes)

The requirement *maxC* is, among others, a consequence of the need for minimisation of production effort on the mother constituent level. This requirement can be met on the sentence level, e.g., by an additional attribute instead of a subordinate clause, with the effect that this economisation at the sentence level is achieved at the expense of an increased complexity. The following example illustrates this.

(3) a. S [$_{NP}$ The students] did not understand anything because they were unprepared]

b. S [$_{NP}$ The unprepared students] did not understand anything].

The first sentence has a length of 10 words, the second one only 7. On the other hand, the subject of the first sentence has only two and the subject of the second sentence three immediate constituents. length (measured in words), on the other hand, is stochastically proportional to complexity: the more immediate constituents a construction contains, the more terminal nodes it will consist of. Figure 4.22 illustrates, in addition to the interrelation of complexity/length and frequency, that degree and variation of complexity are a consequence of the requirement of optimal coding; the dotted lines represent the effect of *minP* as an order parameter for the distributions of the frequency and complexity classes.

The *average* complexity of the syntactic constructions finally depends on the number of the necessary constructions in the inventory and on the number of elementary syntactic categories. This dependence results from a simple combinatorial consideration: every construction consists of a linear sequence of daughter nodes (immediate constituents) and is determined by their categories and their order. On the basis of G categories, G^K different constructions with K nodes can be generated, of which only a part – the "grammatical" one – is actually formed, in analogy to the only partial use of the principally possible phoneme (sound) combinations in the formation of syllables or morphemes – to phonotactic restrictions. Figure 4.24 shows the complexity distribution of all 90821 occurrences of constituents in the Susanne corpus.

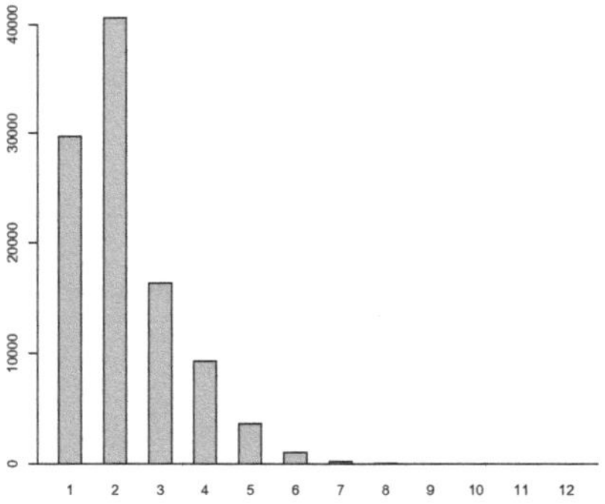

Figure 4.24: Empirical frequencies of constituent complexity in the Susanne corpus

The empirical test of the hypotheses on the interrelation between frequency and complexity and complexity and length is shown in Figures 4.25, 4.26, and 4.27.

The findings described in this section possess a potentially important practical impact. Of the 4621 different constituent types with their 90821 occurrences, 2710 types (58.6%) occur only once in the corpus, 615 types (32.3% of the rest, or 13.3% of the whole inventory) occur twice, 288 types (22.2% of the rest, or 6.2% of the inventory) three times, 176 (17.5% of the rest, or 3.8% of the inventory) four times, etc. Less than 20% of the rules in the corresponding grammar can be

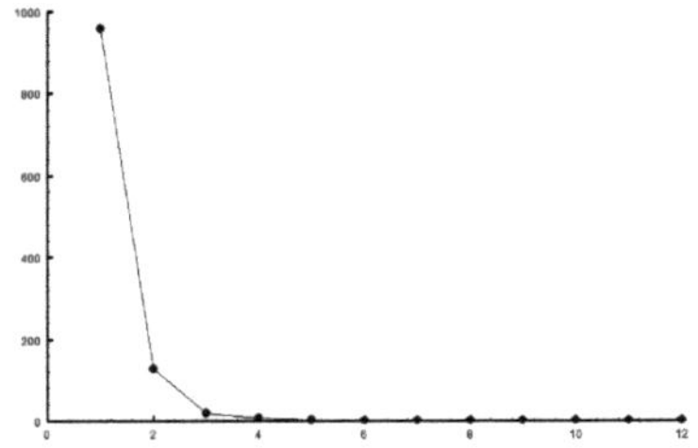

Figure 4.25: Average constituent frequency as a function of constituent complexity, fitting the function $F = 858.83K^{-3.095}e^{0.00727K}$, resulting in $R^2 = 0.99$

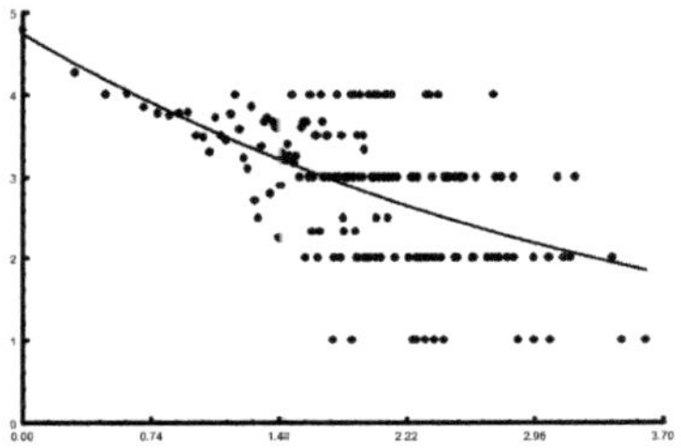

Figure 4.26: Average constituent complexity as a function of frequency (logarithmic *x*-axis), fitting the function $C = 4.789F^{0-.1160}$, resulting in $R^2 = 0.331$

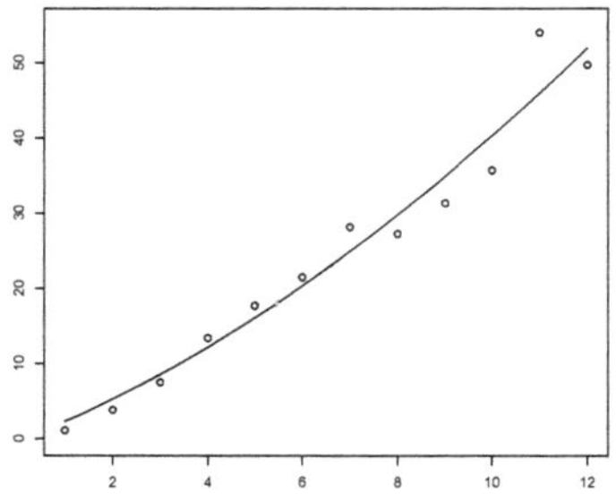

Figure 4.27: The empirical dependence of complexity and length, fitting the function $L = 2.603K^{0.963}e^{0.0512K}$, resulting in $R^2 = 0.960$

applied more than four times and less than 30% of the rules more than two times.

We can expect that investigations of other corpora and of languages other than English will yield comparable results. Similarly to how lexical frequency spectra are applied to problems of language learning and teaching, in compiling minimal vocabularies, in determining the text coverage of dictionaries, etc., the frequency distribution of syntactic constructions and also the interdependence of complexity and frequency could be taken into account, among others, when parsers are constructed (planning the degree of text coverage, estimation of the expenditure needed for setting up the rules, calculation of the degree of a text which can be automatically analysed etc.).

Another property of syntactic units which can easily be determined is their position in a unit on a higher level. Position is in fact a quantitative concept: the corresponding mathematical operations are defined and meaningful; differences and even products between position values can be calculated (the scale provides an absolute Zero).

There are two classical hypotheses concerning position of syntactic units. The earliest one is Otto Behaghel's "Gesetz der wachsenden Glieder" (Behaghel 1930). After Behaghel, word order variation has been considered, in the first place, from the point of view of typology. In linguistics, theme-rheme division and topicalisation as a function of syntactic coding by means of word order have to be mentioned and, in contrast, Givón's discourse pragmatic "the most important first" principle. As discussed in Section 4.1.2, Hawkins introduced a plausible hypothesis on the basis of assumptions about the human parsing mechanism, which replaced Behaghel's idea of a rhythmic-aesthetic law and also some other hypotheses (some of them also set up by Hawkins). We will refer to Hawkins' hypothesis briefly as "EIC principle". The other hypothesis concerning position is Yngve's "depth saving principle" (Yngve 1960; cf. Section 4.1.1). We will integrate both hypotheses into our synergetic model of a subsystem of syntax.

We modify Behaghel's and Hawkins' hypothesis in two respects:

1. Instead of length (in the number of words) as in Hawkins (1994), complexity is considered as the relevant quantity, because the hypothesis refers to nodes in the syntactic structure, not to words[10];

2. We make the hypothesis more vulnerable: we do not only claim that more complex units tend to follow the less complex ones and perform pairwise tests as has been done in earlier studies, but predict a monotonous dependence of position on complexity (or vice versa):

Figure 4.28 shows this interrelation in a form appropriate for our purposes.

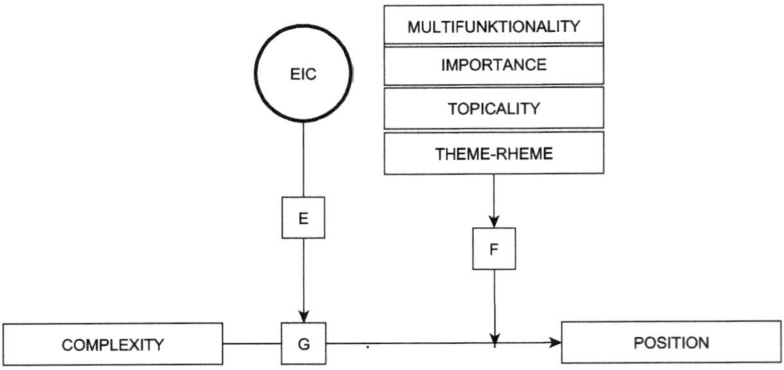

Figure 4.28: Hawkins' EIC principle (modified: complexity instead of length)

The structure contains, besides the variables complexity and position, the requirement which corresponds to Hawkins' hypothesis and the links between these elements a new quantity which combines the effects of four (and possibly more) factors. They have been pooled because their impact on the dependence of position on complexity is assumed to have the same form, i.e. that they may be modelled as a term in the (logarithmic) structure (their values may be added). The function which corresponds to this structure is, as shown above (cf. p. 182), $p = fc^g$. This specific hypothesis was tested on data from the Susanne corpus. Whereas the previous investigations took into account only constituent pairs of 'equal status', in the present study, length, complexity, and absolute position data were collected and evaluated for all constituents in the corpus in two ways: on the sentence level and recursively on all levels.

10. The fact that the phenomenon is also observable when length in words is considered seems to be an indirect effect.

Fitting the power law function $p = fc^g$ to the data from the Susanne corpus yielded a good result (cf. Table 4.12, and Figures 4.29a and 4.29b) for both, length in words and complexity in the number of immediate constituents. Positions with less than ten observations ($f < 10$) have not been taken into account; classes with rare occurrences are not reliable enough.

Table 4.12: Result of fitting the power law function to the data from the Susanne corpus

	Position as a function of length	Complexity as a function of position
Parameter f resp. h	2.5780	0.1179
Parameter g resp. k	0.6236	0.0455
Coefficient of determination	0.9383	0.9186

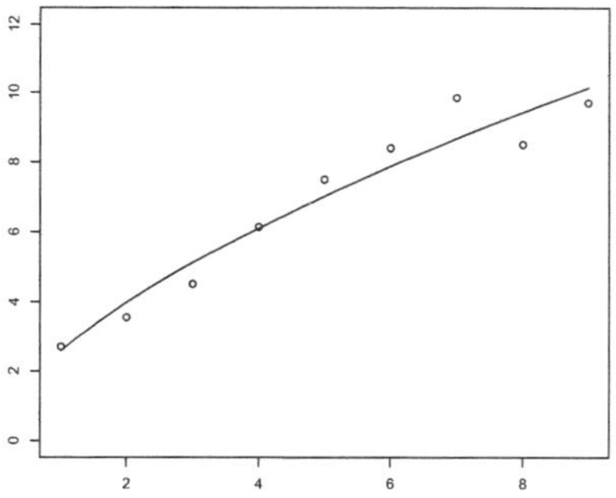

(a) Average constituent length (in the number of words) on position in the mother constituent

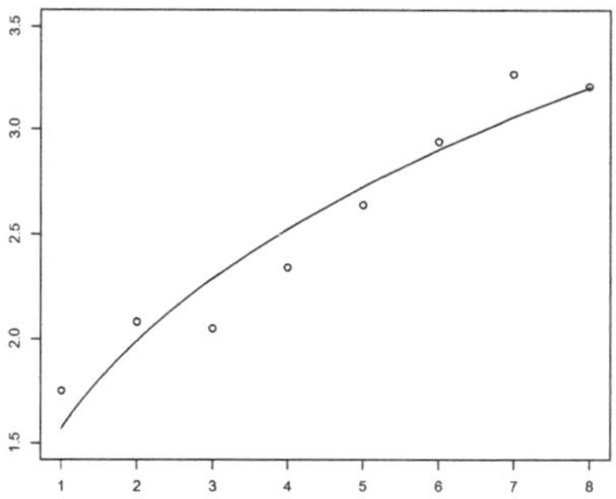

(b) Average constituent complexity (in the number of immediate constituents) on position in the mother constituent

Figure 4.29: Fitting the power law function to the data from the Susanne corpus

The second hypothesis concerning position, Yngve's Depth Saving principle , can be considered as a system requirement in our synergetic framework. In Section 4.1.1, a mathematical formulation – a power law function combined with an exponential function – of a hypothesis which corresponds to the (extended) basic ideas presented by Yngve was set up and tested.

Here, this function is included into the synergetic model by introducing a further system requirement, viz. right-branching preference (*RB*), which controls the influence of constituent position on depth . Additionally, another axiom is set up which represents the necessary limitation of the increase of depth (*LD*) – an order parameter of the distribution of the variable depth. The three requirements *EIC*, *RB*, and *LD* can be subsumed under the general requirement of minimisation of memory effort (*minM*). Here, we have also to take into account that the requirement of maximal compactness (*maxC*) has an effect opposite to the depth limitation requirement, because more compactness is achieved by embedding constituents.

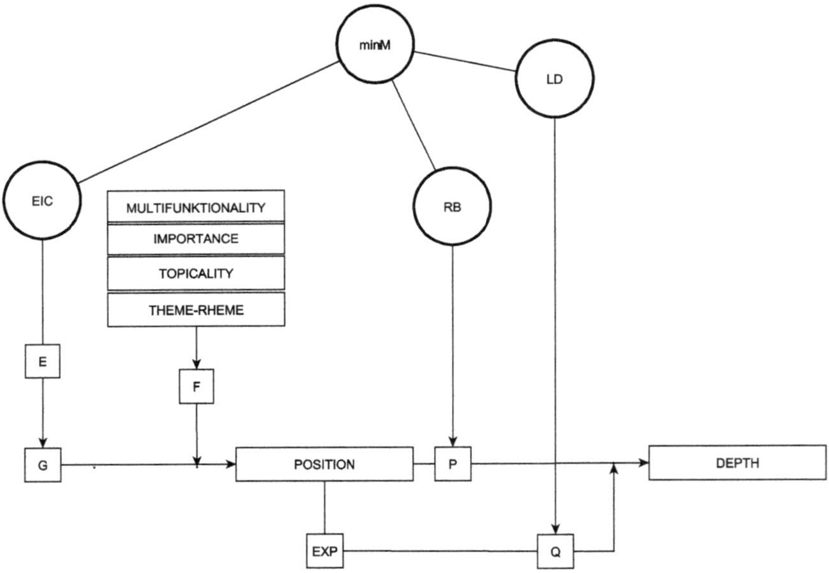

Figure 4.30: Model section containing the quantities complexity, position, and depth with the relevant requirements

This model is a variant modifying the corresponding structure hypothesis in Köhler (1999). The modification is necessary because the exact form of our hypothesis and the empirical data call for the additional exponential part in the formula. This part cares for a reduction of the increase of depth with increasing position; it damps down the steepness of the curve.

In Section 3.4.8, a study on the amount of information conveyed in dependency on position in the mother constituent was presented. A specific hypothesis about the form of the dependency was not given, neither in the original investigation in Köhler (1999) nor later. Here, we will integrate a corresponding hypothesis in our synergetic model and conduct an empirical test using the data given on pp. 88f.). A certain amount *R* of structural information is inevitably connected with any syntactic construction; syntax carries that part of the linguistically conveyed information that exceeds the lexical part and delivers, together with morphology, the logical relations. On the sentence and clause levels, this quantity *R* is influenced by the Menzerath-Altmann law (cf. Section 4.1.3): The longer (or more complex) a construction the smaller (less complex) its constituents.

It is plausible to assume that the structural information within a construction is not evenly distributed over the positions. Each functor has a limited number and fixed types of arguments; therefore, the uncertainty about which of the actants or other parts of a construction will turn out to be the next one decreases with the number of already processed parts. Consequently, information must follow a monotonously decreasing function of position. This and the simple fact that information is always a positive quantity is why the function must start with a positive number at position 1. A linear diagram resulting from a logarithmic transformation as used so far is not possible with an additive term in the original equation. We introduce a new operator *LN* as a special form of junction to connect *R* to the rest of the structure. This junction cares for the correct result after applying the anti-logarithm.

Another new element in the structure (Figure 4.31) is the requirement *minS*, a sub-requirement or aspect of the requirement *minM* (minimisation of memory effort), which controls the operator *S*, which controls the effect of position on information. Table 4.13 shows the number of syntactic alternatives for each position in all the constructions on all levels in the complete Susanne corpus. The first column gives the positions, the second one the number of alternatives, and the third column the logarithm of the values in column two.

The function $\log_{10} y = t + rx^s$ is fitted to the data from columns one and three. The result is an extremely good fit (coefficient of determi-

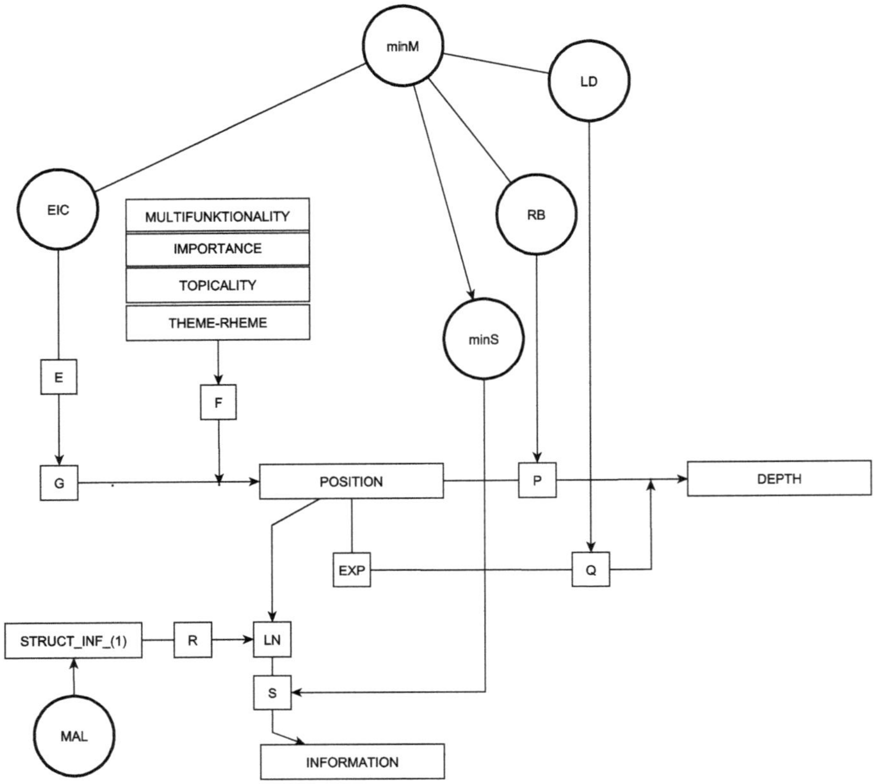

Figure 4.31: Integrating a hypothesis about the dependency of information on position. A new requirement is introduced: *minS* represents the requirement of minimisation of structural information, an aspect of the requirement of *minM* (minimisation of memory effort). The quantity *R* stands for the amount of structural information on position 1, which is connected with the Menzerath-Altmann law

nation $R^2 = 0.9945$) and yields the parameter estimations $t = 1.5916$, $r = -0.00256$, and $s = 2.5958$ (cf. Figure 4.32). This empirical test is a first support of our hypothesis and calls for follow-up studies, of course.

As in earlier models of linguistic subsystems, a requirement of minimisation of inventory size (*minI*) is postulated. In a syntactic subsystem, at least the following interrelations between inventories and other system variables must be investigated: an increase in the size of the

Table 4.13: Number of syntactic alternatives in dependency from their positions in their mother constituents in the Susanne corpus

Position x	Number of alternatives y	$\log_{10} y$	Position x	Number of alternatives y	$\log_{10} y$
1	38	1.58	7	16	1.20
2	38	1.58	8	12	1.08
3	35	1.54	9	7	0.85
4	33	1.52	10	3	0.48
5	25	1.38	11	2	0.30
6	22	1.34	12	1	0.00

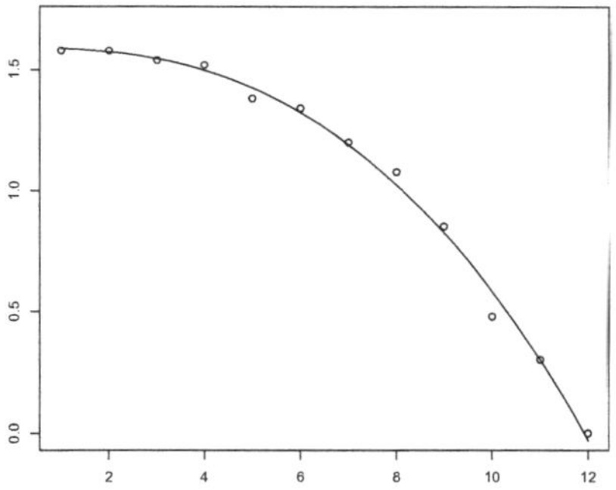

Figure 4.32: The dependency of information (the logarithm of the number of alternative syntactic constituents which can follow the given position) on position; plot of the function $\log_{10} y = t + rx^s$

inventory of syntactic constructions has an increasing effect on the mean complexity of the constructions, whereas mean complexity is the smaller the larger the inventory of categories. The smaller the inventory of categories the greater the functional load (or, multifunctionality). The requirement *minI* has a decreasing effect on all inventories, among others on the mean number of functional equivalents associated with a construction.

The frequency distributions within the inventories are controlled by order parameters (Figure 4.33). The model of a syntactic subsystem developed so far is, as emphasised, only a first attempt to analyse a part of the syntactic subsystem of language in the framework of synergetic linguistics and remains, at the moment, incomplete in several respects. Besides extensions of the model by further units and properties, a broader empirical basis and studies of data from other languages than English and German is needed. A particularly interesting question is the relation between the model structure described in this draft analysis and the Menzerath-Altmann law.

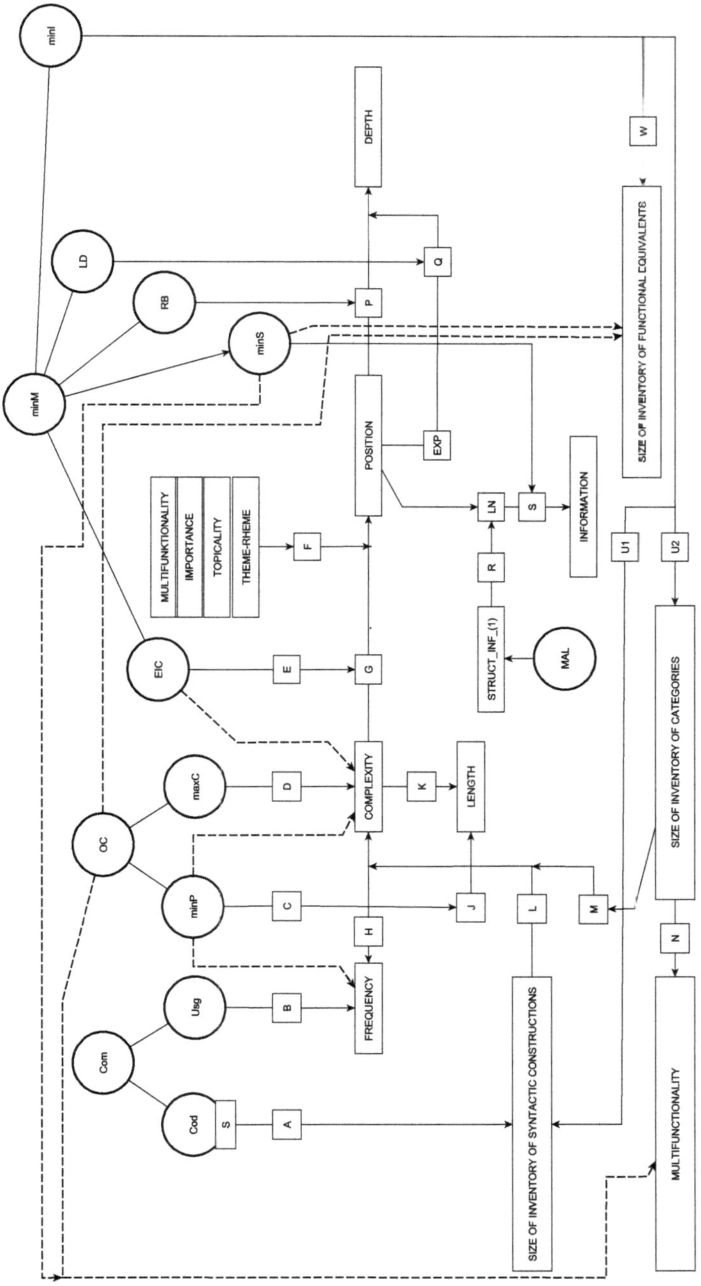

Figure 4.33: The structure of the syntactic subsystem as presented in this volume

4.3 Perspectives

There are, of course, many aspects and fields of syntactic analyses, intra- and cross-linguistic ones, which have not been addressed in this volume. Among them, to name only a few, are the following ones:

Typology: Some of Greenberg's implicative universals could be reinterpreted as hypotheses in the form of mathematical functions. A universal of the type "A language with the property *P* has, with [overwhelmingly...] probability, also property *Q*" could, e.g., be transduced into a new typological hypothesis if quantitation of at least one property is possible. In this case, functional hypotheses could be formulated, e.g. "The more instances of property *P* can be observed (or, the more frequently property *P* occurs) in a language, the greater the probability that the language has also property *Q*". Variants are "[...] the more frequently occurs property *Q* in that language" and "[...] in the more contexts (paradigms, specific forms, uses, etc.) occurs property *Q*" and others. There are countless other ways to form, on the basis of established assumptions or observations, hypotheses with quantitative concepts.

Grammar: Functional linguistic approaches provide a wealth of observations and concepts which could be tackled in a quantitative way. Not few of them have addressed ideas and questions using methods of counting and measuring[11] which could be promising for theoretical and empirical research with the aim to find explanations for what has been observed, i.e. for the quest for universal language laws and, ultimately, for a theory of syntax (in the sense of the philosophy of science, of course).

Pragmatics/discourse analysis: These linguistic fields are dedicated to the study of the ways how linguistic objects are applied. Application, however, is not only the one and only source of frequency – a central property of every linguistic unit – but also the realm where any linguistic object has to prove its usefulness and its usability. Consequently, at least from the point of view of synergetic linguistics, pragmatics plays the role of an important factor in the selection process

11. Cf., e.g. publications by Bybee, Givón, Haiman, and many others in the fields of typology, universals research, historical, and functional linguistics. It is not possible to provide a bibliography of these wide areas in this place.

within the self-organising mechanism of language development, language change, or language "evolution". The fact, that language use forms language structure is well-known in many linguistic sub-disciplines but the attempts at explaining form in terms of function and change in terms of usage must fail without sufficient knowledge in the philosophy of science, in particular on the nature of scientific explanation and the role of laws.

A final remark concerns the empirical aspect of what has been discussed in this volume. We emphasize the fact that in many cases of the presented hypotheses only very few empirical studies have been performed. As a consequence, a large number of subsequent investigations on data from as many and typologically diverse languages as possible will be needed to obtain satisfying empirical support. The same holds for text types and other extra-linguistic variables. At the same time, the theoretical background should be extended by new hypotheses and connecting them to the established network of laws and hypotheses. Extensions of the presented model can be done by adding variables to the ones already discussed here (frequency, complexity, ...) and connecting them to at least ones of the others via a new hypothesis on an effect of one quantity on the other one. Alternatively, consequences of an already described interrelation or of changes of an individual quantity can be found and integrated into the model. One of the most challenging ways to extend the model concerns interfaces to neighbouring domains such as the psycholinguistic, neurophysiological, sociolinguistic, phonetic (acoustic and articulatory), ethnological etc. ones.

References

Altmann, Gabriel

1981 "Zur Funktionalanalyse in der Linguistik." In: Esser, Jürgen; Hübler, Axel (eds.), "Forms and Functions." Tübingen: Narr, 25–32.

Altmann, Gabriel

1991 "Modelling diversification phenomena in language." In: Rothe, Ursula (ed.), *Diversification Processes in Language: Grammar.* Hagen: Rottmann, 33–46.

1993 "Science and linguistics." In: Köhler, Reinhard; Rieger, Burghard B. (eds.), *Contributions to quantitative linguistics.* Dordrecht: Kluwer, 3–10.

1996 "The nature of linguistic units." In: *Journal of Quantitative Linguistics*, 3/1; 1–7.

1980 "Prolegomena to Menzerath's Law." In: Grotjahn, Rüdiger (ed.), *Glottometrika 2.* Bochum: Brockmeyer, 1–10.

1983 "Das Piotrowski-Gesetz und seine Verallgemeinerungen." In: Best, Karl-Heinz; Kohlhase, Jörg (eds.), *Exakte Sprachwandelforschung.* Göttingen, Herodot, 54–90.

1988a *Wiederholungen in Texten.* Bochum: Brockmeyer.

1988b "Verteilungen der Satzlängen." In: Schulz, Klaus-Peter (ed.), *Glottometrika 9.* Bochum: Brockmeyer, 147–170.

Altmann Gabriel; Altmann, Vivien

2008 *Anleitung zu quantitativen Textanalysen. Methoden und Anwendungen.* Lüdenscheid: RAM-Verlag.

Altmann, Gabriel; Beőthy, Erzsébeth; Best, Karl-Heinz

1982 "Die Bedeutungskomplexität der Wörter und das Menzerathsche Gesetz." In: *Zeitschrift für Phonetik, Sprachwissenschaft und Kommunikationsforschung*, 35; 537–543.

Altmann, Gabriel; Burdinski, Violetta

1982 "Towards a law of word repetitions in text-blocks." In: Lehfeldt, Werner; Strauss, Udo (eds.), *Glottometrika 4.* Bochum: Brockmeyer, 146–167.

Altmann, Gabriel; Buttlar, Haro v.; Rott, Walter; Strauss, Udo

1983 "A law of change in language." In: Brainerd, Barron (ed.), *Historical linguistics.* Bochum, Brockmeyer, 104–115.

Altmann, Gabriel; Grotjahn, Rüdiger

1988 "Linguistische Meßverfahren." In: Ammon, Ulrich; Dittmar, Norbert; Mattheier, Klaus J. (eds.), *Sociolinguistics. Soziolinguistik.* Berlin: de Gruyter, 1026–1039.

Altmann, Gabriel; Schwibbe, Michael H.
1989 *Das Menzerathsche Gesetz in informationsverarbeitenden Systemen.* Hildesheim: Olms.

Altmann, Gabriel; Köhler, Reinhard
1996 "“Language forces” and synergetic modelling of language phenomena." In: Schmidt, Peter (ed.), *Glottometrika 15.* Trier: WVT, 62–76.

Altmann, Gabriel; Lehfeldt, Werner
1973 *Allgemeine Sprachtypologie.* München: Fink.

Altmann, Gabriel; Lehfeldt, Werner
1980 *Einführung in die Quantitative Phonologie.* Bochum: Brockmeyer.

Andersen, Simone
2005 "Word length balance in texts: Proportion constancy and word-chain-lengths in Proust's longest sentence." In: Hrebíček, Luděk (ed.), *Glottometrika 11.* Bochum: Brockmeyer, 32–50.

Andres, Jan
2010 "On a conjecture about the fractal structure of language." In: *Journal of Quantitative Linguistics*, 17/2; 101–122.

Baayen, R. Harald; Tweedie, Fiona
1998 "Sample-Size Invariance of LNRE model parameters. Problems and opportunities." In: *Journal of Quantitative Linguistics*, 5/3; 145–154.

Behaghel, Otto
1930 "Von deutscher Wortstellung." In: *Zeitschrift für Deutschkunde*, 44; 81–89.

Bertalanffy, Ludwig van
1968 *General system theory. Foundations, development, applications.* New York: George Braziller.

Best, Karl-Heinz
1997 "Zum Stand der Untersuchungen zu Wort- und Satzlängen." In: *Third International Conference on Quantitative Linguistics.* Helsinki, 172–176.

1994 "Word class frequencies in contemporary German short prose texts." In: *Journal of Quantitative Linguistics*, 1; 144–147.

1997 "Zur Wortartenhäufigkeit in Texten deutscher Kurzprosa der Gegenwart." In: Best, Karl-Heinz (ed.), *Glottometrika 16.* Trier: Wiss. Verlag Trier, 276–285.

1998 "Zur Interaktion der Wortarten in Texten." In: *Papiere zur Linguistik*, 58; 83–95.

2000 "Verteilungen der Wortarten in Anzeigen." In: *Göttinger Beiträge zur Sprachwissenschaft*, 4; 37–51.

2001 "Zur Gesetzmäßigkeit der Wortartenverteilungen in deutschen Pressetexten." In: *Glottometrics*; 1; 1–26.

2005 "Satzlänge." In: Köhler, Reinhard; Altmann, Gabriel; Piotrowski, Rajmond G. (eds.), *Quantitative Linguistik. Ein internationales Handbuch. Quantitative Linguistics. An International Handbook.* Berlin, New York: de Gruyter, 298–304.

Boroda, Moisei

1982 "Häufigkeitsstrukturen musikalischer Texte." In: Orlov, Jurij K.; Boroda, Moisei G.; Nadarejšvili, Isabela S. (eds.), "Sprache, Text, Kunst. Quantitative Analysen." Bochum: Brockmeyer, 231–262.

Bunge, Mario

1967 *Scientific Research I, II.* Berlin, Heidelberg, New York: Springer.

1998 "Semiotic systems." In: Altmann, Gabriel; Koch, Walter A. (eds.), *Systems. A new paradigm for the human sciences.* Berlin, New York: Walter de Gruyter, 337–349.

1998a *Philosophy of science. From problem to theory.* New Brunswick, London: Transaction Publishers. 3rd ed. 2005.

1998b *Philosophy of science. From explanation to justification.* New Brunswick, London: Transaction Publishers. 4th ed. 2007.

Čech, Radek; Mačutek, Ján

2010 "On the quantitative analysis of verb valency in Czech." In: Grzybek, Peter; Kelih, Emmerich; Mačutek, Ján (eds), *Text and Language. Structures, Functions, Interrelations.* Wien: Praesens Verlag, 21–29.

Čech, Radek; Pajas, Petr; Mačutek, Ján

2010 "Full valency. Verb valency without distinguishing complements and adjuncts." In: *Journal of Quantitative Linguistics*, 17/4; 291–302.

Chomsky, Noam

1965 *Aspects of the theory of syntax.* Cambridge: The MIT Press.

1986 "Knowledge of language. Its nature, origins and use." New York, Westport, London: Praeger.

Cohen, Clifford A.

1960 "Estimating the parameters of a modified Poisson distribution." In *Journal of the American Statistical Association*, 55; 139–143.

Comrie, Bernard

1993 "Argument structure." In: Jacobs, Joachim; Stechow, Arnim von; Sternefeld, Wolfgang; Vennemann, Theo (eds.) *Syntax. Ein internationales Handbuch zeitgenössischer Forschung. Halbband 1.* Berlin, New York: de Gruyter, 905–914.

Conway, Richard W.; Maxwell, William L.

1962 "A queuing model with state dependent service rates." In: *Journal of Industrial Engineering*, 12; 132–136.

Cramer, Irene

2005 "Das Menzerathsche Gesetz." In: Köhler, Reinhard; Altmann, Gabriel;

Piotrowski, Rajmond G. (eds.), *Quantitative Linguistik. Ein internationales Handbuch. Quantitative Linguistics. An International Handbook.* Berlin, New York: de Gruyter, 659–688.

Croft, William
1990 *Typology and universals.* Cambridge: Cambridge University Press.

Dressler, Wolfgang; Mayerthaler, Willi; Panagl, Oswald; Wurzel, Wolfgang
1987 *Leitmotifs in Natural Morphology.* Amsterdam, Philadelphia: Benjamins.

Eigen, Manfred
1971 "Selforganization of matter and the evolution of biological macromolecules." In: *Die Naturwissenschaften*, 58; 465–523.
1999 *Everett, Daniel L.*1999 *A língua pirahã e a teoria da sintaxe: descrição, perspectivas e teoria.* Campinas: Editora de Unicamp.

Frumkina, Revekka Markovna
1962 "O zakonach raspredelenija slov i klassov slov." In: Mološnaja, Tatj'ana N. (ed.), *Strukturno-tipologičeskie issledovanija.* Moskva, Akademija nauk SSSR, 124–133.
1973 "Rol' statističeskich metodov v sovremennych lingvističeskich issledovanijach." In: Piotrovskij, Rajmund G.; Bektaev, Kaldybay B.; Piotrovskaja, Anna A. (eds.), *Matematičeskaja lingvistika.* Moskva: Nauka, 166.

Gödel, Kurt
1931 "Über formal unentscheidbare Sätze der *Principia Mathematica* und verwandter Systeme I." In: *Monatsheft für Mathematik und Physik*, 38; 173–198.

Greenberg, Joseph Harold
1957 "The nature and uses of linguistic typologies." In: *International Journal of American Linguistics*, 23; 68–77.
1960 "A quantitative approach to the morphological typology of languages." In: *International Journal of American Linguistics*, 26; 178–194.
1966 *Language universals.* The Hague: Mouton.

Guiter, Henri
1974 "Les relations fréquence – longueur – sens des mots (langues romanes et anglais)." In: *XIV Congresso internazionale di linguistica e filologia romanza.* Napoli, 15–20.

Haken, Hermann
1978 *Synergetics.* Berlin, Heidelberg, New York: Springer.

Haken, Hermann; Graham, Robert
1971 "Synergetik. Die Lehre vom Zusammenwirken." In: *Umschau*, 6; 191.

Hammerl, Rolf
1990 "Untersuchungen zur Verteilung der Wortarten im Text." In: Hřebíček, Luděk (ed.), *Glottometrika 11.* Bochum: Brockmeyer, 142–156.

Hauser, Marc D.; Chomsky, Noam; Fitch, W. Tecumseh
2002 *The Faculty of Language: What Is It, Who Has It, and How Did It Evolve?* In: emphScience, 298; 1569–1579.

Hawkins, John A.
1983 *Word order universals.* 2nd pr., 1988. San Diego u.a.: Academic Press.
1990 "A parsing theory of word order universals." In: *Linguistic inquiry*, 21/2; 223–261.
1992 "Syntactic weight versus information structure in word order variation." In Jacobs, Joachim (ed.), "Informationsstruktur und Grammatik." Opladen: Westdeutscher Verlag, 196–219.
1994 *A performance theory of order and constituency.* Cambridge: University Press.

Helbig, Gerhard; Schenkel, Wolfgang
1991 *Wörterbuch zur Valenz und Distribution deutscher Verben.* 8., durchgesehene Auflage. Tübingen: Max Niemeyer Verlag.

Hempel, Carl Gustav
1952 "Fundametals of concept formation in empirical science." In: *International encyclopedia of unified science II.* Chicago: University of Chicago Press.

Hengeveld, Kees; Rijkhoff, Jan; Siewierska, Anna
2004 "Parts-of-speech systems and word order." In: *Journal of Linguistics*, 40; 527–570.

Herdan, Gustav
1966 *The advanced theory of language as choice and chance.* Berlin, Heidelberg, New York : Springer.

Heringer, Hans Jürgen
1993 "Basic ideas and the classical model?." In: Jacobs, Joachim; Stechow, Arnim von; Sternefeld, Wolfgang; Vennemann, Theo (eds.), *Syntax. Ein internationales Handbuch zeitgenössischer Forschung. Halbband 1.* Berlin, New York: de Gruyter, 293–316.

Heringer, Hans Jürgen; Strecker, Bruno; Wimmer, Rainer
1980 *Syntax. Fragen–Lösungen–Alternativen.* München: Wilhelm Fink Verlag. [= UTB 251]

Heups, Gabriela
1983 "Untersuchungen zum Verhältnis von Satzlänge zu Clauselänge am Beispiel deutscher Texte verschiedener Textklassen." In: Köhler, Reinhard; Boy, Joachim (eds.), *Glottometrika 5.* Bochum: Brockmeyer, 113–133.

Hoffmann, Christiane
2002 "Word order and the principle of 'Early Immediate Constituents' (EIC)." In: *Journal of Quantitative Linguistics*, 6/2; 108–116.

1999 “‘Early immediate constituents’ – ein kognitiv-funktionales Prinzip der Wortstellung(svariation).” In: Köhler, Reinhard (ed.), *Korpuslinguistische Untersuchungen zur quantitativen und systemtheoretischen Linguistik.* Trier. http://ubt.opus.hbz-nrw.de/volltexte/2007/413/, 31–74.

Hřebíček, Luděk

1994 “Fractals in language.” In: *Journal of Quantitative Linguistics*, 1; 82–86.

1999 “Principle of emergence and text in linguistics.” In: *Journal of Quantitative Linguistics*, 6; 41–45.

Hunt, Fern Y.; Sullivan, Francis

1986 “Efficient algorithms for computing fractal dimensions.” In: Meyer-Kress, Gottfried (ed.), *Dimensions and entropy in chaotic systems.* Berlin: Springer, 83–93.

Kelih, Emmerich; Grzybek, Peter; Antić, Gordana; Stadlober, Ernst

2005 “Quantitative Text Typology. The Impact of Sentence Length.” In: Spiliopoulou, Myra; Kruse, Rudolf; Nürnberger, Andreas; Borgelt, Christian; Gaul, Wolfgang (eds.), *From Data and Information Analysis to Knowledge Engineering.* Heidelberg, Berlin: Springer, 382–389.

Kelih, Emmerich; Grzybek, Peter

2005 “Satzlänge: Definitionen, Häufigkeiten, Modelle (am Beispiel slowenischer Prosatexte).” In: *Quantitative Methoden in Computerlinguistik und Sprachtechnologie.* [Special Issue of: *LDV-Forum. Zeitschrift für Computerlinguistik und Sprachtechnologie. Journal for Computational Linguistics and Language Technology*, 20]; 31–51.

Kendall, Maurice G.; Babington Smith, B.

1939 “The problem of *m* rankings.” In: *The Annals of Mathematical Statistics*, 10/3; 275–287.

Köhler, Reinhard

1982 “Das Menzerathsche Gesetz auf Satzebene.” In: Lehfeldt, Werner; Strauss, Udo (eds.), *Glottometrika 4.* Bochum: Brockmeyer, 103–113.

1984 “Zur Interpretation des Menzerathschen Gesetzes.” In: Boy, Joachim; Köhler, Reinhard (eds.), *Glottometrika 6.* Bochum, 177–183.

1986 *Zur linguistischen Synergetik. Struktur und Dynamik der Lexik.* Bochum: Brockmeyer.

1987 “Systems theoretical linguistics.” In: *Theoretical Linguistics* 14/2-3; 241–257.

1990a “Linguistische Analyseebenen. Hierarchisierung und Erklärung im Modell der sprachlichen Selbstregulation.” In: Hřebíček, Luděk (ed.), *Glottometrika 11.* Bochum: Brockmeyer, 1–18.

1990b “Elemente der synergetischen Linguistik.” In: Hammerl, Rolf (ed.), *Glottometrika 12.* Bochum: Brockmeyer, 179–188.

1999 "Syntactic structures: properties and interrelations." In: *Journal of Quantitative Linguistics*, 6/1; 46–57.

2001 "The distribution of some syntactic constructions types in text blocks." In: Altmann, Gabriel; Köhler, Reinhard; Uhlířová, Ludmila; Wimmer, Gejza (eds.), *Text as a linguistic paradigm: Levels, Constituents, Constructs. Festschrift in honour of Luděk Hrebíček.* Trier: WVT, 136–148.

2003a "Zur Type-Token-Ratio syntaktischer Einheiten. Eine quantitativ-korpuslinguistische Studie." In: Cyrus, Lea; Feddes, Henrik; Schumacher, Frank; Steiner, Petra (eds.), *Sprache zwischen Theorie und Technologie.* Wiesbaden: Deutscher Universitäts-Verlag, 93–101.

2003b "Zur Wachstumsdynamik (Type-Token-Ratio) syntaktischer Funktionen in Texten." In: Kempgen, Sebastian; Schweier, Ulrich; Berger, Tilman (eds.), *Rusistika · Slavistika · Lingvistika. Festschrift für Werner Lehfeldt zum 60. Geburtstag.* München: Otto Sagner, 498–504.

2005a "Korpuslinguistik – zu wissenschaftstheoretischen Grundlagen und methodologischen Perspektiven." In: *Zeitschrift für Computerlinguistik und Sprachtechnologie*, 20/2; 2–16.

2005b "Synergetic linguistics." In: Köhler, Reinhard; Altmann, Gabriel; Piotrowski, Rajmond G. (eds.), *Quantitative Linguistik. Ein internationales Handbuch. Quantitative Linguistics. An International Handbook.* Berlin, New York: de Gruyter, 760–774.

2006a "The frequency distribution of the lengths of length sequences." In: Genzor, Josef; Bucková, Martina (eds.), *Favete linguis. Studies in honour of Viktor Krupa.* Bratislava: Slovak Academic Press, 145–152.

2006b "Frequenz, Kontextualität und Länge von Wörtern – Eine Erweiterung des synergetisch-linguistischen Modells." In: Rapp, Reinhard; Sedlmeier, Peter; Zunker-Rapp, Gisela (eds.), *Perspectives on Cognition – A Festschrift for Manfred Wettler.* Lengerich: Pabst Science Publishers, 327–338.

2008a "Word length in text. A study in the syntagmatic dimension." In: Mislovicová, Sibyla (ed.), *Jazyk a jazykoveda v prohybe.* Bratislava: VEDA vydavatel'stvo SAV, 416–421.

2008b "Sequences of linguistic quantities. Report on a new unit of investigation." In: *Glottotheory*, 1/1, 115–119.

Köhler, Reinhard; Altmann, Gabriel

2000 "Probability distributions of syntactic units and properties." In: *Journal of Quantitative Linguistics*, 7/3; 189–200.

Köhler, Reinhard; Galle, Matthias

1993 "Dynamic aspects of text characteristics." In: Altmann, Gabriel; Hřebíček, Luděk (eds.), *Quantitative Text Analysis.* Trier, 46–53.

Köhler, Reinhard; Martináková-Rendeková, Zuzana
1998 "A systems theoretical approach to language and music." In: Altmann, Gabriel; Koch, Walter (eds.), *Systems. New paradigms for the human sciences.* Berlin, New York: Walter de Gruyter, 514–546.

Köhler, Reinhard; Naumann, Sven
2008 "Quantitative text analysis using *L*-, *F*- and *T*-segments." In: Preisach, Burkhardt, Schmidt-Thieme, Decker (eds.), *Data Analysis, Machine Learning and Applications.* Berlin, Heidelberg: Springer, 637–646.
2009 "A contribution to quantitative studies on the sentence level." In: Köhler, Reinhard (ed.), *Issues in Quantitative Linguistics.* Lüdenscheid: RAM-Verlag, 34–57.
2010 "A syntagmatic approach to automatic text classification. Statistical properties of *F*- and *L*-motifs as text characteristics." In: Grzybek, Peter; Kelih, Emmerich; Mačutek, Ján (eds.), *Text and Language. Structures, Functions, Interrelations.* Wien: Praesens Verlag, 81–90.

Krupa, Viktor
1965 "On quantification of typology." In: *Linguistics*, 12; 31–36.

Krupa, Viktor; Altmann, Gabriel
1966 "Relations between typological indices." In: *Linguistics*, 24; 29–37.

Kutschera, Franz von
1972 "Wissenschaftstheorie Bd. 1." München: Fink.

Lamb, Sydney M.
1966 "Outline of Stratificational Grammar." Washington D.C.: Georgetown University Press.

Legendre, Pierre
2011 "Coefficient of concordance." In: *Encyclopedia of Research Design.* SAGE Publications. [In print].
Cf. electronic source: http://www.bio.umontreal.ca/legendre/reprints/Coefficient_of_concordance.pdf (Feb. 9, 2011).

Liu, Haitao
2007 "Probability distribution of dependency distance." In: *Glottometrics*, 15; 1–12.
2009 "Probability distribution of dependencies based on Chinese dependency treebank." In: *Journal of Quantitative Linguistics*, 16/3; 256–273.

Menzerath, Paul
1954 *Die Architektonik des deutschen Wortschatzes.* Bonn: Dümmler.

Miller, George A.; Selfridge, Jennifer A.
1950 "Verbal context and the recall of meaningful material." In: *American Journal of Psychology*, 63; 176-185.

Mizutani, Sizuo
1989 "Ohno's lexical law: it's data adjustment by linear regression." In: Mizutani, Sizuo (ed.), *Japanese quantitative linguistics*. Bochum: Brockmeyer, 1–13.

Naumann, Sven
2005a "Probabilistic grammars." In: Köhler, Reinhard; Altmann, Gabriel; Piotrowski, Rajmond G. (eds.), *Quantitative Linguistik. Ein internationales Handbuch. Quantitative Linguistics. An International Handbook*. Berlin, New York: de Gruyter, 292–298.
2005b "Probabilistic parsing." In: Köhler, Reinhard; Altmann, Gabriel; Piotrowski, Rajmond G. (eds.), *Quantitative Linguistik. Ein internationales Handbuch. Quantitative Linguistics. An International Handbook*. Berlin, New York: de Gruyter, 847–856.

Nemcová, Emília; Altmann, Gabriel
1994 "Zur Wortlänge in slowakischen Texten." In: *Zeitschrift für empirische Textforschung*, 1; 40–43.

Nuyts, Jan
1992 *Aspects of a cognitive pragmatic theory of language: on cognition, functionalism, and grammar.* Amsterdam: Benjamins.

Ord, J. Keith
1972 *Families of frequency distributions*. London: Griffin.

Osgood, Charles E.
1963 "On Understanding and Creating Sentences." In: *American Psychologist*, 18; 735–751.

Pajunen, Anneli; Palomäki, Ulla
1982 *Tilastotietoja suomen kielen muoto – ja lauseo-pillisista yksiköista.* Turku: Käsiskirjoitus.

Pawłowski, Adam
2001 *Metody kwantytatywne w sekwencyjnej analizie tekstu*. Warszawa: Universytet Warszawski, Katedra Lingwistyki Formalnej.

Pensado, José Luís
1960 *Fray Martín Sarmiento: Sus ideas linguísticas*. Oviedo: Cuadernos de la Catédra Feijóo.

Popescu, Ioan-Iovitz; Altmann, Gabriel; Köhler, Reinhard
2010 "Zipf's law – another view." In: *Quality & Quantity*, 44/4, 713–731.

Popescu, Ioan-Iovitz; Kelih, Emmerich; Mačutek, Ján; Čech, Radek; Best, Karl-Heinz; Altmann, Gabriel
2010 *Vectors and codes of text*. Lüdenscheid: RAM-Verlag.

Popper, Karl R.
1957 *Das Elend des Historizismus*. Tübingen: Mohr.

Prigogine, Ilya
1973 "Time, irreversibility and structure." In: Mehra, Jagdish (ed.), *Physicist's conception of nature.* Dordrecht: D. Reidel, 561–593.
Prigogine, Ilya; Stengers, Isabelle
1988 *Entre le temps et l'éternité.* Paris: Fayard.
Prün, Claudia
1994 "About the validity of Menzerath-Altmann's Law." In: *Journal of Quantitative Linguistics*, 1/2; 148–155.
Sampson, Geoffrey
1995 *English for the computer.* Oxford.
1997 "Depth in English grammar." In: *Journal of Linguistics*, 33; 131–151.
Schweers, Anja; Zhu, Jinyang
1991 "Wortartenklassifizierung im Lateinischen, Deutschen und Chinesischen." In: Rothe, Ursula (ed.), *Diversification processes in language: grammar.* Hagen: Margit Rottmann Medienverlag, 157–165.
Sherman, Lusius Adelno
1888 "Some observations upon the sentence-length in English prose." In: *University of Nebraska Studies I*, 119–130.
Sichel, Herbert Simon
1971 "On a family of discrete distributions particularly suited to represent long-tailed data." In: Laubscher, Nico F. (ed.), *Proceedings of the 3rd Symposium on Mathematical Statistics.* Pretoria: CSIR, 51K97.
1974 "On a distribution representing sentence-length in prose." In: *Journal of the Royal Statistical Society (A)*, 137, 25K34.
Temperley, David
2008 "Dependency-length minimization in natural and artificial languages." In: *Journal of Quantitative Linguistics*, 15/3; 256–282.
Teupenhayn, Regina; Altmann, Gabriel
1984 "Clause length and Menzerath's Law." In: Köhler, Reinhard; Boy, Joachim (eds.), *Glottometrika 6.* Bochum: Brockmeyer, 127–138.
Tesnière, Lucien
1959 *Éléments de syntaxe structural.* Paris: Klincksieck.
Tuldava, Juhan
1980 "K voprosu ob analitičeskom vyraženii svjazi meždu ob"emom slovarja i ob"emom teksta." In: *Lingvostatistika i kvantitativnye zakonomernosti teksta.* Tartu: Učenye zapiski Tartuskogo gosudarstvennogo universiteta 549; 113–144.
Tuzzi, Arjuna; Popescu, Ioan-Iovitz; Altmann, Gabriel
2010 *Quantitative analysis of italian texts.* Lüdenscheid: RAM.
Uhlířová, Ludmila
1997 "Length vs. order. Word length and clause length from the perspective of word order." In : *Journal of Quantitative Linguistics*, 4; 266–275.

2007 "Word frequency and position in sentence." In: *Glottometrics*, 14; 1–20.

2009 "Word frequency and position in sentence." In: Popescu, Ian-Iovitz et al., Word Frequency Studies. Berlin, New York: Mouton de Gruyter, 203–230.

Väyrynen, Pertti Alvar; Noponen, Kai; Seppänen, Tapio
2008 "Preliminaries to Finnish word prediction." In: *Glottotheory*, 1; 65–73.

Vulanović, Relja
2008a "The combinatorics of word order in flexible parts-of-speech systems." In: *Glottotheory*, 1; 74–84.

2008b "A mathematical analysis of parts-of-speech systems." In: *Glottometrics*, 17; 51–65.

2009 "Efficiency of flexible parts-of-speech systems." In: Köhler, Reinhard (ed.), *Issues in quantitative linguistics.* Lüdenscheid: RAM-Verlag, 155–175.

Vulanović, Relja; Köhler, Reinhard
2009 "Word order, marking, and Parts-of-Speech Systems." In: *Journal of Quantitative Linguistics*, 16/4; 289–306.

Williams, Carrington B.
1939 "A note on the statistical analysis of sentence-length as a criterion of literary style." In: *Biometrika*, 41; 356–361.

Wimmer, Gejza; Altmann, Gabriel
1999 *Thesaurus of univariate discrete probability distributions.* Essen: Stamm.

2005 "Unified derivation of some linguistic laws." In: Köhler, Reinhard; Altmann, Gabriel; Piotrowski, Rajmond G. (eds.), "Quantitative Linguistik. Ein internationales Handbuch. Quantitative Linguistics. An International Handbook." Berlin, New York: de Gruyter, 760–775.

Wimmer, Gejza; Köhler, Reinhard; Grotjahn, Rüdiger; Altmann, Gabriel
1994 "Towards a theory of word length distribution." In: *Journal of Quantitative Linguistics*, 1; 98–106.

Wimmer, Gejza; Witkovský, Viktor; Altmann, Gabriel
1999 "Modification of probability distributions applied to word length research." In: *Journal of Quantitative Linguistics*, 6/3; 257–270.

Yngve, Victor H.
1960 "A model and an hypothesis for language structure." In: *Proceedings of the American Philosophical Society*, 104; 444–466.

Zhu, Jinyang; Best, Karl-Heinz
1992 "Zum Wort im modernen Chinesisch." In: *Oriens Extremus*, 35; 45–60.

Ziegler, Arne
1998 "Word class frequencies in Brazilian-Portuguese press texts." In: *Journal of Quantitative Linguistics*, 5; 269–280.
2001 "Word class frequencies in Portuguese press texts." In: Uhlířová, Ludmila; Wimmer, Gejza; Altmann, Gabriel; Köhler, Reinhard (eds.), *Text as a linguistic paradigm: levels, constituents, constructs. Festschrift in honour of Luděk Hřebíček.* Trier: Wissenschaftlicher Verlag Trier, 295–312.

Ziegler, Arne; Best, Karl-Heinz; Altmann, Gabriel
2001 "A contribution to text spectra." In: *Glottometrics*, 1; 97–108.

Zipf, George Kingsley
1935 *The psycho-biology of language. An Introduction to Dynamic Philology.* Boston: Houghton-Mifflin. Cambridge: M.I.T. Press. 2nd ed. 1968.
1949 *Human behavior and the principle of least effort.* Cambridge: Addison-Wesley. New York: Hafner. Reprint, 1972.

Subject index

I

L

M

N

T

V

W

Z

Author index

Bei Fragen zur Produktsicherheit wenden Sie sich bitte an:
If you have any questions regarding product safety,
please contact:

Walter de Gruyter GmbH
Genthiner Straße 13
10785 Berlin
productsafety@degruyterbrill.com